Tantric

Mastery the Secrets of Pleasure

Awakening Your Sexual Energy with the Teachings of Tantra Illuminated. A guide through Sex positions for Couples, Massage and Meditation

2 Books in 1

Avaya Alorveda

Table Of Contents

Tantra

TANTRA

Introduction Guide to Tantra Philosophy, Traditions and Practices

Avaya Alorveda

Chapter One

Samsara (The Cyclic Existence)

Whenever we discuss the world, we for the most part mean all the numerous things that make up the stuff of human experience, explicitly the earth and the exercises of our earth and our bustling species. Conversely, the related words universe and universe have an unmistakably increasingly conceptual, generic ring to them. Hardly any individuals realize that the word world gets from the Old Norse word verold, which means actually "man age" (ver being identified with Latin vir, signifying "man"), or human period. Along these lines in its unique sense, world means "world age," that is, a specific stage or cycle inside the unfurling story of the universe as it identifies with mankind. To the people of old, it would have looked bad to think about the world separated from its significance to human presence. "The world" signified "the world as humankind's abode."

The conventional thought of world ages served the people of old as a helpful gadget for seeing enormous social settings from a deep point of view. As I clarified in the presentation, the Indic see is that we live amidst the kali-yuga, a world age portrayed by spiritual and moral decay. This is terrible news just in the short run. Taking an adaptive perspective on history, the conventional cosmologists of India didn't capitulate to cynicism. For, toward the finish of a dull age, they imagined the introduction of another brilliant age. They saw this cyclic progression of world ages (yuga) as a basic part of time-bound presence in which people and different creatures are allowed the chance to mature ethically and deeply in rehashed manifestations.

The Sanskrit language has various words that indicate "world," however none catches this unending reusing of human experience through the system of time more strikingly than the term samsara. It implies truly "that which streams together" (from the prefix sam, relating to the Greek syn, and the verbal root sri, "to stream"), implying the unending motion of presence that unites subjects and items in pivotal mixes. Now and again the Sanskrit expression is ventured into mixes like samsara-mandala (round of cyclic presence), samsara-cakra (wheel of cyclic presence), samsara-sagara (sea of cyclic presence), or samsara-vriksha (tree of cyclic presence). Samsara is regularly to some degree straight rendered as "molded presence" or "ordinary presence." These two English reciprocals neglect to pass on the musical or cyclic nature of our individual common lives, which ride on the current of time, presently submerging into the imperceptible, "unpretentious" domains, presently reappearing into material perceivability. Samsara is the round of birth, life, demise, resurrection, recharged life, and afterward again passing, ceaselessly. It is presence controlled by destiny (daiva), the many-sided and sacred snare of karmic obligation that exists between creatures. Samsdra is karma. This implies, as the contemporary Tantric capable Vimalananda called attention to, that it is for the most part memory. Cyclic or adapted presence is administered by a wide range of laws (which are the solidified recollections of nature), the most significant of which is the law of circumstances and logical results. Newton caught its physical viewpoint in his detailing that each activity has an equivalent however inverse response. India's sages guarantee us that this law applies with equivalent power in the domain of the psyche to our meditations and volitions. Since science takes a gander at the material domain, it neglects to welcome the far reaching nature of causation and subsequently likewise takes into consideration negligible possibility occasions. From a more deep, spiritual viewpoint, in any case, all occasions are administered by causation. Presence is an endlessly perplexing system of conditions offering ascend to different conditions. This is the thing that karma means.

Samsara, as the British mathematician and logician Alfred North Whitehead would say, is "process." And what is being prepared is the human mind (jiva), which must experience rehashed world involvement with request to understand its actual predetermination past all appearance, comprising in the acknowledgment of Being-Consciousness, or Spirit. The world is a school, which is a thought given articulation in non-Indic spiritual conventions too. If human life can be said to have a general reason by any means, it is to graduate through the enlivening of intelligence (vidya, jnana).

From one more point, samsara is maya. In other words, it is a finely woven work of deceptions, established in our key misunderstanding of ourselves and the world. The misguided judgment about ourselves comprises in viewing ourselves as self image characters as opposed to the resolute pure Being-Consciousness. The misguided judgment about the world comprises in viewing it as an outside reality as opposed to as being indistinguishable with our own temperament. This root blunder (avidya), which involves spiritual visual impairment, is the thing that keeps the karmic nexus going. It is at the base of our restricted and constraining experience of reality and is the essential driver of our experience of affliction (duhkha) as apparently individuated creatures.

The Hindu writings depict in realistic terms the idea of cyclic presence. Therefore the Mahabharata, one of India's two extraordinary national stories, contains a critical entry that for simple understanding I will reword instead of decipher truly.

When a brahmin roamed in a rich wilderness possessing large amounts of perilous creatures and plants, which would have startled even Yama, the Lord of Death. Little miracle that poor people brahmin was seized with alarm. Anyway much he attempted to slash himself a way out of the brush, he just prevailing concerning going further and more deep into it. Looking into, he understood that the wilderness was secured with an impervious net, past which he witnessed a goliath female with outstretched arms. Five-headed serpent beasts lingered in the sky.

Then the scared brahmin fell into a pit that had been hidden with brushwood. Hanging topsy-turvy with his legs entrapped in the greenery, he saw a tremendous serpent at the base of the pit and a gigantic elephant with six heads and twelve legs close to the opening. Huge honey bees swarmed around him, and the honey that streamed from their honeycombs dribbled into the brahmin's mouth, expanding his thirst continuously.

High contrast rodents were bothering the tree close to the edge of the pit, and it was obvious to him that after a short time it would topple and pound him under its weight. Practically insane with dread, and with no expectation of salvage, he all things considered still urgently clung to life.

This nightmarish picture is a depiction of the world in its entire ludicrousness and guile. The wilderness obviously speaks to life, and the savage monsters are images of the ailments and setbacks that can come upon us. The goliath female represents the transiency of life. The pit is the human body. The serpent in the pit speaks to time. The brushwood where the brahmin becomes ensnared is our covetousness for presence. The elephant symbolizes the year, his six heads and twelve legs portraying the six Indic seasons and a year separately. The rodents troubling the tree of life are the days and evenings, envoys of death. The honey bees are our wants, and the honey drops symbolize the transient joy that can be gotten from their satisfaction.

The sort of speculation communicated in the above section isn't remarkable to the Mahabharata or its time. It additionally offers a vital aspect for understanding the Tantras, which were made a huge number out of years after the fact. For example, in the Kula-Arnava-Tantra, Shiva announces:

Samsara is the foundation of torment. He who exists [in this world] is [subject to] languishing. However, O Beloved, he who practices renunciation (tyaga), and none other, is cheerful.

O Beloved, one should surrender samsara, which is the origin of all misery, the ground of all difficulty, and the homestead all underhanded.

O Goddess, the psyche that is connected to samsara is bound without ties, cut without weapons, and presented to a frightening strong toxic substance.

Since enduring is along these lines wherever toward the start, the center, and the end, one should relinquish samsara, live in Reality, and accordingly become cheerful.

To be caught in samsara intends to be destined unendingly to rehash oneself, that is, one's karmic designs. Those delicate to this reality have constantly looked to get away from samsara by consuming the karmic seeds of future resurrections into the adapted domains of presence. This is likewise the perspective on the experts of Tantra. As I will appear, however, their amazing quality of time doesn't appear as simple break from the round of spatiotemporal presence yet of real dominance of existence. Impelled by the karmic powers set moving by their own past activities or volitions, the person who is bound to the domain of cyclic presence is called samsarin. The most well-known interpretation of this Sanskrit expression is "worldling"; another rendering is "migrator." By differentiation, the individual who has succeeded getting away from karma and the transition of time through the intensity of liberating awareness is known, in addition to other things, as a mahasiddha, or "incredible skilled" who has risen above or "cheated" time. It is to such a one, that samsara uncovers its hidden, divine nature.

THE ARCHITECTURE OF THE WORLD

Like other customary cosmologies, Hinduism imagines samsara as an immense, progressively sorted out field of understanding, including numerous levels or manors of presence, each containing endless creatures of various types. The obvious material world is believed to be just one of fourteen degrees of indication stretching out above and underneath the earth. Both the domains over the earth and those loosening up beneath it, however undetectable to the normal eye, can be seen by those talented with special insight (dura-darshana, or "remote survey"). As some Hindu writings demand, and as shamans around the globe say also, it is even conceivable to visit these different domains in the unobtrusive body. Indeed, we can see such paranormal capacities as the chief wellspring of information whereupon customary cosmologies are constructed.

Numerous Western translators, however, want to view these cosmologies as simple results of the creative mind. The numerous varieties found in the customary portrayals of the higher and lower domains are commonly taken as verification of their beginning in pure dream, yet we realize that a depiction is just in the same class as an individual's function of perception and phonetic corner. Twelve individuals seeing a similar occasion likely will yield twelve unique depictions of it, as in the notable story of the visually impaired men and the elephant.

Whenever we look at the cosmologies of the different deep customs, however, we locate a surprising cover. We can either clarify this as being because of an acquiring of thoughts from one convention by another, or, all the more sensibly, consider this to be proof that real perception based information was associated with their creation. It is not necessarily the case that inventive creative mind doesn't become an integral factor in the conventional depictions of the world, similarly as it is an element of mode m cosmology and without a doubt any part of information.

Why is it essential to talk about cosmology regarding Tantra? The Tantric objective, similar to the objective of every single spiritual custom, is to rise above the experienced world, which is both outer and inward.

However, to have the option to rise above the world, we first need to know the domain.

The sacred writings of Tantra overall buy in to a similar cosmography that can likewise be found in the Puranas. The Puranas, as the name recommends, are "antiquated" legend, consolidating fantasy with history (particularly dynastic history), religion with fables, and transcendentalism with commonsense good guidance. They are broad in style and indicate to portray the unfurling of life from the earliest starting point of time to the hour of their own time. The Puranas have a plmaster with a surge of information that runs corresponding to the Vedic disclosure. Initially, they accumulated all the information that was not saved in the Vedas, the Brahmanas, the Aranyakas, and the Upanishads, just as the broad analytical writing dependent on these uncovered sacred texts. Afterward, as the Vedic disclosure turned out to be increasingly more acquired by the brahmins, the spiritual specialists and imaginative personalities outside the conventional center delivered their own writing - the Puranas, Agamas, Samhitas, and Tantras. These elective writing, thought about consecrated by their individual networks, share numerous lessons, thoughts, and etymological articulations with the Vedic corpus while from multiple points of view speaking to a particular direction and style. In conventional terms, they all have a plmaster with the kali-yuga. There are additionally various shared characteristics between these different writing themselves, cosmography being one of them.

As indicated by the Puranic-Tantric image of the world, our earth is at the focal point of an immense multidarkensional and multilayered universe, which is known as the "brahmic egg" (brahma-anda, wrote brahmanda). Convention discusses endless such universe-islands skimming in the unbounded vast sea. The detectable material earth is simply the coarsest and least astounding part of the universe. The universe uncovers its actual wonder just too prepared thoughtful vision. As the Puranas and Tantras portray it, the earth is actually part of a tremendous roundabout plane called bhu-mandala (earth round), with a width of 500 million yojanas (c. 4 billion miles). This inquisitively compares with the size of our close planetary system if we think about Pluto's mean good ways from the sun, which is roughly 3.6 billion miles.

The bhu-mandala contains seven concentric rings of land, or mainlands, which are isolated from one another by similarly concentric incredible seas. The deepest island, or landmass, is known as jambu-dvipa, or "Jambu Island," which has a measurement of 100,000 yojanas (c. 800,000 miles). It is named after the Jambu tree that develops over Mount Meru, or Sumeru, which is staged as the focal point of the landmass and in this way at the core of the whole bhu-mandala. Mount Meru, the astronomical mountain made of strong gold, is said to be 84,000 yojanas (c. 672,000 miles) high. It is in some cases depicted as a cone that extends with expanding stature. The Vedic diviners and the visionaries of different conventions and societies talk about this as the tree of life. The Jambu Island is subdivided into nine locales (varsha), eight of which are semiheavenly domains, while the ninth is the heardand of bharata-varsha. This term is commonly applied to India, yet initially may have alluded to the whole earth. In any case, since sacred texts like the Bhagavata-Purana give bharata-varsha's north-south hub as being 9,000 yojanas (c. 72,000 miles), plainly the earth imagined by the antiquated specialists was significantly greater than the earth that is noticeable by the five detects.

Underneath the colossal higher-darkensional earth plane are the seven progressive planes of the black market, every one of which is possessed by different sorts of creatures. Beginning at the base, they are individually known as patala, rasatala, mahatala, talatala, sutala, vitala, and atala (the word tola meaning basically "plane" or "level"). Some of the time different hells (naraka) are said to be staged between the earth plane and patala.

Over the earth plane (likewise called bhur-loka) are the six higher planes, or "domains" (loka), every one of which has its own types of creatures - diving beings and gods relating to the pecking orders of holy messengers perceived in the Middle Eastern religions. In rising request, these divine domains are bhuvar-loka, svarga-loka, mahar-Ioka, jana-loka, tapo-loka, and satya-loka. The most noteworthy plane, occupied by the Creator (be he called Brahma, Vishnu, or Shiva), is the main part of the brahmic egg that endures the intermittent breakdown (pralaya) of the various planes, for the satya-loka fills in as the seed for the following vast development. However, even the Creator detests genuine interminability and relinquishes his life after 42,200 kalpas, comparing to 120 brahmic years. Since one kalpa (or brahmic daytime) is 4,320,000,000 human years long, Brahma's life expectancy converts into a stunning 453,248,000,000,000 human years. The present Brahma is said to be in his fifty-first year. His possible passing will agree with the complete demolition of the brahmic egg itself. This is the minute when our present universe will flicker out of presence totally. Therefore, the spiritual customs of India all consider the accomplishment of satya-loka as at last ugly. Actually, the Indic lessons acclaim human existence with its force of understanding as a special stage for getting away from the pattern of birth, life, and passing, which is discovered attractive even by the divinities themselves. Past the massiveness of the brahmic egg lies the incomprehensible component of the amorphous Divine, which, as the Mundaka-Upanishad puts it, is "subtler than the subtlest." The Divine, compared in the Tantras with Shiva/Shakti, is outside the domain of causation or predetermination and is the incomparable object of the freedom lessons. This aspatial and atemporal Reality, which alone is eternal, all the while and incomprehensibly interpenetrates the universe in the entirety of its degrees of sign and is in this manner additionally a definitive deep center of the individual. Without the characteristic of the Divine, freedom would be unimaginable. Without its amazing quality, freedom would be good for nothing.

Since the different degrees of the universe, aside from the obvious part of our earth world, are open just through the pathway of reflection or inward vision, the three-darkensional cosmographic portrayals found in the Tantras and Puranas are minimal more than (maybe even rather deceptive) disentanglements of what in truth is a gigantically unpredictable higher-darkensional reality. Regardless, it is a reality that is a vital piece of the experience of Tantric experts and that in this manner ought not to be rejected simply based on our insight into the tactile world.

The higher and lower planes are very similar to the layers of an onion, and they are to the world what the "sheaths" (kosha) are to the individual person as a microcosm. This parallelism is principal to Tantric spiritual practice, and I will have event to examine its imagery in resulting sections regarding the forms of the unobtrusive body, (for example, the cakras and nadis).

To enter, in meditation, the unobtrusive covers of the physical body intends to rise above the noticeable and the imperceptible domains and understand the heavenly Self, a definitive Reality.

LEAVING THE PRISON OF THE WORLD

The objective of Tantra Yoga, starting at any Yoga, is to split the inestimable egg, to utilize Joseph Chilton Pearce's obliging representation. To do so infers the amazing quality of the texture of room time. Since the world isn't something that is only outside to us however is a piece of our awareness, and the other way around, there is no doubt of any spatial direction out of the world. Freedom is an intrapsychic occasion. Subsequently Pearce was correct when he offered a metaphorical, mental understanding of the vast egg:

Our enormous egg is the whole of our ideas of what the world is, thoughts which characterize what reality can be for us. The break, then, is a method of thoroughly considering which creative mind can get away from the unremarkable shell and make another enormous egg.

For our situation, the break is the way of Tantra Yoga. It makes the vital opening in cyclic presence. However for the yogin it isn't creative mind that get away, on the grounds that creative mind has a plmaster with the domain of the psyche and in this way to the world. Creative mind, however, has the ability to get a handle on the idea of the truth wherein we are up to speed and show us an exit from it. When it has done so it must be discarded for freedom to happen. The psyche, driven by creative mind, doesn't itself escape. It is a piece of our common things. Actually, nothing actually ever gets away from the limits of the world. The break in the inestimable egg is just a split in our restricted understanding, a gap in our creative mind through which certifiable astuteness can show. In a specific sense, freedom is something of a nonevent, for there is neither loss nor gain in it. Or maybe, when astuteness completely shows, the world gets straightforward, uncovering our actual nature, which is characteristically free. The possibility that we are bound is the first and the last dream.

Nor is it the jogin's aspiration to make another enormous egg in the wake of surrendering the former one. Despite what might be expected, experts of Tantra do their most extreme to enter all cover of hallucination, that is, all psychological builds of Reality. Right now can make certain to be freed of all conceivable subjugation to infinite presence now and for eternity.

From a yogic point of view, the brahmic or enormous egg is a jail. Numerous individuals, affected by maya (basic fantasy), are not at all mindful of their self-sustained condition of detainment. Yet, those in whom insight has unfolded can see that the world, or rather how they experience it, is keeping. They additionally are touchy to the way that common presence is suffused with misery (duhkha). From the outset, they may not see an exit from the inestimable jail, however as astuteness expands, there is a developing feeling of a Reality that rises above the universe. Then they comprehend that the Divine, however rising above existence, stays inside themselves as the everlasting Self (atman) and that it is the shrouded entryway to freedom. As it were, the jail doors were never bolted. As Shankara, the incredible preceptor of Advaita Vedanta, plmasters it in his mainstream Viveka-Cudamani:

Dolts wrongly venture servitude and freedom, which are traits of the psyche, upon Reality, similarly as the shade provide reason to feel ambiguous about the eyes by a cloud [is anticipated upon] the Sun itself. For this unchanging [Reality] is nondual, unattached Consciousness.

When we understand the perpetual Self, recently darkened by karmic habit designs, we defeat the world, which implies we beat our specific confined world experience. Right then and there the world loses its antagonistic quality and rather uncovers itself to us as the amiable ever-present Reality itself. Until that snapshot of metanoia, in any case, we are entangled by our own portrayals of Reality, our peculiar (however to a great extent shared) mirrorings of Truth. This is the importance of subjugation (bandha) in the Hindu freedom lessons, including Tantra.

What is so shocking about cyclic presence is that it is shot through with affliction. What's more, enduring is principally brought about by the experience of fleetingness, showing as change and passing. These, thusly, are an element of time (kala), which is the subject of the following part.

Chapter Two

Time, Bondage And The Goddess Kali

Samsara signals both spatial and worldly control. Most importantly, notwithstanding, samsara is time. The Maitrayani-Upanishad talks about epitomized time as the incredible sea in which all animals (counting the time-pacing solar diety, Savitri, himself) have their being and are "cooked," or aged. Time implies change, be it as characteristic rhythms or sudden advances. A large portion of us Westerners are so used to staying in urban areas that we have gotten moderately careless in regards to the common rhythms of nature. The quick pmaster of life and the substitute reality made through both the broad utilization of power for light and warmth and the utilization of medications (particularly torment executioners) have distanced us from our own physical cycles, or biorhythms. Our awareness is ruled by a straight origination that comprehends the progression of time as a bolt pointing from the past to the future instead of as comprising of self-rehashing cycles. Correspondingly, we are always pursuing time, either by trying after the future or by finding the recollections of the past, while frequently neglecting to be careful in the present. The conventional awareness, paradoxically, fears to be trapped in the patterns of time, which at last bring minimal more than physical and mental torment.

Time (kala) has been a most loved topic of the Indic

sages since the time the early Vedic period. In the Atharva-Veda, two deeply figurative songs are devoted to the secret of time. One psalm talks about time as the primary god among the gods, "throned in the loftiest domain," maker all things considered and of energy (tapas) itself.

The other song, in a comparable vein, reads as follows:

From Time the grandiose waters developed.

From Time came pious reflection (brahman), energy (tapas), and the spatial bearings.

As a result of Time the Sun rises and in Time it sets once more.

As a result of Time the breeze purges [everything]. As a result of Time the Earth is incredible.

Upon Time the extraordinary paradise is fixed.

Quite a while in the past, Son Time caused the past and what's to come. Through Time the psalms of applause appeared.

Through Time the conciliatory recipes appeared.

Time introduced the penance giving the divine beings oblation. In Time are the gandharvas and apsarases.

In Time the domains are built up.

In Time are set these brilliant Angiras and Atharvan. For both this domain and the most elevated domain, the ethical domains, and the upright interspmasters - all domains vanquished through devout meditation, this Time proceeds onward as the most noteworthy god.

I have cited this Vedic psalm in full since it additionally catches the way of thinking of time found in the Tantras, created a few centuries later. Since the Atharva-Veda anticipates the Tantric legacy from multiple points of view, a few researchers and followers of Tantra respect this Vedic hymnody, or the social condition where it was made, as one of the chronicled underlying foundations of Tantra.

Time as the "most elevated god," however, must not be confused as alluding to minor regular time. It is simply the preeminent Reality in its nurturing, continuing, and requesting viewpoint - what in Buddhist Tantra is known as kala-cakra. A comparable thought is available in the Devi-Mahatmya, prevalently known as the Candi, after the name of the goddess to whom it is tended to. This song is to devout Shaktas (admirers of Shakti, the incredible goddess) what the Bhagavad-Gita is to votaries of Vishnu in his natural manifestation as the god-man Krishna. The two psalms comprise of 700 refrains and are recited day by day.

The Candi is an ardent tribute to the goddess as the general framework, or heavenly mother. Even though she is unceasing, she shows in innumerable ways, is the early stage reason for everything, bolsters the universes, causes change by showing as time (kala) in its different divisions, and has the ability to pulverize the universe; however she likewise prompts freedom. She is the storehouse of the Vedic songs of acclaim and the conciliatory recipes, is worshiped even by the Lord of Gods himself, lights up the spatial headings, claims all the fortunes of the divinities, gandharvas, and nagas,6 and tolerates as higher comprehension (buddhi) in the heart. Yet, as is obvious from the center story of this psalm, the goddess likewise has her damaging side. She vanquishes every single satanic power as well as obliterates the universe at the fitting time. To her aficionados, however, she shows her most favorable maternal perspective, securing and at last freeing them. Subsequent to having been satisfied with acclaim, the goddess reacts:

Whosoever with focus venerates Me continually with these [hymns], all his challenges I will evacuate definitely.

KALI , SHIVA, AND THE COSMIC DANCE

Indeed, even a short abstract of the Tantric perspective on schedule, as endeavored here, would be deficient without presenting the Divine Female, or Shakti, in her most starding appearance as the goddess Kali. The name is the ladylike type of kala, signifying "time," "passing," and "dark." These three undertones are completely melded in the imagery of the goddess Kali. Dark outcomes from the assimilation all things considered, while white is their copresence. The pious Ramakrishna, master of Swami Vivekananda, offered an aficionado's corresponding clarification of the name Kali when he commented, "You consider her to be dark since you are far away from her. Go close and you will locate her without all color." In The Gospel of Sri Ramakrishna, which accounts the life and lessons of this incredible nineteenth-century master, we locate the accompanying song:

In thick haziness, O Mother, Thy nebulous excellence shines; Therefore the yogis contemplate in a dull mountain cavern.

In the lap of limitless dark, on Mahanirvana's waves

upborne, Pemaster streams quiet and endless.

Appearing as the Void, in the robe of obscurity wrapped, who art Thou, Mother, situated alone in the plmaster of worship of samadhi? From the Lotus of Thy dread dispersing Feet streak Thy love's lightning;

Thy Spirit-Fmaster sparkles forward with chuckling awful and noisy!

To retain, eat up, or demolish the universe is one of the alarming elements of the dark goddess. She brings passing to the person as well as to the astronomical egg itself in which people, high and low, experience their particular separative lives again and again. In the Mahanirvana-Tantra the goddess is tended to as the incomparable yogini on the grounds that toward the finish of time she eats up the devourer of time himself, Shiva in his form as Mahakala.

In numerous sanctuaries in Bengal and Nepal, Kali is portrayed as a dark or dull blue block of stone. In her humanoid form, Hindu iconography pictures Kali as a wild looking female whose bare, full-breasted body stands on the back of or straddles the prostrate naked body of her heavenly accomplice Shiva, with powder-colored skin and erect penis. Her eyes are all the way open and her long red tongue juts from her teeth-uncovering mouth trickling with blood. Around her neck she wears a wreath of fifty human skulls, around her abdomen a support of human hands. The skulls represent the basic energies of the universe (likewise spoke to by the fifty letters of the Sanskrit letters in order); the hands symbolize activity and its karmic fulfillment. In her temple is a third eye, showing her omniscience. She typically has four arms, yet two-, six-, eight-, and ten-equipped adaptations are likewise known. One remaining hand holds a cut off human head by the hair, proposing the demise of the sense of self character that must go before freedom; the other left hand holds a wicked sword that trims all subjugation to the world. One right hand is in the dread dissipating motion, the other in the signal of gift. Encompassing her lower legs, wrists, and upper arms are serpents, which are images of both worldly cycles and the arcane information that frees the start from existence yet is perilous to the unenlightened. The serpents are additionally connected with the secretive kundalini-shakti, the serpentine psychospiritual energy living in the human body as the instrument of both subjugation and freedom. Aesthetic creative mind has made various varieties of Kali's fear imparting picture.

Kali's lovers, however, experience her as an adoring, sustaining, and ensuring mother. With tear-filled eyes and an aching heart, they summon her as Kali Ma, approaching her for wellbeing, riches, and joy, just as freedom. Like a gushing mother, she gives all aids to her human kids. Sri Ramakrishna, who was an incredible aficionado of the goddess, appealed to Kali for the product all things considered and, as he affirmed, "She has given me everything that is in the Vedas, the Vedanta, the Puranas, and the Tantra." Toward her enthusiasts, Kali consistently shows her most amiable perspective. Indeed, even her damaging side is regulated in a kind manner, as a power that expels all inward and external hindrances, particularly deep visual impairment, and awards the most noteworthy acknowledgment past existence. "Since You eat up Time (kala), You are called Kali," pronounces the Mahanirvana-

Tantra.

Toward the finish of time, the incomparable Goddess additionally gobbles up all the bunch forms occupying spmaster. Then only she stays, in personal association with her celestial Beloved, Shiva - until the following Big Bang, when the vast egg recently emerges from its own remains.

The Feminine Divine and the Masculine Divine are rarely truly independent. Thus Kali's ruinous function is additionally regularly ascribed to the preeminent god Shiva. He is likewise called Mahakala, signifying "Extraordinary Time." Thus the Mahanirvana-Tantra has this appropriate refrain, spoken by a fan of the goddess:

I venerate the base Kalika [i.e., Kali] whose appendages resemble a [dark] downpour cloud, who has the moon in her crown, is triple-looked at, dressed in red, whose lifted hands are [in the motions of] favoring and dissipating dread, who is situated on an open red lotus with her wonderful grinning fmaster moved in the direction of Mahakala [i.e., Shiva], who, tipsy on sweet wine, is moving before her.

Like Kali's horrifying picture, Shiva's move is one of the fantastic prime examples of Hinduism. The moving Shiva is known as Nataraja, or "Lord of Dancers." His exhibition stretches out all through the universe. His collection, or move steps, incorporate the creation, protection, and obliteration of the world, just as camouflage of reality and beauty by which a definitive Reality is uncovered in its actual form. What isn't regularly refreshing outside India is that Shiva's move has a few forms, each passing on an unmistakable however related message. Its most popular form is that of the tandava, which Shiva moves in wild forsake in the graveyard and incineration ground.

As indicated by Hindu folklore, Shiva once visited a gathering of sages in their timberland cottages. Oblivious of his actual character, they started to revile him. When their condemnations had no impact, they set a fierce tiger upon him. Shiva destroyed the creature and put its cover up around his midriff. Still blinded by their own dream, the sages next set a gigantic serpent upon him. Shiva just held onto it and hung it around his neck like an innocuous neckband. Finally, the woodland recluses set an awful dark midget upon him, however with a solitary blow Shiva thumped him to the ground and afterward planted his correct foot on the smaller person's back. The devilish midget, named Muyalaka, speaks to the karmic energies that must be quelled to accomplish freedom.

Then Shiva began his infinite move, pulling in even the gods from the most elevated domains to watch the display. As he moved, he musically beat his drum, which exuded a blinding light. A little bit at a time the universe around him began to break up. At the appropriate time, notwithstanding, his move reestablished the world out of nothingness. The cardinal observer of Shiva's move was Kali, the incomparable Goddess in her savage form. As indicated by one legend, she was even the reason for his ruinous move. She had would have liked to crush him however wound up venerating him. After her agreeable motion, Shiva disclosed to her that he had played out the move not in light of her test to him but since he needed to give a dream of the move to the sages of the backwoods.

Normally, Shiva Nataraja is portrayed with four, six, or ten arms and cobralike strands of uncontrollably streaming hair, the smaller person caught under his correct foot, the left foot brought up in a moving advance, and encompassed by a ring of fire, speaking to the holocaust toward the finish of time. In his four-equipped form, Nataraja holds a drum (damaru) in his upper right hand and a fire in his upper left hand. The lower right hand is in the dread dispersing motion, while the lower left hand centers to the raised leg that presents freedom.

For the Shaktas, it is Kali who plays out the musical move that weaves and unravels the gossamer strings of grandiose presence. As indicated by one fantasy, the goddess Durga once battled the evil spirit Raktabija (Blood Seed), yet anyway much she cut off his appendages with her sword, she couldn't slaughter him, for each drop of the devil's blood that fell on the ground instantly offered ascend to a thousand new evil presences as ground-breaking as Raktabija. When Durga's wrath arrived at its pinnacle, the dull goddess Kali sprang from her temple and hardheartedly assaulted the evil presences, spinning about suddenly of movement. Between the reliable strikes from her sword, she licked the blood that had spilled to the ground, forestalling the age of new evil presences. Finally she obliterated Raktabija himself.

In triumph, she began to move, and the more she moved the more she lost all feeling of self. Her excited move made the earth tremble and before long took steps to obliterate the universe itself. At the command of the frightened divinities, the preeminent god Shiva asked the goddess to quit moving. When she overlooked his solicitation, Shiva lay prostrate before her. She speedily hopped on his body, setting one leg on his chest and the other on his all-encompassing legs, proceeding with her move. After some time she understood that she was moving on her significant other's body, became embarrassed, and halted. The pulverization of the universe was ended, and gods, people, and every single other being had the option to continue their particular lives represented by the beat of time.

Chapter Three

Samsara Equals Nirvana (The Other World)

Since the time the development of strict and social pluralism in the Western side of the equator, an ever increasing number of individuals have been pondering, what is reality with regards to anything? Under the spell of Einstein's relativity hypothesis, many have embrmasterd the radical view that reality itself is relative and totally reliant on the situation of the spectator. This perspective isn't totally without merit since it might lead one to practice modesty and resilience toward different points of view. However, it isn't extremely agreeable when one is searching for a higher reason in life that can bring enduring joy. All things considered, one must go past the person on foot level of understanding that takes truth to be variable. As the extraordinary spiritual conventions of the world certify, truth is constantly one, however there are numerous pathways to it. Truth is Reality, which is solitary. What is relative are our edges of observation and understanding.

The bosses of Tantra in this way recognize two degrees of understanding, comparing to two degrees of the real world. First there is the common (laukika) perspective, which trusts in a strong material universe and which will in general be fractional and frequently tainted. And afterward there is the spiritual (adhyatmika) perspective, which is educated by insight and leads one to reality, that is, a definitive Reality. The common understanding, shot through with want and fancy, is not really a dependable guide for those looking for enduring joy. It is obviously extremely helpful in common issues, however it is insufficient in deep issues. Additionally, astuteness doesn't empower us to fix a bike, yet it enables us to carry on with an amicable life that is helpful for higher acknowledge. It adds to our treatment of material information and aptitudes by liberating us from negative feelings and mentalities. In this way even from an unremarkable point of view, astuteness can be said to make us increasingly practical. That shrewdness is higher ranking than common information is evident from the way that without managing intelligence, common information very effectively turns ruinous. Numerous pundits of our postmodern mechanical society have contended absolutely thusly.

THE DIVINE NATURE OF CYCLIC EXISTENCE

To the normal, unenlightened psyche, the world is a position of blended encounters, bearing both delight and agony. On occasion it even offers ascend to the feeling that it is the most ideal all things considered - until ailment, loss, or passing come to their meaningful conclusion once more. This portrays the credulous, unexamined disposition to life.

To an increasingly insightful knowledge, however, the world is a long way from a perfect spot, for it can give no tolerating joy. Everything is dependent upon temporariness, the bleeding tooth of time. People particularly are very fleeting and collect various unsavory encounters. As Gautama the Buddha put it basically, "Birth is languishing. Life is languishing. Passing is languishing. Everything is languishing." This well-known announcement is resounded in numerous Tantric and different writings. Therefore

Patanjali, the creator of the Yoga-Sutra, pronounces in one of his apothegms: "To the perceiving individual everything is languishing." But past this acknowledgment of the inescapability of enduring in the circle of limited reality, and a long ways past the innocent disposition of the negligent individual, there is a third, astonishing chance in understanding the idea of presence. This is the Tantric view, as per which, as one contemporary proficient put it, our contingent universe (samsara) is the "other" world. In increasingly customary (Buddhist) terms, samsara rises to nirvana.

I'm not catching this' meaning? It is plainly not the credulous viewpoint that views standard life as though it were heaven. No fancy or self-double dealing is included here. Or maybe, the equation "samsara rises to nirvana"" suggests an absolute intellectual move by which the exceptional world is rendered straightforward through prevalent knowledge. Never again are things seen as being carefully isolated from each other, as though they were separate real factors in themselves, however everything is seen together, saw together, and lived respectively. Whatever qualifications there might be, these are varieties or indications of and inside the similar Being. As Lama Anagarika Govinda clarified:

Along these lines, great and awful, the sacrosanct and the profane, the sexy and the spiritual, the common and the supernatural, numbness and Enlightenment, samsara and nirvana, and so on, are not supreme contrary energies, or ideas of completely various classifications, yet different sides of a similar reality.

Carefully, the condition of samsara with nirvana has a

plmaster with the language and applied form of Buddhism. Both the word nirvana and the idea for which it stands are additionally found in Hinduism, nonetheless. In like manner, the possibility that the world is none other than a definitive Reality is as much at home in Hinduism for what it's worth in Buddhism. As right on time as the Chandogya-Upanishad, which is presently thought by certain researchers to have been made in the second thousand years BCE, we locate a veteran sage announcing: "Verily, this is the Absolute." That is to say, this whole universe is nothing other than the particular Being, which contains inside itself each possible thing.

This old thought arrived at its peak in the medieval Sahajiya development, straddling both Hinduism and Buddhism. Sahaja implies actually "conceived (ja) together (saha)" and alludes to the fundamental character between the limited and the unending, the marvelous and the noumenal reality. The term has differently been interpreted as "the intrinsic," "the regular," or "immediacy" - all meaning the indissoluble Reality. The Sahajiya development is completely Tantric in direction and solidifies the most noteworthy spiritual knowledge of Tantra. The Tantric adroit Sarahapada (800 CE?), one of the Buddhist maha-siddhas, described sahaja consequently:

Even though the house-lights have been lit, the visually impaired live on in obscurity.

Even though immediacy is widely inclusive and close, to the cheated it remains constantly far away.

Honey bees that know in blossoms Honey can be found.

That Samsara and Nirvana are not two how will the

cheated ever get it?

There's not something to be invalidated, nothing to be affirmed or got a handle on; for it can never be considered. By the fractures of the insight are the bamboozled Fettered; unified and pure remains immediacy.

As per the Ratna-Sara, a book of the medieval Vaishnava Sahajiya convention, creatures are conceived out of sahaja, live in sahaja, and again disappear into sahaja. In the two surviving renditions of the Akula-Vira-Tantra, a sacred text of the significant Kaula convention, sahaja is portrayed as a condition of being described by omniscience, inescapability, and goodness. When the deep expert achieves, everything insight converge into it and the psyche turns out to be totally quieted. Then all duality is exiled, all enduring is disposed of, and all karmic seeds are scorched to cinders, so the tree of unenlightened presence can't grow once more.

The Tantric affirmation that samsara rises to nirvana can be read on at any rate two levels. To begin with, it very well may be deciphered to imply that the limited world is actually the vast Reality and that, as it were, what we see to be the restricted universe is in a general sense a hallucination. Second, it very well may be comprehended to imply that the savvy who made the presentation encounters the world to be none other than the enduring, constant Reality. The two readings are right and go together. A third understanding is take the announcement to be a solution, and this also is suggested in the customary equation. The remedy or caution is this: since world and Reality are not genuinely unmistakable, subsequently understand this to be so in your own case. This epitomizes the methodology of Tantra, which is earnestly down to earth. As noted in the presentation, the Tantras are above all else pitiful hana-shastras, or lessons intended to help deep order. Our actual nature, sahaja, is consistently with us. It resembles honey in our mouth. However, out of numbness, we ceaselessly search for it outside ourselves. Tantra instructs us to appreciate the sweet-tasting honey that is as of now on our tongue by upgrading our mindfulness.

VERTICALIST, HORIZONTALIST, AND INTEGRAL TEACHINGS

In another book, I have made a differentiation between verticalist, horizontalist, and essential ways to deal with life. The Sanskrit counterparts for the initial two are nivritti-marga (way of discontinuance) and pravritti-marga (way of movement) individually. The third direction can be named purna-marga (way of completeness).

The horizontalist approach portrays the regular outgoing way of life of the worldling (samsarin), who is engrossed with their activity, family, possessions, status, and possibilities. At a specific phase of deep improvement, these horizontalist concerns are suitable enough, and the Hindu specialists have created reading material (shastra) on a wide scope of points empowering common disapproved of individuals to carry on with a superior life. In the West maybe the most popular such work is the Kama-Sutra, which manages the nuances and details of sexuality and was initially intended for the advantaged class of Hindu society.

To the class of horizontalist lessons has a plmaster likewise the tremendous legitimate writing of Hinduism, known as dharma-shastra. Here the most popular work is the incorporating Manava-Dharma-Shastra (or Manu-Smriti), which comprises of 2,685 stanzas attributed to the amazing Manu. All such Sanskrit sacred writings try to give direction on the initial three objectives or quest for human presence, in particular, material welfare (artha), enthusiastic self-articulation (kama), and good prudence or legality (dharma).

Manu, who is recognized as the forebear of the present human rmaster, partitioned the course of human life into four phases - those of a student, householder, renouncer, and freed being. Each stage is thought to reach out over a time of twenty-one years, yielding a perfect aggregate of eighty-four years. In the principal stage the establishments for a strong scholarly, good, and spiritual life are laid. In the subsequent stage, the Vedic preparing is applied in regular day to day existence. Then when one's youngsters are developed and have their own kids, the time has come to revoke the way of life of a householder and resign to the woodland or a comparative remote region. This is the start of the verticalist approach. The renouncer in the third phase of life strengthens their ceremonial practices, reflection, and petition, progressively concentrating on a definitive perfect of freedom. This perfect is customarily perceived as the fourth and most noteworthy human interest (purusha-artha, wrote purushartha). When one's renunciation has conceived foods grown from the ground has understood the supernatural Reality, or deepest Self of oneself and all creatures and things, it is fitting to embrmaster the unconstrained way of life of a freed being. The way of life of the completely lit up sage is inherentiy coordinated yet may incline toward verticalism or horizontalism without, however, being bound to either direction.

In the West, which is driven by the way of thinking of horizontalism, we have no comparable to the last two phases of human life as imagined in Hinduism. Our idea of retirement does exclude the perfect of endeavoring to understand our higher human potential. Or maybe, we normally consider it to be an expansion of the quest for joy that additionally oversees a lot of our dynamic life. Our realist approach doesn't allow the thought of internal work, it doesn't mind the fabulous perfect of freedom. Exceedingly scarcely any individuals take advantage of the lucky break of retirement to develop their self-information and devote themselves to investigating the spiritual element of presence. Our advanced society is commanded by horizontalist concerns. It offers a lot of information yet valuable little shrewdness. Endeavors at verticalist lessons, as we discover them for example in the New Age development, frequently stay on the degree of insignificant intellectualization, advancement, psychologization, and quasireligious admonishment. All these are substitute's for real spiritual practice that points not at information, joy, self-improvement, or good goodness yet at the amazing quality of oneself and the total change of human instinct.

Certified freedom and the freed life are the focal point of the assemblage of knowledge known as moksha-shastra, which includes sacred texts having a plmaster with both impactful position (shruti) and customary power (smriti). To the previous have a plmaster the Vedas, Upanishads, Brahmanas, Aranya-kas, and - for disciples of Tantra at any rate - the Tantras. The classification of customary lessons is tremendous and broadened. It incorporates, in addition to other things, such functions as the Mahabharata epic (of which the Bhaga-vad-Gita is a section), the various Puranas (however a few, similar to the Bhaga-vata-Purana, are considered uncovered writing by specific gatherings), and the Sutras (prominently the Yoga-Sutra) and their numerous analyses and subcommentaries.

An enormous extent of India's freedom writing admits lessons that fall into the class of what I have called "verticalism." They show a pathway out of the karmic traps of the flat, common life. Their proclaimed objective is some powerful condition of opportunity. They see freedom as being against the say of customary life, which is compared with one of subjugation (bandha). All their prescribed systems are intended for freeing the searcher from their purposeful constrainment in a human body and a limited world. The illustration that best portrays this direction is that of a departure from the world straight up into a measurement past the restrictive universe.

The verticalist way to deal with freedom has been colossally powerful on Indian culture. Its beginnings can be seen in the early Upanishads, for example, the Brihad-Aranyaka and the Chdndogya. It arrived at its top in the lessons of Advaita Vedanta, as prevalently communicated, for example, in the Viveka-Cudamani, credited to the incredible preceptor Shankara. Here the target world is portrayed as being more destructive than the toxic substance of a cobra and the body as being deserving of minimal more than judgment. Since the body and the world overall are esteemed irrelevant, the deep searcher is additionally encouraged to concentrate solely on the Self, forsaking every single customary interest. That Self is said in section 132 to be brilliantly present in the "cavern of the brain" (dhiguha), that is, inside oneself, in the heart. The way to it is portrayed in section 367 as comprising in restriction of discourse, nongrasping, nonhoping, nonwilling, and continually developing isolation. These methods involve the preeminent passage of Yoga - unmistakably comprehended here as the vertical quest for illumination.

Had India created just verticalist freedom lessons, its blessing to current searchers would maybe not be as appropriate and important as it truly seems to be. In any case, quite a while in the past the Indic sages additionally won through to an indispensable direction that holds exceptional hugeness for now. Integrative patterns can be recognized, for example, in the previously mentioned two Upanishads, and the prior refered to explanation "Verily, this is the Absolute" is an exemplary articulation of these early patterns. A fuller sign of integralism can be found in the Bhagavad-Gita, which portrays itself as a yoga-shastra yet has picked up the status of an uncovered sacred writing.

The blossoming of the vital direction happened with the rise of Tantra. Even though the Tantric sacred writings are not liberated from thoughts and works on having a plmaster with the verticalist approach, a large number of them plainly incline toward integralism. Most importantly, they see the world as an indication of a definitive Reality and the body as a sanctuary of the Divine. Hence, they take a gander at the sort of outrageous plainness supported by verticalism and censured as of now by the Buddha around 500 BCE. Subsequently in the Kula-Arnava-Tantra Shiva tends to the goddess in the accompanying manner:

Morons betrayed by your function of dream (maya) seek to the Invisible (paroksha) by such methods as austerity of the body and abstention from food.

How can there be freedom for the uninformed through the discipline of the body? What incredible serpent has ever kicked the bucket from striking an ant colony dwelling plmaster?

Are asses and so forth yogins on the grounds that they wander on the planet bare without disgrmaster and for whom house and backwoods are the equivalent?

O Goddess, if individuals could get freed by covering themselves with mud and cinders, then townspeople who live in the midst of mud and remains should all be freed.

O Goddess, are parrots and myna flying creature's extraordinary researchers since they talk and continue interesting things before individuals?

Fundamental lessons underscore the inward work, or internal penance (antar-yaga), as opposed to any outward custom, however without expelling outer love through and through. The Kula-Arnava-Tantra puts it along these lines:

Similarly as a lord favors the individuals who move inside [the palmaster] over the individuals who are outside it, along these lines, O Goddess, you favor the individuals who develop the internal penance over others.

The revelation of the internal penance was shown up of Tantra. However, it remained the region of a chosen few due to the deep rooted inclination in people to disregard the internal universe of cognizance and be excessively dynamic in the outside domain. Numerous Tantric teachers responded against this inclination, which was emphatically present in the standard holy culture of Hinduism. They additionally responded against the equal habit, powered by the holy way of thinking of nondualism (advaita), which fled the Many to accomplish the One. Even though in numerous regards Tantra proceeded with the power and language of nondualism, it regularly tried to communicate new implications through them. The Tantric One (eka), for example, isn't the life-refuting Singularity of some brahmanical teachers however the sweeping Whole (purna), which is available as the body, the brain, and the world yet rises above these. At its best, Tantra is integralism. This is indicated in the word tantra itself, which, in addition to other things, signifies "continuum."

This continuum is the thing that the edified adepts acknowledge as nirvana and what unenlightened worldlings experience as samsara. These are not unmistakable, inverse real factors. They are completely the equivalent Being, a similar embodarkent (samarasa). That pith just seems distinctive to various individuals due to their karmic inclinations, which resemble cloak or mental channels darkening reality. To customary worldlings, the one remains totally covered up. To deep searchers, it appears to be a far off objective, maybe feasible after numerous lifetimes. To starts, it is a dependable internal guide. To the Self-acknowledged sages, it is the one in particular that exists, for they have become the Whole.

Chapter Four

The Secret Of Embodarkent

P robably the best commitment of Tantra to spirituality is its way of thinking of the body. Not at all like the vertical lessons going before and encompassing it, Tantra has paid attention to the human body. A great articulation of the verticalist perspective on the body can be found, for example, in the MaitrayanT-Upanishad, a work most likely having a plmaster with the third century BCE:

O Venerable one, what great is the satisfaction in wants right now, pitiful body, an insignificant combination of bones, skin, ligaments, muscles, marrow, tissue, semen, blood, bodily fluid, tears, rheum, excrement, pee, wind, bile, and mucus? What great is the happiness regarding wants right now, is harassed with want, outrage, ravenousness, daydream, dread, wretchedness, begrudge, partition from the attractive, association with the bothersome, hunger, thirst, feebleness, malady, distress, passing, and so forth?

Philosophical verticalism sees the body as a rearing ground for karma and a programmed impedarkent to illumination. The regular Sanskrit word for "body" is deha, which comes from the verbal root dih ("to spread" or "be dirty"). It alludes to the contaminated idea of the body. However the equivalent verbal root can likewise imply "to bless," which gives the thing deha the undeniably increasingly commendatory significance of "that which is blessed." The more seasoned Sanskrit word for "body" is sharira, gotten from the verbal root shri ("to settle upon" or "to help"), which has a progressively positive implication: the body fills in as the prop, or form, by methods for which the Self can encounter the world. This thought prompted the still increasingly positive translation of the body as a sanctuary of the Divine - a thought insinuated in the early Upanishads however not completely expounded until the development of Tantra a lot later.

Tantra's body-positive methodology is the immediate result of its integrative transcendentalism as indicated by which this world isn't simple deception however an appearance of the incomparable Reality. If the world is genuine, the body must be genuine also. If the world is fundamentally divine, so should be the body. If we should respect the world as a creation or a part of the heavenly Power (shakti), we should in like manner respect the body. The body is a bit of the world and, as we will see, the world is a bit of the body. Or on the other hand, rather, when we really comprehend the body, we find that it is the world, which basically is divine.

Since the human body has a complex sensory system permitting higher articulations of awareness, it is particularly important. Undoubtedly, the Tantric sacred texts regularly help understudies to remember the value of human life. Along these lines in the Kula-Arnava-Tantra Lord Shiva pronounces:

Subsequent to acquiring a human body, which is hard to get and which fills in as a stepping stool to freedom, who is more evil than he who doesn't traverse to the Self?

Along these lines, after acquiring the most ideal living thing, he who doesn't have a clue about his own great is just murdering himself.

How might one come to know the reason for human existence without a human body? Subsequently having gotten the endowment of a human body one ought to perform exemplary deeds.

One ought to totally secure oneself without anyone else. One is the vessel for everything. One should put forth an attempt in ensuring oneself. In any case the Truth can't be seen.

Town, house, land, cash, even favorable and ominous karma can be gotten again and again, however not a human body.

Individuals consistently put forth an attempt to ensure the body. They don't wish to relinquish the body in any event, when debilitated with sickness and different infections.

To accomplish information, the ethical individual should safeguard the body with exertion. Information centers on the Yoga of meditation. He will be freed rapidly.

If one doesn't monitor oneself against that which is unfavorable, who, expectation on the great, will ever traverse to the Self?

He who doesn't mend himself from awful infections while here on earth, what would he be able to do about an ailment when he goes to a plmaster where no cure exists?

What moron begins burrowing a well when his home is ablaze? Inasmuch as this body exists, one ought to develop the Truth.

Mature age resembles a tigress; life runs out like water in a wrecked pot; ailments strike like adversaries. In this way one ought to develop the most noteworthy great at this point.

One ought to develop the most elevated great while the faculties are not yet fragile, enduring isn't yet solidly established, and difficulties have not yet gotten overpowering.

When we unload the calculated substance of the above stanzas, we locate that human life is so remarkably valuable since it can fill in as a stage or stepping stool for Self-acknowledgment. It blesses us with adequate mindfulness to consider our reality and in this manner give us important alternatives throughout everyday life. One of the essential decisions we have is in truth to go past the karma - creating automatisms, past the oblivious standards of conduct, by which life will in general propagate itself. We can decide to become perpetually aware of the powers pushing and pulling us and along these lines to turn out to be progressively equipped for forming our fate. Finally, we can select to relate to the very rule of mindfulness, the Self (atman), instead of the different showcases of the body-mind. Solidly, we can decide to quit considering ourselves simply as a person of a specific rmaster, belief, sexual orientation, age, social setting, or instructive and proficient foundation.

Hindus, including practically all instructors of Tantra, accept that passing isn't the end yet that we experience various resurrections and rehashed passings. They additionally accept that this cycle can be intruded on just by interceding in the procedures of the psyche itself, by moving our feeling of personality from the body-brain to the Self. When this move is finished and irreversible it is called freedom. Since our present life is the aggregate of all our past unenlightened volitions (samkalpa) and activities, it is difficult to say which seeds planted in past lives have as of now borne leafy foods are as yet anticipating realization. This additionally implies we can't know with total sureness the specific nature of a future epitome. As we as a whole know, life is loaded with amazements, and a considerable lot of these shocks originate from our exercises in previous existences both on the material plane and on progressively inconspicuous planes of presence. As indicated by certain schools of Hinduism, we can't be certain that our next manifestation will fundamentally be into human form. Henceforth it is customarily viewed as generally promising to have accomplished a human birth. Increasingly blessed despite everything is a human life wherein we experience a deep teacher and encouraging that conceivably can liberate us from the whole pattern of rehashed manifestations.

As valuable as human life seems to be, it is likewise amazingly delicate and short. Along these lines all freedom schools are concurred that we should take advantage of each lucky break to build up the craft of self-understanding, self-change, and self-greatness - which is called spiritual order, yoga, or tantra. In the Bhagavata-Purana, the sage Prahlada clarifies the essentialness of human life in these words:

When still youthful, the insightful individual ought to develop the ideals dear to the Divine. A human birth is hard to acquire here on earth, and even though human life is temporary, it is brimming with criticalness.

Consequently one should move toward the Lord's feet, for he is simply the acceptable hearted leader of the all things considered and is of high repute to them.

Tactile joys, similar to torment, are collected easily by epitomized creatures all over, essentially by virtue of their fate.

One should put forth no attempt to get joy, for that would be a misuse of life and would not bring the preeminent harmony that springs alone from the Lord's lotus feet.

Subsequently, an astute individual who is up to speed on the planet should battle for harmony while the human body is as yet prospering instead of coming up short.

The range of human life is a hundred years. Half of this is squandered by an individual lacking restraint, since he dozes hazily in the corner of night.

Twenty years pass by in early youth when one is stupefied and in youth when one is distracted with playing; an additional twenty years pass by in mature age when one is truly weakened and ailing in assurance.

The rest of the years are squandered by that individual who, out of incredible disarray and voracious want, is frantically connected to family life.

By what method can an individual who is joined to family life, with his faculties uncontrolled and bound by solid ties of love, free himself?

Freedom surmises the radical inward demonstration of renunciation of every single common article and relations. It must be joined by a similarly extreme spotlight on the celestial Reality. Prahlada's "definitive concern" was Vishnu, who, after numerous preliminaries, allowed him the most elevated acknowledgment.

Prahlada's dad, King Hiranyakashipu, moreover converged with Vishnu, since his brain was continually fixed on the Divine. For Hiranyakashipu's situation, notwithstanding, it was not cherish however exceptional scorn of Vishnu that demonstrated freeing. This is a Tantra-style showing story, and no one but Tantra can offer a conceivable clarification for this astonishing accomplishment: Whether the psyche is engaged by adoration or scorn, inasmuch as its objective is simply the Divine, the catalytic procedure of comprehend et coagula can happen. For the brain must point past itself to blast through its confinements by converging with a higher rule. As the Shata-Patha-Brahmana expressed quite a while in the past, one turns into that which one mulls over. Tantra investigated and explained on the more deep ramifications of this arcane truth.

AGELESS BODY, TIMELESS MIND

If we seek to enduring satisfaction, which concurs with our full arousing in edification, we should focus on our real presence at this very moment. Very much of the time deep searchers search for extreme satisfaction separated from their physical presence. And very as often as possible they end up not in certifiable conditions of higher being and awareness however in mental says invoked by the intensity of creative mind, which obviously are neither freeing nor at last fulfilling. On the other hand, Tantra pays attention to the body - not in the feeling of giving it an absolution that it doesn't have, yet in understanding it as the ground for every single higher acknowledgment.

The Tantric methodology is communicated well in the Yoga-Vasishtha, a surprising and enormous Sanskrit work by a Kashmiri adroit who likely lived in the eleventh century CE and was impacted by Tantra. He put the accompanying words into the mouth of the extraordinary sage Vasishtha:

For the uninformed individual, this body is the wellspring of unending affliction, however to the savvy individual, this body is the wellspring of vast pleasure.

For the astute individual, its loss is no loss by any stretch of the imagination, however while it endures it is totally a wellspring of enjoyment for the savvy individual.

For the insightful individual, the body fills in as a vehicle that can ship him quickly right now, it is known as a chariot for accomplishing freedom and ceaseless delight.

Since the body manages the savvy individual the experience of sound, sight, taste, contact, and smell just as thriving and fellowship, it brings him gain.

Even though the body opens one to an entire string of excruciating and blissful exercises, the omniscient sage can calmly tolerate all encounters.

The shrewd individual rules, liberated from hot misery, over the city known as the body, even as Vasava [the god Indra] stays in his city liberated from trouble.

It doesn't cast him into the pit of pride like a high-mettled horse, nor does it cause him to relinquish his "little girl" of astuteness to malicious voracity, etc.

The body, then, is the field wherein we develop and reap our encounters, which might be sure or negative, agonizing or lovely. While negative, difficult encounters don't bring us prompt happiness, they do as such over the long haul because - if we are insightful - we identify with them properly by seeing them as valuable exercises. No experience need be without merit. Individuals have had significant deep leaps forward because of deep torment and weakening disease. Indeed, even physical torment doesn't need to be a just upsetting encounter. Truth be told, it can once in a while be an entryway to bliss. I once experienced an agonizing three-hour session at the dental specialist. The Novocaine infusions were not working appropriately, and subsequent to squirming in the seat during a convoluted method, I finally was brought to the point of essentially giving up to the circumstance. Out of nowhere, as my protection from the agony was evacuated, I wound up in a condition of joy, which went on for the rest of the activity. I had found the disposition fundamental a great part of the world's parsimony, referred to in India as tapas. Rather than avoiding the agony, I had permitted myself to give full consideration to it and along these lines go past it. Ladies have announced making a comparable revelation during labor.

In their generally read book In the Zone, Michael Murphy and Rhea A. White notice notable football players and fighters who proceeded in a challenge regardless of broken bones, totally negligent of the agony. However, more than that, a few competitors - particularly separation sprinters - welcome agony to change over it into happiness and surplus energy. As Gerald Heard, one of the early representatives for Vedanta in the West, called attention to in his interesting book Pain, Sex, and Time, torment is unquestionably in excess of an unimportant notice signal; it is a marker of the store of accessible developmental energy in us:

Conventional and current supposition expect that man's development is finished. Any sensation he encounters, regardless of whether difficult or charming, must be for protection and solmaster, for reestablishing an upset steadiness, for keeping him where he is. Intense sensation can't be planned to prod him to imagination and to encourage him to another degree of being. It should then be indicated that there is unquestionable verification that we are creating genuine limits and resources which so draw out and utilize our crucial energy that when this is done we are rendered easy. Odd as it might appear, enough proof has just aggregated to make this exceptionally plausible.

The new guideline is basic. It might be expressed as a suggestion: The more intellectually dynamic anybody is, the less is he equipped for torment. The half-alert endure most; the most seriously mindful are least mindful of agony.

The guideline expressed in the last sentence has been abundantly shown by yogins and fakirs, who appear to be safe to torment on account of their serious mental focus. Heard appropriately accepted that the energy, or imperativeness, that commonly makes us experience torment centers to the chance of our further advancement - not on the physical level however on the degree of cognizance. This chance is in truth a test to us, for so as to make an interpretation of it into fact we should react to it deliberately. Furthermore, this is unequivocally the reason for all Yoga and Tantra.

Tantra doesn't prescribe that starts seek after torment. Its objective is that of all Indie freedom lessons: to move past all misery and find the unbelievable happiness of Being. However, Tantra comprehends that life on earth and in the other restrictive domains brings us blended encounters to which we should apply a proportion of impartial, understanding acknowledgment and self-restraint. Dreadful shirking of what we believe are negative encounters simply strengthens the very disposition - in particular, the restrictive recognizable proof with a constrained body-mind - that breeds negative encounters. In like manner, dazzle connection to what we consider positive encounters only makes another sort of karmic tie by which we endure in our condition of unenlightenment.

Significantly, Tantra requests that we go past the conventional position of the cool, absolutely isolates eyewitness of every one of our encounters. It prescribes the more refined situation of seeing while simultaneously understanding that eyewitness and watched are not decisively unmistakable. The Tantric methodology is to see all educational encounters as the play of a similar One. Regardless of whether positive or negative, all encounters are implanted in supreme happiness, the extraordinary pleasure (maha-sukha) of Reality. When we have comprehended that what we fear the most - be it loss of wellbeing, property, connections, or life itself - isn't happening to us however inside our bigger being, we start to see the gigantic cleverness of exemplification. This knowledge is really freeing.

The Tantric sacred writings hammer on what might be the most significant disclosure of old otherworldliness, in particular, that we are the world. The world is our actual body. Along these lines we are really imperishable, for as per Hindu cosmology the Big Bang that brings forth the world is, after the end of our present universe, trailed by another Big Bang, forever. Grandiose presence unfurls and envelops itself unendingly. In addition, since body and brain are just thoughtfully discrete and in reality form parts of a similar world procedure, our psyche is immortal too. This significant finding is enunciated in the bygone instructing of the character of microcosm and cosmos.

THE MYSTERY OF MICROCOSM AND MACROCOSM

The deep rooted isomorphic training that the microcosm is an impression of the world is crucial not exclusively to all enchantment yet additionally to arcane expressions like soothsaying, just as to the spiritual customs, including Tantra. An oft-cited articulation of the Vishva-Sara-Tantra puts it along these lines: "What is here is somewhere else; what isn't here is nowhere." Western understudies of esoterica know about this standard from the well-known saying of Hermes Trismegistus, "As above, so underneath." Moreover, without this hermetic knowledge, which has been rediscovered by present day science in the possibility of the "holographic universe," we can't sufficiently comprehend the Vedas and quite a bit of later Hindu sacrosanct literature. For example, it is a master key to a more deep understanding of the imagery of numerous accounts contained in the

Mahabharata and the Turanas, which have a spiritual criticalness. It is surely major to Tantric hypothesis and practice.

It is inside the microcosm (body-mind) that, as per the Tantras, we discover the entryway to the external universe. The whole engineering of the universe is dependably reflected in our own body-mind. As the Shiva-Samhita, a seventeenth-century Hatha Yoga manual made impaired out of Tantra, says:

Inside this body exist Mount Meru, the seven mainlands, lakes, seas, mountains, fields, and the defenders of these fields.

In it additionally abide the soothsayers, the sages, all the stars and planets, the hallowed waterway intersections and journey centers, and the divinities of these centers.

In it spin the sun and the moon, which are the reasons for creation and obliteration. In like manner, it contains ether, air, fire, water, and earth.

All creatures exemplified in the three universes, which are associated with Mount Meru, exist in the body together with the entirety of their exercises.

He who realizes this is a yogin. There is no uncertainty about this.

We can get to the universe by going inside ourselves since objective and emotional real factors coevolve from and consistently subsist in a similar Reality. In the supernatural measurement, they are completely indistinguishable. In the unobtrusive domains, they are scarcely unmistakable, and they show as apparently separate lines of development just in the obvious material measurement. This makes no difference obviously to realists, who accept just in the presence of material components and (reluctandy) in cognizance as a result of issue (i.e., the mind). The Tantric view is substantially more thorough and modern since it gives due consideration to mankind's mental and spiritual limits.

As per one noticeable school, Kashmir's Pratyabhijna, Tantra's philosophy (model of presence) includes thirty-six standards or classes (tattva). These advance out of a definitive Reality, or Parama-Shiva, who or which is known as a metaprinciple (atattva). In plummeting request, these are as per the following:

1. General Principles

1. Shiva (the Benevolent) - the manly or cognizance part of a definitive bipolar Reality
2. Shakti (Power) - the ladylike or force part of a definitive bipolar Reality, which enraptures Consciousness into "I" (aham) and "this" (idam), or subject and article, however without isolating them dualistically
3. Sadakhya (That which is named Being [sat]) or Sada-Shiva (Ever-Benevolent) - the supernatural will (iccha) that perceives and certifies "I am this," with the accentuation still on the emotional "I " as opposed to the goal "this" of the general bipolar One
4. Ishvara (Lord) - the Creator, relating to the acknowledgment of "this I am," unobtrusively stressing the target side of the One and in this manner making way for grandiose development
5. Dismal Vidya (Knowledge of Being) or Shuddha-

Vidya (Pure Knowledge) - the condition of harmony between the emotional and the goal, which are currently plainly recognizable inside the One

II. Constraining Principles

1. Maya (She who measures) - the intensity of fancy inborn in a definitive Reality by which the One gives off an impression of being restricted and quantifiable through the division of subject and article, which denotes the start of the debased request of presence
2. The Five "Covers" (Kancuka) Associated with Maya:
3. Kala (Part) - the rule by which the boundless maker boat of Consciousness gets constrained, causing restricted viability
4. Vidya (Knowledge) - the standard by which the omniscience of Consciousness is darkinished, causing limited information
5. Raga (Attachment) - the standard by which the completeness (purnatva) of Consciousness is disturbed, offering ascend to the longing for incomplete encounters
6. Kala (Time) - the rule by which the unfathomable length of time of Consciousness is darkinished to fleeting presence set apart by past, present, and future
7. Niyati (Necessity) - the rule by which the autonomy and inescapability of Consciousness is abridged, achieving restriction comparative with cause, spmaster, and form

III. Standards of Individuation

1. Purusha (Man) or Anu (Atom) - the cognizant

subject, or Self, which encounters the target reality

2. Prakriti (Creatrix) - the completely externalized reality, or nature, which is specific to each cognizant subject

IV. Standards of the "Internal Instrument" (Antahkarana)

1. Buddhi (Understanding) - the intellectual function of insight, which is described by the limit with respect to making differentiations
2. Ahamkara (I-creator) - the guideline of individuation by which an individual appropriates encounters ("I am such and such," or "I have such and such")
3. Manas (Mind) - the intellectual function that orchestrates the approaching tactile impressions into entire ideas and pictures

V. Standards of Experience

The Five Powers of Cognition (Jndna-Indriya, wrote Jnanendriya):

1. Ghrana (Smell) - the olfactory sense
2. Rasa (Taste) - the gustatory sense
3. Cakshus (Eye, i.e., Sight) - the visual sense
4. Sparsha (Touch) - the material sense
5. Shravana (Hearing) - the sound-related sense
6. The Five Powers of Conation (Karma-Indriya, wrote Karmendriya):
7. . Vac (Speech) - the staff of correspondence
8. Hasta (Hand) - the staff of control
9. Pada (Foot) - the staff of headway
10. Pdyu (Anus) - the stomach related staff
11. Upastha (Genitals) - the procreative staff

The Five Subtle Elements (Tanmatra):

1. Shabda-Tanmatra (Subtle Element of Sound) - the potential for sound-related recognition
2. Sparsha-Tanmatra (Subtle Element of Touch) - the potential for material recognition
3. . Rupa-Tanmdtra (Subtle Element of Sight) - the potential for visual recognition
4. Rasa-Tanmatra (Subde Element of Taste) - the potential for gustatory recognition
5. Gandha-Tanmatra (Subtle Element of Smell) - the potential for olfactory observation.

VI. Standards of Materiality

1. Vayu-Bhuta (Element of Air) - the guideline of motility created from the unobtrusive component of touch
2. Agni-Bhuta (Element of Fire) - the guideline of development created from the unobtrusive component of sight
3. Apo-Bhuta (Element of Water) - the guideline of liquidity created from the unobtrusive component of taste
4. Prithivi-Bhuta (Element of Earth) - the guideline of strength created from the unobtrusive component of smell

Tantric metaphysics looks to respond to the topic of how the One can get Many, or how a definitive Reality, which is particular, can offer ascent to the endless articles that we see through our faculties. All freedom lessons give an a response to the conundrum of creation, because so as to be freed we should follow our way from the Many back to the

One. In Advaita Vedanta, as verbalized by the eighth-century teacher Shankara, the universe of assortment is basically the result of our deep numbness (avidya). The world is a ghost created by the unenlightened brain. When the root obliviousness is expelled, the world uncovers itself in its actual nature, which is none other than the all-inclusive particular Being-Consciousness-Bliss (saccid-ananda), According to Shankara, the sensational world isn't inexistent (on the grounds that in the last examination it is the unceasing extreme Reality); in any case, it is stunning (asat) because it shows up as an option that is other than what it genuinely seems to be. To portray this inquisitive condition the Vedantic sages frequently summon the term maya, which means hallucination. What is inferred by this idea is, in addition to other things, the possibility that the change from the One to the Many is definitely not an authentic transmission yet just an evident advancement (vivarta).

Like Advaita Vedanta, most schools of Tantra likewise keep up that a definitive Reality is particular. In any case, they incline toward the view that the Many really and not simply clearly advances out of the One (while as yet being contained inside the One as the unceasing setting of grandiose presence). They dismiss any power of illusionism. This emanationism is actually known as sat-karya-vada, which indicates that the impact (karya) is prior (sat) in the reason: the world couldn't appear if it didn't as of now exist in potential form in a definitive Being. Maybe 4,000 years prior - well before the ascent of Tantra - the sage Aruna showed his twenty-four-year-old child Shvetaketu this powerful guideline. He brought up that an earth pot, a mud container, or a dirt statue all are produced using mud, however they are given various names to show their particular capacities. Then Aruna explicitly tested the magical philosophy that something can leave nothing (creatio ex nihilo):

Darling, to start with [all] this was as a rule in particular, solitary, without a second. Some say that [all] this was nonbeing just, particular, without a second and that out of nonbeing being was created.

He sayd: But how to be sure, darling, could this be? How could being be delivered from nonbeing? Undoubtedly, darling, first and foremost [all] this was as a rule in particular, solitary, without a second.

Over a thousand years after the fact, the Bhagavad-Gita followed up on this thought, extending it as follows:

Nonbeing (asat) doesn't appear (bhava); being doesn't vanish (abhava).

Regardless, the significance of the Tantric emanationism lies not in the circle of theory however in the domain of deep practice. For the existential classes serve the yogins or tantrikas as a guide by which they can discover out of the labyrinth of assortment back to the straightforwardness of the nondual Reality.

The essential classifications of Tantric philosophy were turned out quite a while in the past by the Samkhya way of thinking, the fundamentals of which can be discovered as of now in the Rig-Veda. In its traditional form, as outlined in the Samkhja-Karika of Ishvara Krishna, Samkhya perceives twenty-four ontological standards, the twenty-fifth being the rule or class of the remarkably cognizant Self (purusha). The twenty-four standards have a plmaster with the territory of nature (prakriti), and they are basically equivalent to those given by the Tantric thinkers (and outlined previously). In any case, they included twelve additional standards based a cautious examination of their encounters in the most inconspicuous conditions of meditation and joy.

A definitive guideline is pure Consciousness, the final Identity all things considered and things. The Pratyabhijna school calls it Parama-Shiva, or "He who is remarkably benevolent." as opposed to Ad-vaita Vedanta, notwithstanding, the Pratyabhijna framework fights that a definitive Reality, however solitary, incorporates the guideline of supernatural Power (called shakti). The two are indistinguishable. As the Tantras say, Shiva without Shakti is frail, and Shakti without Shiva is similarly barren.

This is a quintessentially Tantric tenet. As the Shaiva tantrikas are partial to bringing up, their comprehension of the idea of reality has a particular favorable position over the transcendentalism of Advaita Vedanta. For they don't need to invoke a different corner - to be specific, maya - to clarify the presence of the world, nor do they need to prevent the truth from claiming the world. From their perspective, their nondualism is more self-predictable than that of Advaita Vedanta. For the Shaiva metaphysicians, both maya and world are essential to the One, and the world isn't a shadow to be deserted however a brilliant sign of Shiva. In any case, Advaita Vedanta in their eyes isn't genuinely nondualistic because notwithstanding the presence of the One it additionally asserts the start ningless effectivity of maya, which is independent from the One and is the reason for the Many. Shankara foreseen this analysis when he clarified maya as being neither a reality in itself nor an apparition (which would be incapable) however as characteristically indeterminable (anirvacaniya).

Working with the force or energy part of Reality is the claim to fame and phenomenal quality of the Tantric adepts. Consequently Tantra is some of the time wrongly related to Shaktism. Both are extremely unmistakable authentic floods of otherworldliness, however they have gready affected each other throughout the hundreds of years. I will talk about the teaching of Shiva - Shakti in the following part. Get the job done it to say here that a definitive Reality, which has two viewpoints (Consciousness and Energy), shows as the universe. It is consequently that we, who are that Reality, can stir to our actual nature even while we are in the typified say.

We are the world, as present day biological disapproved of thinkers have rediscovered, and we additionally are what rises above, makes, and continues the world and again pulls back it into its unending and immortal scope.

Chapter Five

Divine Play Of Shakti And Shiva

The Tantric perspective certifies the presence of gods - extensive higher creatures on unobtrusive planes who are invested with uncommon forces. The tantrikas search out their assistance through conjuring, supplication, custom, reflective perception, and not least mantra recitation. Simultaneously, notwithstanding, they comprehend that these gods, in spite of their raised status, are not yet completely develop deep creatures like the culminated experts (siddha). The divine beings and goddesses are ground-breaking however not freed. As per a generally held view in Hinduism, they can achieve freedom just by first embodying as a person. The Tantric pantheon incorporates an enormous number of divinities, some of which can likewise be found in Vajrayana Buddhism. They are commonly summoned for assurance against obstructions and karmic hindrances. The Western brain will in general hurriedly expel this part of Tantra as unimportant superstition or, best case scenario, as a projection of original symbolism occupant in the human mind. For the Tantric experts the gods are genuine, notwithstanding, each relating to a specific fiery nearness that can be discernibly felt in meditation and even at different occasions. The tantrikas tap into those enthusiastic existences to achieve their objective of self-change, to block or disperse negative powers impinging upon them, and furthermore to help other people in their deep life or material battles.

The Tantric sadhakas are altogether at home in the inconspicuous component of presence, and the adepts are experts of the lively powers present in the imperceptible domains. From their vantage point, conventional individuals are purblind, uninformed of the numerous powers that invade and control the flatland universe in which they live. As the Bhagavad-Gita puts it:

That which is night for all creatures, in that is oneself controlled expert (samyamin) conscious. That where creatures are alert is night [i.e., irrelevant] for the seeing sage.

Terms like "crude polytheism" that have been applied to Tantra and Hinduism as a rule are instant marks that neglect to do equity to the genuine circumstance. The manly and female gods revered in the Tantric customs are embodarkents of explicit keen energies present in the unpretentious measurement. Past this, the Tantric specialists additionally comprehend that the divine beings and goddesses are figures, images that point past their quick types of sign to the supreme Godhead, the particular Being. In the sacred texts, and in custom love, the limits between clever energy, represented image, and the celestial foundation are regularly obscured. In this manner the Tantric adepts likewise see the divinities as such a large number of unmistakable however related parts of a similar Reality. When they conjure a specific god, they intellectually connect the bay between the individual and the unoriginal, the solid and the dynamic, just as the mental and the ontological. They are discerning of the particular Being loom• ing huge behind or radiating through a particular divinity. It is in actuality the brilliant ubiquity of Being that pervades a god with holiness and exceptional importance. However the tantrikas are very much aware that a divinity is a restricted being and not simply a definitive Reality. Divine beings and goddesses can, nonetheless, become entries to that Reality.

In the Tantras, which include the two general classes of Agamas and Nigamas, different gods loan their name to the solitary unceasing Being. For example, in the Agamas, it is regularly Shiva - yet in addition Bhairava, Ganesha (Ganapati), and Vishnu - who is praised and loved as the Ultimate. In the Nigamas, the pure Being-Consciousness is typically recalled in its ladylike pretense as the Mother Goddess, or Power (shakti), under a decent variety of names - Devi, Kali, Durga, Uma, Lakshmi, Kubjika, and others. Together with the name, a divinity's differing traits frequently are additionally gave on the Absolute, however consistently with the understanding that in its pith the Godhead is past all conceivable spellbinding names and classes. Such embodarkents of the Divine are in the administration of commitment (bhakti), which Tantric specialists develop to differing degrees. Particularly most Shaiva schools of South India - the Siddhanta custom - stress a reverential methodology and demand that there is an unobtrusive yet positive separation between a definitive Lord and the supraconscious Spirits. However even the professionals of all the more carefully nondualist Tantra are saturated with the well-established folklore related, for example, with Shiva. They may draw on it for their reverential life, while simultaneously being mentally persuaded of the featureless peculiarity of a definitive

Reality.

Right now, Tantras are displayed as immediate correspondences from Lord Shiva. They portray him as being situated over the paradisiacal Mount Kailasa, the world mountain, in the organization of his cherished companion, beneficiary of his lessons. The Mahanirvana-Tantra, which is a generally ongoing book, starts with these reminiscent words:

At the wonderful summit of the first mountain, radiant with different diamonds, secured with different trees and creepers, reverberating with the tunes of different winged animals, aromatic with the scent of blossoms from all the seasons, generally great, fanned by abundant cool, sweet-smelling, slow-breezes, . . . inhabited by hosts of adepts, minstrels, heavenly fairies, and adherents of Ganapati, there was the quiet God, world instructor of moving and fixed things, who is ever kindhearted, ever ecstatic, an expanse of ambrosial empathy, white like camphor or jasmine, comprising of pure sattva, all-inescapable, spmaster-dressed [i.e., naked], ruler of the down and out, master of yogins, darling of yogins, upon whose topknot the Ganges sprinkles, who is decorated with locks of hair, besmeared with remains, quiet, wearing a festoon of serpents and skulls, with three eyes, who is master of the three domains, holding a trident, who is effortlessly assuaged, brimming with astuteness, bestower of the product of freedom (kaivalya),1 amorphous, intrepid, undifferentiated, untainted, the robust practitioner of good to all, God of divine beings. Seeing Shiva with his tranquil fmaster, Goddess Parvati bowed deferentially and to assist the whole world asked him [to educate her].

Then follow Shiva's lessons and further inquiries from his celestial life partner, with yet more answers. This lovely abstract gadget is intended to pass on to the readr that the substance of this Tantra is legitimate, life-changing, and consecrated. As Shiva pronounces at the finish of his lessons:

In answer to your inquiries I have totally uncovered right now was the most mystery discipline (sddhana) and the most magnificent information. (14.200)

Then Shiva makes this guarantee:

By tuning in to this extraordinary Tantra, he who is figuratively speaking blinded by obliviousness, who is dull, or who is tricked by activity is discharged from the obligations of karma.

The Mahanirvana-Tantra isn't one of a kind in making such a case. The investigation of the Tantric writing is thought to stir the will to freedom, which thusly propels the starts to put forth a concentrated effort steadily to the different Tantric practices. At the appropriate time their endeavors will prove to be fruitful, and afterward Shiva's guarantee will have been satisfied.

All Tantras share this nature of faith. They additionally consistently declare that their uncovered lessons are to be stayed quiet, as they should not fall under the control of ill-equipped people who might neither acknowledge nor advantage from them and for whom they might even demonstrate unsafe. This exhortation ought to be borne as a top priority by Westerners who endeavor to practice Tantra without appropriate inception and the deep rooted duty and obligation this involves.

PARAMA-SHIVA: the Ultimate Reality

When the Tantras notice Shiva, they regularly mean the Godhead, a definitive Reality, or Parama-Shiva. They portray it as sac-cid-ananda, or Being (sat), Consciousness (cit), and Bliss (an-anda). What is implied by this? Being is the totality of presence, the Whole (purna). As we can promptly acknowledge, we experience just a tiny cut of what there is. Our recognition is limited to a genuinely tight scope of recurrence. We don't hear the full scope of the beat screams of bats or the ultrasound echolocation of dolphins, nor the low-recurrence calls of elephants. We don't have the visual keenness of a falcon, nor would we be able to see into the infrared or the bright spectrum. Our taste buds are not as productive as those of fish, which have taste buds over their whole skin surfmaster, and contrasted with a canine, our feeling of smell is exceedingly poor. Justifiably, we will in general respect the bit of presence we experience through our faculties as though it were the whole universe. If we neglect to check this gullible mentality, in any case, we end up with a ruined realist theory that stunts our deep development and keeps us entangled in samsara. To keep away from this trap, we should fall back on reason and instinct.

The Tantric adepts talk about a definitive Reality as cit ("cognizant" or "awareness"), caitanya (that which is cognizant), or para-samvid (incomparable knowing), or hridaya (heart). The last assignment is especially intriguing, as it associates with a deep rooted deep convention that views the human heart as the seat of cognizance. In this manner the heart is the door to the

Heart. To a deep professional, the expression "heart" passes on "that which I really am," which isn't the body and not the psyche, however pure Being-Consciousness-Bliss.

The supernatural Consciousness or Awareness is obviously very unmistakable from what we mean by these terms in customary settings, for in a definitive Being there is no separation into subject and item. Our everyday experience of mindfulness is the nearest guess that we have to oneself lighting up nature of Being. Cit is endless, pure, glowing Intelligence, which consistently lights up the bunch shapes that make up its endlessness and are not the same as it.

Parama-Shiva is depicted as being established of prakasha and vimarsha. The previous term signifies "iridescence," while the last term means "assessment." Prakasha is the Light of lights, which has no source however is the wellspring of everything. Vimarsha (from the verbal root mrish, "to contact") is the awesome "reflect" in which the everlasting Light is reflected. Without it, the incomparable Light could never sparkle into any universes or human hearts. It would be feeble. Vimarsha, oneself reflecting nature of Being, is answerable for making the multidarkensional universe in which the preeminent Light shows as lesser lights, or items. To utilize another representation, it is a gem parting the particular Light into its innate range of bright light that makes up the universe in the entirety of its numerous layers. Our own mindfulness recreates this reflecting limit inside Being itself. This permits us to remain over from our exercises, inspect them, and, eventually, follow our way back to the Source Light.

Parama-Shiva is boundlessly strong, the holder all things considered (shaktimat). The five most significant forces (shakti) characteristic for a definitive Reality are self-uncovering Consciousness (cit), total Bliss (ananda), boundless Will (iccha), all out Knowledge (jnana), and widespread Dynamism (kriya). The thought of the inherendy euphoric nature of Reality is especially alluring to those of us who are enmeshed in the restrictive domains, which are loaded with misery. This euphoria, no doubt, has no item. When we are upbeat we are, all things considered, cheerful about something. Our joy is subject to an outside organization and along these lines is somewhat restricted and fleeting. Just when we have built up a proportion of happiness do we become autonomous of outside enthusiastic sustenance. Our hunt slows down, and we start to find the delight inside ourselves, which is an implication of the fantastic rapture of Being.

Parama-Shiva's boundless Will represents transcendence, while absolute information represents omniscience. By widespread Dynamism is implied Parama-Shiva's ability to accept any form at all. Together the five forces (shakti) innate in a definitive Reality are simply the establishment for both covering and self-disclosure, the two parts of Being by which it gets inalienable while yet staying supernatural and entirety.

SHIVA: The Principle of Consciousness

Shiva, rather than Parama-Shiva, is that part of a

definitive Reality which is Consciousness. It is pure subject, pure "I, "without the scarcest idea of "I am" or "I am this," or "I am here." Hence the rationalists of Kashmiri Shaivism additionally call this perspective ahamta, or "I-ness." The incomparable Tantric capable and researcher Abhinava Gupta allots to Shiva, positioned at the heart, the mantric sound worth aham (signifying "I"). From the point of view of development, the Shiva rule (shiva-tattva) is the principal rising inside a definitive Reality. It contains possibly all other consequent standards or classes of presence, yet shows just the part of Consciousness without an item. This absolute first ontological guideline must be painstakingly recognized from the "I-maker" (ahamkara), which comes a lot later in the developmental procedure from the One to the Many. In a specific sense, the inner self is a ventured down form of the supernatural "I. "Shiva is the consequence of a transcendence of the crucial intensity of awareness (cit-shakti) innate in Parama-Shiva. In fact, "overwhelming nature" is to some degree misdirecting, because it inspires spatial symbolism, though Shiva exists preceding reality. In any case, when discussing these mystical real factors, we should surrender to the impedarkents of language and be happy to fall back on mystery and not so much fitting similitude.

In his Tantra-Aloka, Abhinava Gupta talks about Shiva as the "Mother and Father" of the universe and as the widespread operator. It is Shiva who (or which) is the seed of the multidarkensional universe, offering ascend to all other ontological classes. In any case, there is no duality in Shiva, since he is still totally submerged in delighted association with Shakti.

SHAKTI: The Principle of Energy

Shakti, the subsequent angle or guideline inside a definitive Reality, is the standard of innovativeness. Despite the fact that it is commonly recorded after the Shiva rule, Shakti exists together with Shiva and cocreates the universe. It would in this way be erroneous to think about it as a new guideline, or evolute. In this manner, in certain schools Shakti isn't recorded as a different rule however is portrayed together with the Shiva standard.

Whenever tallied independently, Shakti is comprehended to be an appearance of the Bliss part of a definitive Reality. On that preeminent level, it is the mirror wherein Consciousness, the Shiva rule, is reflected. Accordingly it additionally is the seed for the consequent division into subject and object, experiencer and experience. It is otherwise called spanda-shakti or extreme vibratory energy. As Shakti triggers the procedure of advancement or dynamic appearance, she clouds Consciousness. This bears the specialized term nimesha, or "shutting," rather than unmesha, or "opening," which portrays the procedure associated with uncovering the genuine idea of Shiva going with the disintegration of the universe either macrocosmically (toward the finish of a world cycle) or microcosmically (in reflection).

Disguise and disclosure, or shutting and opening, are relative terms that are basically important to the Tantric professionals in reorienting their life. Rationally, we have to value that the advancement or spread of the tattvas happens inside a definitive Reality. As Jaideva Singh, one of the best contemporary mediators of Kashmiri Shaivism, clarifies in his discourse on the Spanda-Karika:

The world isn't contained in Him as a pecan in a sack where the pecan has its own autonomous presence and the pack for the present contains it. The world has no different presence from Siva as the pecan has from the sack. So likewise when we say that the world has turned out from Him, it isn't implied that the world has turned out from Him as a pecan turns out from a sack where both the pecan and the pack are independent from one another. The world and Siva are not two separate substances. Siva is the world from the perspective of appearance, and the world is Siva from the perspective of Reality.

Another point that should be completely refreshing is that the veiling impact of Shakti doesn't block Shiva from our view totally, or else deep life would be outlandish. As an animal types, we can see enough of our actual nature - as Being-Consciousness-Bliss - that we can devote ourselves to its full recuperation. We are allowed to rediscover our basic being, similarly as we are allowed to deny it and carry on with the inauthentic existence of the normal worldling, who follows the direct of self-hallucination (moha), voracity (lobha), and animosity (krodha), just as the various karma-causing negative feelings and mentalities. We are liberated to be free, similarly as we are liberated to be in subjugation to our karmic molding. Tantra is a way to realness, respectability, and straightforwardness past all psychological constraint or passionate blockage. It is a way to understanding our intrinsic opportunity and quality as Shiva-Shakti.

THE DIVINE LOVE PLAY AND CREATION

Hindu iconographers have made different endeavors to portray in three-darkensional form the zero-darkensional connection among Shiva and Shakti. One well known picture is that of ArdhanarTshvara (lit. "Half-Woman-Lord"), which is once in a while wrongly portrayed as bisexual. The left 50% of this figure is delineated as a female with one abundant bosom, while the correct half is portrayed as a male, frequently holding Shiva's trident. Clearly, this picture is just a flawed delineation of the "association" among Shiva and Shakti, which is a consistent coherence of Consciousness and Power inside one and a similar Reality. Indeed, even the expression "extremity" doesn't depict this supernatural circumstance precisely. A fairly all the more fitting similarity would be that of a multi-darkensional image that yields one picture when seen from a specific edge and another picture when seen in an unexpected way.

A similar constraint intrinsic in the Ardhanarlshvara picture likewise applies to Tantric canvases or statues portraying Shiva and Shakti in close grasp. Normally amble Shakti sits on the back of her dearest's lap, folding herself over him like a creeper in what the Tibetans call the yab-yum (mother-father) position, fmaster turned ecstatically upward. This realistic theme recommends sexual love, which bodes well, since for some individuals sexual association bears the main experience of solidarity.

When they lose themselves in the arms of their sweetheart, they involvement with least a similarity to the personality rising above awareness of the Tantric adroit. It is along these lines not amazing that such a large number of Neo-Tantrics in the West view Tantra as a sexual control promising delight past all desire, for the most part as drawn out or various climaxes. Neo-Tantrics look to imitate the celestial couple yet ordinarily overlook that the joining among Shiva and Shakti is supernatural and consequently likewise abiogenetic. The product of their association - and henceforth likewise the objective of Tantra Yoga - isn't real climax, anyway overpowering, yet never-ending happiness a long ways past anything the human sensory system is equipped for delivering.

A third theme frequently misused in works of art and figures is that of the leaning back Shiva, with Shakti (generally as the dread ingraining goddess Kali) transcending above him, with weapons in her grasp, a wreath of skulls around her neck, projecting tongue dribbling with the blood of her exploited people. This picture gives us the most infiltrating look into the Shiva-Shakti imagery. Here Shiva is portrayed with an enormous erection, yet with a body besmeared from toe to crown with remains, obviously proposing that he is apathetic regarding his sexual excitement and the world on the loose. The pale, practically translucent white shade of his skin recommends the iridescence of the Divine. It is no mishap that he looks like a cadaver, lying in what is known as the carcass pose (shava-asana), for the picture unequivocally centers to a training at the very heart of Tantra that numerous Western eyewitnesses have found rather disturbing. This is the old custom of left-hand tantrikas to get commencement from a female adroit in the memorial park. The Tantric male specialist copies Shiva, who is dead to all energy and pure Consciousness. Indeed, even his blood is gone to remains - an image of absolute dispassion.

An unfathomably rearranged type of the awesome intercourse among Shiva and Shakti is the yoni-linga image, which can be drawn, painted, or cut. It comprises of a round or oval shape in whose middle an upstanding linga is put. These speak to the male and female generative organs and their relating imaginative energies. The yoni (vulva) represents Shakti, energy, characteristic; the linga ("imprint" or "phallus") speaks to Shiva, cognizance, amazing quality. Their juxtaposition symbolizes the innovative association because of which assortment can emerge inside the straightforwardness of Parama-Shiva. This specific symbolism has additionally been consolidated into the depiction of the psychoenergetic focus at the base of the spine, the muladhara-cakra. This is the seat of the serpent power, the limited nearness of the nonlocal Shakti. The serpent power is delineated as being curled three and a half times around a shiva-linga. The winding curls again recommend the inborn dynamism of Shakti.

Another solid picture that is generally used in Tantra to portray the correlative connection among Shiva and Shakti is the shri-yantra. Here the five upward-pointing triangles speak to Shiva, the four descending pointing triangles Shakti. Their entwining, offering ascend to a sum of forty-nine triangles, represents enormous presence in general.

What is huge for the present conversation is that in Hindu Tantra Shakti assumes the dynamic job, though Shiva, albeit stirred by Shakti's adoration play, stays aloof and cool. He shows the total stillness of Consciousness; she communicates the boundless strength of Power or Energy. Together they symbolize the play of life and passing, creation and demolition, void and form, dynamism and balance. This exchange is found on all degrees of grandiose presence on the grounds that, as we have seen, it preexists in a definitive Reality itself. As we descend the stepping stool of inestimable presence - from the supernatural to the inconspicuous to the coarse degrees of appearance - the supernatural "extremity" progressively gets one of distinct restrictions. The Sanskrit writings allude to the dvandvas (two-twos), which are matches, for example, light and dark, hot and chilly, clammy and dry, yet in addition commendation and fault, notoriety and haziness, etc. Tantric experts must figure out how to master these by raising their cognizance from the material plane to the supernatural element of presence, which is portrayed as nirdvandva, or past all alternate extremes. Right now Gustav Jung, ideally voicing the Western way to deal with life, offered these important remarks:

The Indian's objective isn't good flawlessness, however the say of nirdvandva. He wishes to liberate himself from nature; with regards to this point, he looks for in reflection the say of imagelessness and vacancy. I, then again, wish to endure in the condition of exuberant examination of nature and of the mystic pictures. I need to be liberated neither from people, nor from myself, nor from nature; for all these appear to me the best of supernatural occurrences.

Jung's perceptions recommend a direction that approximates the perfect of what the Hindu sacred writings call prakritilaya, the condition of ingestion in the ground of nature. This term is additionally applied to those adepts who, by goodness of their single-pointed examination of nature, have converged with the supernatural center of nature instead of with Being-Consciousness-Bliss itself. Jung supported indication and decent variety over the inadequate effortlessness of a definitive Reality. His investigate of the Indian perspective, however, neglects to welcome that Hinduism incorporates not simply verticalist ways yet additionally necessary conventions, for example, Tantra.

The Tantric custom, as we have seen, offers a positive assessment of the show domains, which all emerge inside and as the Divine. Genuine, the Tantric professionals, similar to the followers of what I have called verticalist customs, attempt to liberate themselves from the limitations of the universe of contrary energies. However, they don't look for just to get away from the show domains yet to master them from the vantage purpose of Self-acknowledgment, or freedom. Henceforth the incredible adepts of Tantra are largely bosses of the inconspicuous component of presence. They "have" a definitive force (siddhi) of freedom yet additionally the entire scope of paranormal forces (likewise called siddhi) by which they master says of the different unobtrusive planes. From a Tantric perspective, Jung's picked way stays on the degree of scholarly interest, which in the last investigation is a karmic perspective. In that function it is dependent upon the blinding intensity of maya.

To come back to the fundamental conversation: Ontologically, the "polarization" of a definitive Reality into Shiva and Shakti is the framework for the alternate extremes experienced at the degree of restrictive reality. All polarities and dualities - strikingly male and female - that we can experience on the planet are precontained in the Shiva-Shakti measurement. Mentally, the unitive relationship of Shiva and Shakti can be comprehended as an image for intrapsychic solidarity or, in Jung's terms, the joining of ill will and anima. We could say that since Shiva and Shakti are at last in flawless association, we are fit for accomplishing a comparative association inside our mind. Alternately, because a definitive Reality has these two perspectives, our mind likewise shows a ladylike and a manly side. As above, so beneath. As without, so inside. Tantric mysticism is likewise a metapsychology with extensive down to earth suggestions.

Chapter Six:

Guru Principle

Tantra is carefully an initiatory custom, which implies that its hallowed and mystery lessons are passed on in the well-established design of oral transmission from teacher to train. Right now, is notably not quite the same as Neo-Tantrism, which is very frequently practiced and declared by lovers who have not been appropriately started yet have procured their insight generally from books. In any case, as the Mahabharata expressed quite a while in the past, books are a weight insofar as we don't have the foggiest idea about the truth behind their words. No measure of scholarly learning is freeing. The Yoga-Shikha-Upanishad even talks about the "catch of course books" (shastra-jala). In the Yoga-Bija we can read:

The individuals who through [their study of] interminable rationale, and punctuation, etc, have fallen into the catch of the course readings become intellectually confounded.

The Vina-Shika-Tantra brings up that books are anything but difficult to get a hold of, yet the guidelines for genuine practice are hard to acquire. Without information on the right execution of the Tantric practices, however, particularly mantra recitation, there can be little any expectation of success. It is, in any case, additionally obvious that the Tantric custom has created an enormous number of writings. Clearly the sadhakas and siddhas who formed them more likely than not felt that the written word may be useful to different professionals.

Regardless, the Tantric specialists are resolute that solitary that guidance which has been gotten straightforwardly from the teacher's mouth is potentiated and can bring real inward development. "Commencement," proclaims Shiva himself in the Mantra-Yoga-Samhita, "is the base of all triumph." He goes on:

O Goddess! He who is deprived of commencement can have no success and no lucky fate. Along these lines one should try to look for commencement from a [qualified] instructor.

The Tantric adepts think about inception (diksha) vital to one's advancement on the deep way. What's more, for commencement to be genuinely enabling, it must be allowed by a certified Tantric master. Such a master is known as a master. This Sanskrit word is used both as a thing and as a descriptive word. Etymologically, it is gotten from the verbal root gur, signifying "to be substantial." Thus the master is somebody whose astuteness or insight is, by prudence of their own accomplishment, deep or of conclusive significance to the spiritual procedure as it unfurls in the disciple. Put all the more informally, the master is a deep heavyweight. Eso-terically, the word master is clarified in the Kankala-Malini-Tantra as follows:

The sound gu means "darkness." The sound ra [i.e., ru] indicates "causing the limitation of that [darkness]." Because he expels obscurity, he is known as a master.

The letter ga is said to signify "giving success (siddhi)." The letter ra signifies "evacuation of wrongdoing." The letter u indicates Vishnu, the triple Self, the instructor himself.

Here transgression represents the karmic inclination to propagate egoic presence, instead of being available as the Self. The master is the specialist who scatters spiritual visual deficiency and through their transmission and instructing securely directs the follower to flawlessness (siddhi). Little miracle that the Tantric sacred texts give significant consideration to the figure and job of the master.

Another recondite derivation is given in the Guru-Gita:

The syllable gu [means] "rising above the characteristics (guna)"; the syllable ru [means] "without form." He who gives the quintessence of rising above the characteristics [of Nature] is known as a master.

Nature is made out of three crucial characteristics (guna), speaking to the standards of iridescence, dynamism, and latency individually. Their transaction is answerable for all show presence, including our incessantly overactive brain. Self-acknowledgment, or freedom, surmises amazing quality of these fundamental powers. The teacher's extraordinary blessing to the pupil is the endowment of pure seeing before the play of the gunas. In the Shiva-Sutra-Varttika of Bhaskara, the practiced proficient is said to wear the characteristics like the sacrosanct string worn by brahmins.

One method for clarifying the function of the master is to say that the person plants the seed of edification in the supporter, which then can be made to grow and mature through the delicate consideration of the follower's day by day deep control (sadhana). This function is the thing that the Tantras and Yoga sacred texts call the finesse of the teacher (master kripa or master prasada). The Shiva-Samhita contains these stanzas:

[Only] information conferred from the master's mouth is gainful [of liberation]; else it is unbeneficial, feeble, and the reason for a lot of burden.

He who puts forth an attempt to satisfy the master [through his commitment to self-restraint and service] gets the [secret] information. At the appointed time he will likewise get the product of that information.

The master without a doubt is father, the master is mother, and the master is god (deva). Along these lines one ought to tail him in the entirety of one's activities, considerations, and discourse.

By the master's effortlessness one gets everything favorable. Consequently one ought to consistently follow one's master, or else there will be no advantage.

To practice Tantra Yoga without the initiatory effortlessness of an adroit adds up to a Sisyphean undertaking; unenlightened searchers are occupied with pushing the huge stone of their own karma tough, and what anticipates them at last is either debilitation or self-dream. Just the smooth mediation of a skilled both darkinishes the heaviness of the karmic rock and injects the expert's muscles with the fundamental solidarity to arrive at the highest point of the pile of internal development. Since spiritual commencement isn't an idea in our advanced Western culture, however, hardly any individuals can value the remarkable open door this speaks to. Rather they stress over issues of intensity and abuse. Their interests have been energized as of late by uncovered in the news media about the untrustworthy and even injurious conduct of a few notable deep instructors. However, these frailties say nothing regarding the custom of inception itself, which is as powerful and applicable as ever.

Whatever liabilities exists in the master convention, these relate to people and not to the initiatory framework all things considered. To delineate this point, think about arithmetic. It is a splendidly legitimate image framework. However, there are acceptable and not very great math instructors, who either succeed or fall flat (in some cases totally) to convey that framework and its characteristic scholarly magnificence to their students. When the standards of arithmetic are gotten a handle on, however, the information can be thought to have been effectively conveyed, and from now on any student of a specific fitness can master more elevated levels of the science game.

During inception, regardless of whether formal (in a custom setting) or casual (e.g., by a minor look), the master transmits something of their own fundamental nature - as Being-Consciousness-Bliss - to the pupil. Another, maybe progressively fitting method for putting it is to say that the master makes an opening inside the student through which the individual in question can all the more unmistakably intuit, or become delicate to, a definitive Reality. The initiatory procedure is an underlying refinement of the pupil's psyche, which should then be kept up and without a doubt enlarged through consistent application to spiritual practice. The whole way to freedom can be framed as far as a dynamic cleansing of the student's common being to where it resembles a reasonable precious stone that steadfastly mirrors the light of Consciousness. The representation of filtration is unavoidable in the freedom writing of India, similar to the purificatory practices themselves.

Similarly as with the arithmetic model, the spiritual searcher must bring to commencement a specific fitness. A few people are deeply talented; others are less along these lines, contingent upon the work they have done in past lives. In this way a few starts experience a significant leap forward at the primary snapshot of inception, while in others the procedure unfurls underground so to speak. However, for each situation it definitely dissolves down the dividers of the self-image and makes an expanding reverberation with one's actual nature, giving the supporter genuinely follows the course of orders spread out by the master. Swami Muktananda commented:

The commencement performed by the Guru happens effectively and basically. The Siddhas [adepts] express that when the Guru plants the seed of Shakti, the seed forms normally into a tree with blossoms and organic product.

Regardless of whether commencement will bear a definitive product of freedom right now on numerous conditions, primarily the deep development of the devotee and their application to the given sadhana.

GURU - YOGA

Westerners, who are taught to be individualists, experience issues in getting a handle on the idea that the master isn't such a lot of an individual as a function. Obviously, the master work depends for its exhibition on an individual, and in this manner it generally happens with regards to a specific character. This is what is the most confounding to Western understudies, who will in general become involved with facades. Their trouble is enormously exacerbated by the way that most Eastern instructors additionally have a character type molded by their own way of life, which can conflict seriously with the Western mind. These mental contrasts provoked Carl Jung to totally expel any proposal that yogic and Tantric practices could be valuable for Westerners.

The master, as expressed in the above sayment from the Shiva-Samhita, is to be thought of as father, mother, and divinity. I'm not catching this' meaning? Inside customary Hindu society, masters certainly are pervaded with parental power, and male instructors are broadly tended to as baba ("granddad" in Hindi), though female teachers are called mata (nominative of matri, Sanskrit and Hindi) or mama (Hindi), both signifying "mother." This convention is repelling and once in a while even hostile to free disapproved of Westerner searchers. Hindu instructors working in the West have needed to make changes, and the individuals who have not had the option to do so have definitely experienced issues with their understudies.

While deep parentalism has its natural challenges when transplanted into a Western setting, the condition of the master with God is still increasingly risky. Western understudies, who are familiar with brain research however might not have a top to bottom information on Eastern deep conventions, are able to expel this customary condition as sense of self swelling and as an open greeting to spiritual oppression and abuse. Tending to this issue, His Holiness the Dalai Lama carefully prescribed that master yoga, which rotates around considering one's to be as a definitive Reality, ought not to be locked in by fledglings. Obviously, as a Tantric proficient, he completely embraces this conventional practice at further developed levels.

The master is God not in the feeling of having extended (swelled) their human character to divine extents. Or maybe the master, having risen above (not demolished) the character, is equipped for expecting a freeing function with respect to the pupil. As it were, the master - if the individual is a dismal master, or "genuine teacher" - is completely equipped for suspending individual meditations with regards to helping the spiritual arousing of others. It normally encourages the disciple to realize that the master is oneself freed, or enlightened. In any case, regardless of whether that isn't the situation, the supporter is customarily urged to view the master as though the individual in question were illuminated at any rate. Consequently the supporter's faith (shraddha) assumes a huge job in the success of their teaching.

Obviously, it bodes well to pick one's teacher cautiously. If one can't discover a completely stirred master, then one should in any event verify that one's teacher has outright uprightness and is totally dedicated to help one's own enlivening. The purpose behind treating even an unenlightened teacher as though the person were edified is direct: Without this presumption one would continually scrutinize the instructor's intentions, which thusly would just cripple one's deep practice. Additionally, if one can figure out how to confide in the master's direction, in any event, when it enormously challenges one's close to home inclinations and discernments, then one can figure out how to confide in life itself, create persistence, lowliness, and numerous different ethics.

For most Western understudies, master yoga is the incredible hindrance in their apprenticeship. Having been raised to "have an independent mind" and "be their own individual," they confound submission to the master with immature reliance. Yet, the pitiful master isn't keen on assuming a parental job. The tragic master's parenthood or parenthood toward the pupil is just one of outright consideration for the follower's deep development. The instructor in whom the ""guru work" is alive has no other enthusiasm for the supporter than, as one contemporary skilled put it, to disintegrate the marvel called "pupil."

Shockingly, only one out of every odd instructor is a dismal master, and accordingly it is judicious to utilize one's knowledge and judgment before moving toward a teacher for commencement and apprenticeship. This has clearly been an issue for quite a while. For example, in the Kula-Arnava-Tantra, made just about a thousand years prior, the accompanying words are articulated by Shiva himself:

Masters are as various as lights in each house. Yet, O Goddess, hard to discover is a master who lights up everything like the sun.

Masters who are capable in the Vedas, reading material,

etc., are various. However, O Goddess, hard to discover is a master who is capable in the incomparable Truth.

Masters who know frivolous mantras and home grown inventions are various. In any case, hard to discover here on earth is one who realizes the mantras portrayed in the Nigamas, Agamas, and course readings.

Masters who loot their devotees of their riches are various. However, O Goddess, hard to discover is a master who evacuates the pupils' misery.

Various here on earth are the individuals who are resolved to social class, phase of life, and family. Yet, he who is without all worries is a master hard to discover.

An insightful man ought to pick a master by whose contact the incomparable Bliss is achieved, and just such a master and none other.

The Tantras list extra characteristics to be searched for in a genuine instructor. To refer to the Kula-Arnava-Tantra once more:

O Beloved, he whose vision is steady without object, whose psyche is [equally firm] without help, and whose breath is steady without exertion is a master.

He who truly knows the arrangement of the standards of presence (tattva) from Shiva down to the earth component is esteemed a preeminent master.

O Beloved, he who truly knows the character of the body (pinda) and universe (brahma-anda), [the mystery about] the head, and the quantity of bones and hairs is a master, and none other.

He who is gifted in the eighty-four unmistakable stances, for example, the lotus stance and who realizes the eightfold Yoga is esteemed an incomparable master.

The "master work" fundamentally comprises in continually and steadfastly reflecting the supporters back to themselves, while simultaneously reinforcing their instinct of a definitive Reality, the supernatural Self. In view of this double angle, the master's work with supporters is both a destruction work and a remaking. From the followers' point of view this is troublesome yet in addition fulfilling. In his book Secret of the Siddhas, Swami Muktananda makes reference to how when he finally got the initiatory mantra from his teacher, the incomparable Bhagavan Nityananda, it delivered in him both "internal warmth and the coolness of delight."

The self-image character, braced by duplicate fortified habit designs, is independently impervious to change, particularly the sort of radical change imagined in Tantra. In this way, notwithstanding solid faith in the teacher, all the while, and in themselves, teaches likewise should grasp self-change through persistent control. The master can lead their supporters to the everlasting wellspring, yet can't make them drink the solution. Both beauty and self-exertion are expected to achieve freedom.

Faith in one's instructor develops into affection (bhakti). At whatever point Swami Muktananda, who was himself an incredible proficient, discussed his darling master he would unavoidably break into appreciative recognition and verse:

Just when I lost myself in the bliss of Nityananda did I

understand what his identity was? He is the honey of adoration which emerges when everything, conscious and insentient, gets one. He is the magnificence of the world. He swarms all forms, cognizant and latent. He is the brilliant sun, the moon, and the stars in the sky. He skips and influences with adoration in the blowing of the breeze. His awareness flickers in people. There is just Nityananda, only Nityananda. He is the ecstasy of the Absolute, the joy of the Self, the euphoria of opportunity, and the happiness of adoration. There is just love, love, only love.

To land at such an acknowledgment, Swami Muktananda needed to discharge the grasp of the ordinary self-image character. Just when one is happy to drop all egoic boundaries can the "master work" accomplish its transformative work. Then the master, as Being-Consciousness-Bliss, progressively manifests in oneself. This is the reason Kshemaraja in his Shiva-Sutra-Vimarshini talks about the "teacher as the signifies" (master upaya, writtenguru-paya). This helps one to remember the acclaimed expressions of the organizer of Christianity who, as indicated by the Gospel of John, announced: *"I am the way, reality, and the life."*

The objective isn't being gulped by the teacher's character however converging with their actual nature, which is the solitary Reality that likewise is one's own actual nature. At the end of the day, when the master has prevailing with regards to dispersing one's inward darkness, the qualification among teacher and devotee, way and objective, and even freedom and servitude blurs. There is just the widely inclusive delighted Reality. As the Maha-nirvana-Tantra confirms:

One appreciates freedom when one realizes that the Self is the Witness, the Truth, the Whole (purna), all unavoidable, nondual, incomparable, and however living in the body, isn't body-bound.

Information on the Self (atma-jnana), O Goddess, is the main way to conclusive freedom. He who realizes it is genuinely freed right now. There is no uncertainty about that.

Chapter Seven

Bringing Down The Light (Initiation)

When one has discovered an instructor who motivates faith and expectation, one ought to modestly and officially approach that person mentioning commencement. As per an old Vedic convention, the hopeful ought to bring "fuel sticks" as an indication of his (or, around then incredibly infrequently, her) internal availability to have the sense of self consumed to cinders. However, since this is the absolute most significant advance for an spiritual searcher to take, a portion of the Tantras prescribe that one should first cautiously examine one's imminent teacher, taking, if essential, as long as twelve years to do as such.

The Tantric specialists don't authorize irrationalism in issues of spiritual life, on the grounds that such a great amount of is in question. Apprenticeship includes a deep rooted responsibility, or if nothing else until one has accomplished freedom oneself. The Tantras are very straightforward about the characteristics that one should search for in a master. Consequently the Sharada-Tilaka-Tantra announces:

A decent supporter aim on the most noteworthy human reason [i.e., liberation], who has an pure aura, sanitized comparative with mother and father and with his faculties controlled, should fall back on a gum.

[The instructor should] comprehend the substance of the considerable number of Agamas, know the truth behind all the reading material, and be committed to serving others, just as be caught up in recitation, revere, etc.

[The instructor ought to be] somebody whose words are not futile, quiet, gave to the Vedas and the import of the Vedas, developing the Yoga way, and contacting the core of the gods.

One who is blessed with such characteristics is regarded by the Agamas to be a master.

As indicated by the sixteenth-century ShrT-Tattva-Cintamani, the master ought know mantras and yantras as well as, more significantly, have understood the deepest Self (adhyatman) and consequently have a serene mind and be a completely practiced (siddha). As the Kula-Arnava-Tantra underscores:

A knower of Truth (tattva-vid), despite the fact that he might be deficient with regards to all recognizing qualities, is known as a master. Thus a knower of Truth alone is freed and a savior.

He who knows the Truth, O Great Goddess, can light up even a "monster" (pashu).1 But how might somebody coming up short on the Truth handle reality with regards to the deepest Self?

The individuals who are educated by knowers of Truth without a doubt become knowers of Truth. In any case, those, O Goddess, who are educated by "brutes" are known as "monsters."

Just he who has been punctured [by the Truth] can

penetrate others, O Goddess. But he who has not been penetrated can't be a piercer. Just he who is freed can free one who is bound. In what function can he who isn't freed be a hero?

The Tantric specialists stress the significance of obtaining a master who is a piece of a built up instructing genealogy. "The divinities," expresses the Kula-Arnava-Tantra, give assurance just to those instructors who safeguard a genealogy (parampara). The Sanskrit word parampara implies truly "consistently," alluding to the whole progression of instructors, all connected by the engaged lessons went down the line from teacher to student. A similar Tantra encourages searchers to search for an instructor who has a place with a solid transmission (arichinna-sampradaya) starting with the incomparable Being - Parama-Shiva - itself.

An ancestry resembles a continuous electric flow that doesn't reduce in power, at any rate not except if there is a feeble connection. At times when the transmission has gotten interfered with, an extraordinary ace embodies to restore the lessons and the educating genealogy. A notable model is that of the Buddhist ace Asanga, who, accepting lessons straightforwardly from Buddha Maitreya, prevailing with regards to resuscitating the lessons of Mahayana. Unexpectedly, Asanga's kin Vasubandhu was generally far-fetched of his senior sibling's case to have been educated by Buddha Maitreya himself. However the shrewdness pouring forward from Asanga before long altered Vasubandhu's perspective and mentality.

Another model, inside Hindu Tantra, is that of Matsyendra Natha, the originator of the Yogini part of the Kaula custom.

As indicated by legend, as told in the Kaula-Jnana-Nirnaya, Lord Shiva himself granted the Kaula mysteries to his child Vatuka Karttikeya (the god Skanda), who out of numbness tossed the mysterious content into the sea. Then Shiva protected the heavenly book by executing the fish that had gulped it. He shrouded it in a mystery place, however it was taken by Kruddha (Skanda), accepting the say of a mouse. Again it was thrown into the sea, and this time it was gulped by a fish of immense size. Shiva, expecting the type of the angler Matsyendra Natha, made a net woven by Shakti, got the beast fish, and again recouped the lessons of the kula-agama (custom of the Mama).

The customary accentuation on the significance of genealogy is particularly pertinent in our cutting edge Western setting. As I have said previously, Neo-Tantrism is all around a hand crafted development whose teachers have not gotten the lessons and the going with deep transmission inside a perceived heredity. There is an incredible preferred position in having a place with a settled genealogy, since it contains certain protections against debasement. A genealogy is a chain of bona fide instructors who give their insight and strengthening to qualified pupils (who become teachers thus). The nearby bond among master and supporter, which generally proceeds past the grave, stays flawless just insofar as the devotee (regardless of whether the person has become a spiritual expert in their own right) safeguards the honesty of the transmission, both as to the oral lessons and the deep transmission got. To certify this progression, the tantrikas remember for their day by day practice the proper adoration of their quick master as well as the paramaguru (teacher's instructor), the parapara-master's (teacher's instructor), other heredity teachers, and not least the root master, or author of the ancestry.

At whatever point a master gives a devotee authorization to educate, this implies the individual has been made a decision about skillful to instruct and give the lessons to other people. Every master has a duty toward the ancestry all in all and is in this way anxious to safeguard its uprightness, which is the reason authorization to educate is never given delicately. The destiny of the individuals who defy this norm is said to be not freedom but rather numerous years in the hellfire domains.

Similarly as a hopeful ought to be reasonable in their quest for a master, so the instructor ought to inspect the appealing to searcher with equivalent consideration, because the exclusive lessons must not be bestowed to an unfit wannabe. To offer inception to an inadmissible individual isn't just futile to the pupil yet additionally amazingly perilous to both devotee and teacher. As the Kula-Arnava-Tantra says:

Information granted to false teaches lacking commitment becomes debased like dairy animals' milk blended in with canine's fat.

If one starts - out of dread, ravenousness, or for money related meditations - somebody who is unfit, one welcomes the scourge of divinities and the demonstration is pointless.

The Kula-Arnava-Tantra prescribes testing a searcher for a time of a quarter of a year to a year. The master, this sacred text proceeds to say, ought to during this trial period turn around everything in issues concerning life, cash, surrender, orders, etc. As such, the person should deceive the searcher, who, then again, must comprehend the teacher's insane conduct as beauty. The wannabe ought to never dismiss the genuine purpose behind the teacher's upsetting activities, in any event, when the master has all the earmarks of being brutal, apathetic, and one-sided. The content incorporates being pulled about and beaten by the instructor.

The mysterious arranger of the Kaula-Avali-Nimaya offers the dismal expression that fools who study its lessons without having acquired them from a master will kick the bucket, and every one of their moves will make them directly to hellfire. However, inception offered appropriately to a solid and steady supporter, as indicated by the Shr-Tattva-Cintamani, is equipped for expelling the transgressions collected in heap lives. The content further says that inception will empower a brahmin to accomplish brahma-loka (brahmic domain), an individual from the warrior home to achieve the domain of Indra, an individual from the dealer home to accomplish the domain of Prajapati, and an individual from the servile bequest to achieve the divine domain of spirits. Different Tantras don't separate the product of commencement along these social lines however insist that anybody, paying little heed to their societal position, can arrive at the most significant standard of freedom if properly started. Indeed, the Tantric custom from various perspectives restricted and undermined the inflexible social form of Hinduism, and most early teachers of Tantra originated from lower positions.

As indicated by the Mahanirvana-Tantra, the conventional solicitation for inception may take the accompanying form:

O caring one! Master of the pitiable! To you I have desired shelter. O you who are wealthy in notoriety, cast the shadow of your lotus feet upon my head!

Having along these lines implored and loved the master as per his best function, the follower ought to stay before him peacefully with collapsed hands.

This sort of supplication suggests that the applicant has experienced a lot of heart looking and is presently prepared to submit to a thorough order and the teacher's direction. The individual in question may have had a few contacts with the forthcoming master and may even have been tried in different manners. In any case, in some cases a teacher may choose to test a searcher's responsibility further by over and over declining to start that person. Understudies of Tantric Buddhism know about the notable story of Milarepa, who looked for guidance from Marpa however first needed to achieve one Herculean assignment after another. Marpa's instructor Naropa was in like manner seriously tried by his master, Tilopa. However, these people had incredible spiritual capability (adhikara) and were consequently ready to persevere through all the numerous tests, which in a way were then some portion of their preparation. As a rule, in any case, a master will be unmistakably progressively indulgent and, expecting the supplicant meets the essential capabilities, won't retain inception unduly. All things considered, veritable instructors are rarely selfish yet are ever moved by a longing to advance a definitive welfare of others.

THE INITIATION RITUAL

The Sanskrit word for "inception" is diksha. In his Para-Trishika-Laghu-Vritti, Abhinava Gupta etymologically connects this term with the words dana (giving) and kshapana (wrecking). Inception decimates the bonds that keep the pupil in numbness and gives the person in question self-information (sva-pratiti) prompting freedom. The Kula-Arnava-Tantra clarifies diksha as that which gives the celestial condition (divya-bhava) and wipes away character recolors, the most exceedingly awful of which is deep ignorance. Sometimes the word abhisheka (sanctification) is used synonymously with diksha, however in certain settings it indicates a different function, which held either previously or after inception.

Progress on the deep way is believed to be slow or even

incomprehensible without inception. As Shiva is made to say in the Mantra-Yoga-Samhita:

O Goddess! There can be no success or a decent predetermination for one who needs inception. Along these lines one should bend over backward to get inception from a master.

When a competitor has been acknowledged for inception, the instructor may precipitously start that person on the spot. As the Mantra-Yoga-Samhita reminds us, the master is legitimate (svadhma) and enriched with all forces. It is increasingly normal, however, for an instructor to fix a spot and time for a formal initiatory custom. Frequently inception happens at the teacher's home, however here and there the master inclines toward an exceptional blessed site, for example, a sanctuary, place of worship, cavern, or on the banks of a sacrosanct stream. The banks of the Ganges are believed to be particularly favorable.

Since the time the hour of the Buddha, the graveyard (shmashana) has been another supported spot, especially of the adherents of the left-hand way and certain Kaula schools of Tantra. As Mircea Eliade remarked:

The job that the graveyard (smasana), together with reflections performed while sitting on a body, plays in various Indian austere schools is notable. The imagery is regularly stressed in the writings: the burial ground speaks to the totality of psychomental life, bolstered by awareness of the "I"; the cadavers symbolize the different tangible and mental exercises. Situated at the focal point of his profane understanding, the yogin "consumes" the exercises that feed them, similarly as carcasses are singed in the graveyard. By meditating in a smasana he all the more straightforwardly accomplishes the burning of narcissistic encounters; simultaneously, he liberates himself from dread, he summons the horrible evil presences and acquires dominance over them.

The adepts of the Aghorl faction, a radical left-hand school of Tantra, are acclaimed in India for frequenting burial grounds, taking skulls, and in any event, devouring bits of bodies. Their way of life is a distinct show of the inversion of qualities pushed in Tantra and tries to commute home the point that Reality rises above ordinary ethical quality.

The aghorins, as the experts of this antinomian convention are called, are celibates and for the most part carry on with an existence of radical renunciation. Their precursors, the Kapalikas, in like manner enjoyed whimsical works on including the burial ground, yet they were orgiastic as opposed to plain. The name kapalika signifies "skull conveyor" and alludes to the custom of these starts to convey a skull that capacities as a nourishment bowl. In his collection of memoirs The World of Tantra, Brajamadhava Bhatta-charya remembers an episode that occurred in 1934. While submerging his recently perished sister's body in the Ganges for a last bathing toward the day's end, he saw a skeletal figure of a man distressing the scorched survives from a cadaver he had angled out of the water. Bhattacharya was both stunned and nauseated. Tired from the day's occasions, he slept close to the burial ground doors. Starded by something, he sluggishly opened his eyes and found a similar man, an aghorin, situated before him. Bhattacharya, who had been started into Tantra at an early age, arrived at deep inside himself to stifle the rising dread. Then the aghorin moved him to beat his critical psyche. Abruptly, he pushed Bhattacharya over, situated himself on his chest, and began to recite mantras. Subsequent to spitting on and all around Bhattacharya's body, he vanished into the night as fast as he had come. Bhattacharya never found a clarification for that remarkable episode, yet without a doubt some type of inception or favoring had been given.

It is conceivable that commencements in the burial ground were very normal in the beginning of Tantra. This ought not to shock us, since Tantra began around and around outside the brahmanic universality, at the edges of society, where various ideas of virtue won. Almost certainly, the soonest instructors of Tantra were frequently ladies, particularly the individuals who earned their occupation as washerwomen (dombi).

Bhattacharya's first master and initiator was a lady, the "Woman dressed in Saffron," who was a coconut merchant and clearly a Tantric capable of no little success. His memories read like an experience novel. She lived without anyone else, avoided mingling, however inquisitively developed a close connection with the youthful brahmin kid who numerous years after the fact would compose the previously mentioned book and numerous others, including a two-volume history of Shaivism.

Any place the master may decide to concede the commencement, including the burial ground, that spot ought to be viewed as consecrated, suitable, and lucky. As the Mantra-Yoga-Samhita attests, there is nothing better than the master, whose word is similar to disclosure.

In picking the correct time, a master may turn to soothsaying, which is an antiquated art in India. The Mantra-Yoga-Samhita gives definite guidelines about the propitious and unfavorable visionary signs and yearly seasons. By and large the greatest month is regarded to be Caitra (March), and sun powered and lunar obscurations are viewed as especially favorable. The time must match the particular divinity and its mantra, which will be granted during commencement. The Vina-Shikha-Tantra favors the fourth, fifth, ninth, and particularly the eleventh days of the month.

One day before commencement, the supporter must refrain from sexual movement, and the person in question may likewise be required to watch certain preliminary ceremonies, for example, fasting and meditating the teacher's lotus feet. As per the Mantra-Yoga-Samhita, on the day going before commencement, the teacher should tie the student's topknot (shikha) while discussing a mantra for dreaming (svapa-mantra), which the follower must recurrent thrice before resting. The mantra runs as follows:

Deference, triumph to the Three-Eyed One, to Pingala, the Great Self. Deference to the all inclusive Rama, Lord of Dreams. Come clean with me in my fantasies totally about what can anyone do. By my effortlessness I, Maheshvara [i.e., Shiva], give on you the intensity of activity.

On the morning of the day of inception, the devotee tells the master his fantasies. The accompanying dream pictures are believed to be positive: a young lady, umbrella, chariot, light, royal residence, lotus, waterway, elephant, bull, wreath, sea, tree with organic product, mountain, horse, conciliatory meat, wine, and alcohol. The last three assume a significant job in left-hand Tantra and furthermore on the Kaula way. As dream pictures, they will undoubtedly have a to some degree distinctive noteworthiness in a Western setting, where these substances are generally used in a common manner. The instructor, as well, will plan for the commencement. The individual in question may, as the Vina-Shikha-Tantra stipulates, remain up throughout the night persistently discussing a mantra for security.

In deciding the correct mantra for a forthcoming pupil, the teacher resorts to their natural information on the devotee's character and spiritual fate, yet may likewise utilize different conventional diagrams (called cakra). Since the mantra is the very pith of the god that from this time forward forms the rotate of the supporter's spiritual practice, it is generally essential to grant the right mantra. The Mantra-Yoga-Samhita portrays in some detail the kula-akula-cakra, which organizes the fifty letters of the Sanskrit letters in order as indicated by the five material components.

It permits the instructor to bestow the best possible mantra relating to the follower's character. For example, if the master has verified that the amateur's basic character has a place with the ether component, then it is suitable to start the person in question into the puzzle of Shiva and subsequently grant one of Shiva's mantras, for example, om namah shivaya. The earth and water components are esteemed well, just like the fire and wind components, while the ether component is thought perfect with all others. Hence it is conceivable to give a mantra that isn't drawn legitimately from the letters found in the segment indicating the pupil's trademark component however from any of the letters recorded in the section of the perfect component.

Since specific days and even hours of the day are related with explicit gods, the master may defer commencement until that time. For each situation, however, the crucially significant element of commencement is the teacher's real strengthening of the devotee. Mantras that are not enabled are considered nearly, if not totally, pointless.

The Vina-Shikha-Tantra depicts how the teacher plans a lovely mandala with hued powder, having four doors at the cardinal bearings. The individual then makes different contributions and pictures the fundamental divinity and different gods, just as defenders. When the holy space has been made and the applicant has been appropriately refined, the master welcomes the competitor into the mandala. Typically, the teacher faces east or south, with the start inverse, however the Mahanirvana-Tantra has the instructor confronting east or north, with the pupil on the left.

Further representation and rital revere occur, lastly the instructor trains the novice in the starter methods of love, the basic lessons of the school, and at times likewise in the specialty of breath control and reflection. Subsequent to reprimanding the start to keep the mantra completely mystery, the master at last bestows the mantra the person in question has chosen for the amateur. Typically, the mantra is murmured into the correct ear and is rehashed multiple times. The Mahanirvana-Tantra, in any case, endorses that the mantra ought to be murmured multiple times into the correct ear of a brahmin devotee and into the left ear of followers of every other home or ranks. This is an indica tion of the variety in principle and work on existing between the different schools.

The service frequently finishes with the new devotee

doing a full-body surrender before the teacher who, as indicated by the Mahanirvana-Tantra, should articulate:

Rise, darling, you are freed! Be given to the information on the Absolute (brahma)! May you generally act naturally controlled, honest, solid, and sound!

A similar Tantra clarifies that when the follower has gotten the mantra, their general existence is suffused with the divinity. From now on, loyal to the master, the supporter wanders the world "like a god." This implies the seed for the making of the "divine body" (divya-deha) has been planted.

Subsequent to making a contribution to the master of organic product, cash, or their own being, the supporter once in a while circumambulates the master multiple times clockwise. Then the person in question will get a portion of the nourishment that was offered to the divinities during the service, and finally the pupil is required to go to the sanctuary to love in appreciation.

THE DESCENT OF DIVINE POWER

Commencement has numerous forms, contingent upon its motivation and the specific custom or school. As indicated by Swami Agehananda Bharati, the contemporary Natha request recognizes three sorts of inception: Yoga-diksha is commencement into certain yogic practices in which no mantra is given. Upayoga-diksha is commencement into mantra practice for purposes other than Self-acknowledgment. Jnana-diksha is commencement into astuteness with the assistance of a mantra, prompting ones close to home acknowledgment of a definitive Reality.

Another qualification made in the Tantras is between the

samayi-diksha (ordinary inception) and the putraka-diksha (commencement of a child). The previous centers on the refinement of the supporter and comprises of an assortment of customs, of which the Tantra-Sara portrays no less than forty-eight. The last inception lifts the follower, or spiritual "child" (putraka), on the double into a more significant level of awareness, just by the master's beauty. It is commonly conceded simply after that says of the other kind of commencement have been satisfied.

The Shri-Tattva-Cintamani groups inception into trick bhavi-, shakteyi-, and mantn-diksha. The first is inception that happens unexpectedly just due to the instructor's beauty and by uprightness of their accomplishment of Shivahood (shivata); it gets powerful through the master's insignificant look, contact, or spoken word. A notable model is that of Swami Vivekananda, who entered the condition of transconceptual joy (nirvikalpa-samadhi) when his master, the incomparable Rama-krishna, planted his foot on the clueless supporter's chest. The second type of diksha utilizes the proficient's internal force (shakti). The third and most reduced form is inception by methods for a mantra.

The Sharada-Tilaka-Tantra talks about four sorts of inception:

1. Kriya-vati-diksha - inception by methods for ceremonial exercises for every single common pupil; this all around matches with previously mentioned mantri-diksha.
2. Varna-mayi-diksha - commencement comprising in the teacher's putting the letters of the Sanskrit letter set into the supporter's body and in this way arousing the intensity of sound in that person, prompting the

enlivening of the intensity of Consciousness.

3. Kala-atma-diksha - commencement comprising in the teacher's putting the kalds (inconspicuous types of energy) into the supporter's body and in this way arousing their function.

4. Vedha-mayi-diksha - commencement by "penetrating," in which the master concentrates their brain on the supporter's serpent power (kundalini-shakti), stirs it in the psychoenergetic focus at the base of the spine, and behaviors it securely to the middle at the crown of the head, in this way offering on the devotee the endowment of freedom. As indicated by the Kula-Arnava-Tantra, "penetrating" (vedha) may make the pupil experience extreme joy, real tremor, an impression of reeling, a feeling of being reawakened, abrupt deep rest, or blacking out.

The last three modalities are conceivable just on account of remarkable deep specialists, who have had a lot of readiness right now past lives. Raghava Bhatta, in his critique on the Shar-ada-Tilaka-Tantra, makes reference to that the renowned proficient Utpaladeva was started in the fourth design by the extraordinary ninth-century ace Somananda.

The Kashmiri schools of Shaivism have their own fourfold order conspire, while the Kula-Arnava-Tantra records seven sorts of inception. Different groupings are additionally known, yet these are largely fundamentally the same as. What they share for all intents and purpose is the agile transformative organization of the awesome Shakti. Regardless of whether the start will understand a definitive Reality on the double or just bit by bit relies upon their planning and limit.

The initiatory procedure is commonly depicted as including what is called shakti-pata, which means truly "plunge of the force." This articulation is to some degree misdirecting, on the grounds that the celestial Shakti is inescapable and doesn't have to go anyplace. However, from the perspective of the unliberated individual there gives off an impression of being a plummet of elegance, followed at the appropriate time by the climb of the kundalini-shakti, which likewise is a type of the perfect Power. As the Kula-Arnava-Tantra puts it, through the play of Shakti the "monster" (pashu) is changed into Shiva. A similar book likewise says:

O Beloved! Similarly as iron transforms into gold when infiltrated by mercury, so oneself accomplishes Shivahood when it is entered by commencement.

When karmas are singed by the fire of inception, the shackles of maya are cut off. One who is without [karmic] seed and has achieved the incomparable say of astuteness becomes Shiva.

The start doesn't have to achieve anything through plainness, rules, or promises, nor by going to consecrated spots or by controlling the body.

Yet, O Beloved, the recitation, love, and different customs of the individuals who are unenlightened bear no foods grown from the ground like seed planted on rock.

Due to the superlative significance of inception, the Tantras consistently encourage deep searchers to discover an instructor who will start them. As we have seen, the master is Shiva, and as Shiva the person comes completely outfitted with Shakti. As indicated by the Sadyojyoti editorial on the Svayambhuva-Sutra-Samgraha, a definitive Reality (Shiva) shows as knowledge (jnana) and inception (diksha), and both are of the idea of Shakti. Like the instructor, the pupil is obviously likewise Shiva-Shakti however isn't in contact with this fact. During commencement, because of the puzzling speculative chemistry of Consciousness and Energy, the devotee is reconnected with that more deep degree of their being. From that point on, the Goddess unyieldingly pounds away at the numerous layers of polluting influence clouding the start's inward vision. Dependent upon the follower's cognizant cooperation by methods for consistent control, this cleansing procedure will eventually prompt illumination, or freedom.

The Svayambhuva-Sutra-Samgraha proclaims:

Commencement alone discharges one from the broad subjugation impeding the incomparable Abode and leads upward to the Abode of Shiva (shaiva-dhdman).

However, "upward" signifies additionally "descending" and "corner to corner," since a definitive Reality is wherever simultaneously, or no place whenever. As the Svayambhuva-Sutra-Samgraha itself recognizes:

A way is a street to be voyage. However there is no such street to the Lord, and there additionally is no doable movement for the Spirit (pums = purusha), because both are ubiquitous.

Freedom is consistently the situation, and through the procedure activated by inception this fact will occur to on us when the brain has become worn out on developing an elective reality. Up to that point we will either remain totally trapped in the snare of the extraordinary restricting intensity of maya or battle to remove ourselves bit by bit through deliberate spiritual order.

Chapter Eight:

Discipleship

The Tantras, as we have seen, have firm thoughts regarding the certifications of an authentic teacher. They are similarly explicit about the capabilities or ability (adhikara) of a decent pupil (shishya). The Sharada-Tilaka-Tantra, for example, records the accompanying qualities:

The follower ought to be noble,1 of pure self, aim on the [highest] human reason, very much read in the Vedas, capable, concentrated on being freed at the appropriate time; he ought to be ever generous toward [all] living creatures, conventional, liberated from unconventional perspectives, holding fast to his own obligation (sva-dharma), affectionately endeavoring to regard his dad and mom; he ought to be partial to tuning in to the teacher in issues of body, discourse, and psyche, liberated from vanity about instructors, status, information, riches, etc; what's more, he ought to be set up to yield his life so as to comply with the master's requests, surrendering his own arrangements and continually getting a kick out of working for the teacher.

The last stanza specifically makes stipulations that cutting edge mainstream readrs will discover alarming. Removed from its consecrated setting or followed by sincerely juvenile devotees it without a doubt should caution us. Inside a conventional system, however, such complete compliance to the master is intended to fill in as a vehicle for the catalytic procedure among instructor and follower. The more shishyas drop their egocentric inspirations, feelings, and exercises, the more they can copy the master's inward say for themselves. What's more, this isn't any misfortune yet rather an incalculable addition. The shishyas don't become frail willed, careless zombies who just duplicate the instructor. Or maybe, they are called to understand their actual nature through a procedure of self-understanding, self-greatness, and self-change that is essentially special for every person.

The Kaula-Jnana-Nirnaya supplements the above-refered to depiction by disclosing to us who is undeserving of the initiatic astuteness granted by the master:

O Goddess, my Beloved, this incomparable kaula [teaching] must not be advised to the individuals who need dedication to the kula and are without commitment to the teacher, nor should the fundamental kaulika [Kaula teaching] be given to understudies who are seen as moderate witted, nor to the beguiling, the forlorn, the stupid, the lacking, or those disdaining reality.

One ought not to give this beauty to the individuals who loathe gods, fire, or religious zealots. Those instructors who give this [secret teaching] to such understudies will miss the mark regarding flawlessness.

Yet, proceeds with the Kaula-Jnana-Nirnaya, those teachers who confer the freeing shrewdness upon appropriately qualified followers will be enduring. This announcement implies the incredibly close association among master and shishya. When inception has been in all actuality, instructor and supporter are, in the expressions of a contemporary ace, "joined at the hip." The master in a way bolsters the devotee with their own life substance, and if it is wasted on a contemptible student, the teacher's life is believed to be abbreviated. Hesitant or in any case undeserving supporters are a channel on the master's energies. If the teacher is completely edified, the person will consistently have a boundless store of deep energy (shakti) to draw from, however this energy isn't really unreservedly accessible for the upkeep of the instructor's physical body. Indeed, the negative energy of a disgraceful devotee goes about as an impedarkent for the instructor. If the blockage is sufficiently extreme, the instructor may even desert the body to proceed with their spiritual work somewhere else, giving the devotees on the physical plane the chance to mature through the harsh times of life.

PRECONDITIONS FOR THE TANTRIC PATH

As a result of inception by a certified teacher, the deep searcher gets changed into a pupil. This is a significant change, which requires the devotee to pick mindfulness over obviousness, obligation over carelessness, and reality over self-hallucination. A basic piece of this new life is the appropriation of the deep control prescribed by the master. This is the yogic way or what the Tantras call sadhana. As I have clarified in the presentation, this Sanskrit expression is gotten from the verbal root sidh ("to be cultivated"), which additionally shapes the words siddhi ("success," "fulfillment," or "flawlessness") and siddha ("he who is practiced/culminated").

Etymologically, the word shishya, for the most part deciphered as "student" or "follower," implies somebody who is being educated or taught. The Kula-Arnava-Tantra clarifies it as somebody who commits body, riches, and life energies to the master and learns (shikshate) from the instructor. The word originates from the verbal root shas, which additionally shapes the words sasha ("order"), shasana ("guidance"), shastra ("guidance" or "reading material"), and shastrin ("researcher"). Strangely, the equivalent verbal root likewise means "to reprimand." This passes on the nearby relationship of instruction with preparing and restorative discipline (danda), which is additionally present in the English word "discipline." Most teachers, I would presume, have managed hard-headed trains just by disregarding them or requesting that they leave the withdrawal (ashrama) or religious community (matha). In any case, convention likewise is aware of teachers who didn't stop for a second to manage physical discipline to wayward or sluggish understudies. For contemporary Westerners, who work with solid substantial limits, the possibility of physical rebuke is loathsome. Hence this reformatory strategy is additionally probably not going to be viable. However when concentrating customary records we should value their diverse social setting. All the more critically, we should remember that every single veritable master have consistently been intensely mindful of the amazingness of the ethical uprightness of nonharming (ahimsa). If, in former occasions, they depended on physical discipline by any means, it was with the long-extend vision of intelligence.

This is flawlessly represented on account of the Buddhist Tantric ace Marpa, who is known to have been liberal with blows for his followers. In any case, it was exactly his wild nature that drew out the best in his understudies. His unpleasant treatment of Milarepa even incited Marpa's significant other to dissent, yet it demonstrated helpful to this star student, who is affectionately recognized as probably the best ace. Much after Milarepa had immovably achieved edification, he despite everything kept on applauding his master with significant appreciation. In one of his tunes, hats Marpa therefore:

Implore, consistently recall me, this oblivious supporter! Ask grasp me ever with your incredible empathy!

As indicated by the Sharada-Tilaka-Tantra, the premier commitment of the supporter is to overcome the "six foes," in particular, want, outrage, ravenousness, dream, pride, and jealousy. These are the equivalent qualificab tions that the Tantras determine for an appropriate wannabe. No mystery is included here, on the grounds that the master is completely mindful that if an individual were to have every one of these temperances, the person would as have now be illuminated and never again needing commencement and guidance. What the teacher, in this way, is truly searching for in the pupil is the general nonappearance of negative feelings and mentalities and the nearness of at any rate a small amount of understanding and a solid will to change and develop deeply. A follower ailing in these ideals will, as the Mantra-Yoga-Samhita puts it, simply bring distress (duhkha) to the teacher.

Without in any event the craving for freedom, the student isn't just improbable to embrace the troublesome assignment of self-change however will undoubtedly encounter a lot of dissatisfaction and trivial hardship. The craving for freedom is known as mumukshutva, which is appeared differently in relation to bubhukshutva, or the longing for common experience only. In Tantra, obviously, both these driving forces are not decisively hopeless. The Tantric proficient who has understood a definitive character of the universe of progress and the supernatural Reality - samsara and nirvana - is both freed and able to do deep satisfaction on the planet. In any case, for the apprentice, the test is to conquered experience and find more prominent take pleasure in spiritual facts.

To this end, the Tantric experts recommend for their understudies a pretty much thorough course of controls, called sadhana. This shifts from school to class, or genealogy to ancestry, yet it commonly includes an entire scope of practices, strikingly mantra recitation, supplication, custom love, and representation. These different components of the Tantric way will be talked about in more subtleties in the accompanying sections. Here I am chiefly worried about the subject of how they identify with apprenticeship when all is said in done.

All parts of sadhana are intended to work on the devotee's customary thoughts and intuitive propensities. Consequendy this procedure is of the idea of a sacrosanct difficulty that must be persevered. It is hard for us contemporary Westerners, who will in general fear torment similarly as we are frightful of malady and demise, to get a handle on the basic justification of the initiatory procedure. We are slanted to take a gander at the amazingly grim existence of yogins and joginis somewhat with pompous beguilement and mostly with dread. Why, we ask ourselves, would they need to go to such length to rebuff themselves?

Yet, what we see as insignificant self-embarrassment may be, for the starts, an essential control of self-constraint by which they activate a lot of internal energy coordinated toward the extreme transmutation of the character. The Tantras at times utilize the old term tapas (particular case) to portray this consecrated trial. The word signifies "sparkle" or "heat" and is broadly used in the feeling of "plainness" or "somberness." In Vedic cosmogony, tapas is the procedure whereby the first Singularity (eka) duplicated itself, bringing forth the many-layered universe with its heap forms.

Therefore a definitive Reality itself is thought to have intentionally experienced the trial of selflessness so as to make the universe. All creation includes a component of such selflessness, and in this way it is likewise present in apprenticeship, which can be comprehended as a complete re-formation of oneself, or the making of another character. Carefully, the new character that the follower decides to make or find is truly not new by any means, yet is the first and interminable Identity everything being equal and things, called atman, or "Self." Only for the unenlightened passerby trapped in the relativity of room time is there the presence of progress. For the edified being, illumination is the acknowledgment that there has consistently been and will consistently be just the one equivalent Reality, or Self-Identity.

Apprenticeship, then, is simply the procedure whereby a person who esteems oneself unenlightened, or bound, understands that freedom is consistently the situation. This enlivening is reliant on self-filtration, that is, on cleaning the reflection of the brain. The whole round of freedom or servitude is sanctioned on the phase of the brain. Unenlightenment involves being oblivious of what is in every case valid for us. Apprenticeship involves unlearning how we consider ourselves and reality on the loose.

Another method for talking about this major numbness (avidya) is to say that we are ordinarily trapped in the snare of our thoughts regarding everything. Those thoughts thusly shape our perspectives, which will in general solidify into propensities or inclinations. It very well may be somewhat hard to change a thought, however to free oneself of a habit can now and again represent an apparently unfavorable issue. Regularly we are even very ignorant of our routine perspective and our social inclinations.

Spiritual apprenticeship is intended to bring both into our mindfulness, and the master - suddenly or something else - tries to undermine all the habit designs that dilemma the supporter to the dream of being a different element disconnected from all others by the skin hung around fragile living creature and bones. The instructor isn't essentially keen on whether the devotee likes zesty nourishment or super cold beverages, inasmuch as these inclinations are not constant checks to their enlivening. On a basic level, however, the master anticipates that the follower should totally rebuild their life, since then all the habit designs are tossed into unmistakable alleviation for prepared self-assessment. Not having the option to eat zesty nourishment or appreciate super cold beverages can incite an emergency and lead to noteworthy bits of knowledge into one's character (or habit designs).

The master nudges the supporter any place connection (sanga) makes a block to self-understanding and self-amazing quality. Connection is the huge hindrance, at any rate connection to common things. Tantra doesn't consider common things evil in themselves, as they also are Shiva. The issue with connection to them is essentially that we experience them as outside to ourselves, and consequently they ceaselessly strengthen our bogus self-way of life (as the restricted sense of self character instead of the widespread self). The tantrikas don't look to disperse the energy present in connection in that function, however they divert it to a definitive Reality. When connection to Shiva (or Shakti) surpasses every single other connection, freedom is close within reach.

Tantric experts attempt to accumulate every one of their energies into a laser shaft concentrated on the Divine. All the numerous methods and approaches of Tantra fill this need. They fall into two general classes, as has been plainly articulated in the Yoga-Bhashya, which portrays dispassion (vairagya) and deep practice (abhyasa) as the bipolar methods for achieving freedom. All types of Tantric control (sadhana) contain both these parts of the holy work prompting internal immaculateness (shuddhi). "In the cleaned mind," expresses the Mahanirvana-Tantra, "information on the Absolute is induced." The Absolute (brahman) is Shiva, who is endless Being-Con sciousness-Bliss. Dispassion is nonattachment. In the expressions of the

Kula-Arnava-Tantra:

Nonattachment (nihsanga) alone is [the means] of freedom. All imperfections spring from connection. In this way one gets upbeat by forsaking connection and depending on Reality.

Practice is basically self-decontamination. Until the minute when gnosis first lights, the professional must be totally ready to bear this cleansing procedure, which is sanctioned altogether in the pupil's psyche. It comprises in voiding one's psyche of every unclean idea (ashuddha-vikalpa). In the normal follower, commencement may bring a quick, if just transitory, instinct of the brilliance of a definitive Being, yet won't evacuate unclean ideas for all time. Or maybe, the experience of duality, which denotes the unenlightened say, will speedily return. This, thusly, offers ascend to the various factors by which we keep up ourselves in the condition of unenlightenment.

However the master's effortlessness - spiritual transmission - conferred during inception will have opened the entryway to edification, giving the devotee loyally receives the purificatory disciplines. The master's beauty likewise is accessible to the supporter as immediate guidance. On this point the Mantra-Shiro-Bhairava (as cited in the Shiva-Sutra-Vimarshim says: "The master's function inhabitant in the master's mouth is more prominent than the master himself." at the end of the day, the master is a vehicle of beauty - a gift power that surpasses his individual information and abilities. The Tantras all around recognize progression of training as one of the most significant components of a fruitful sadhana. As the Yoga-Sutra stresses, practice must be developed uninterruptedly and over an extensive stretch of time. Just a prepared teacher can tell how rapidly, or gradually, a devotee may be fruitful on the way. It is, in any case, considered reasonable not to overestimate one's abilities and to be completely arranged to practice for any time allotment.

Tantra regularly introduces itself as the brisk way, and the sacred writings guarantee accomplishment following a specific number of years, regardless in any event during this lifetime. Yet, this consistently surmises the professional has the essential karmic preconditions and is equipped for Herculean effort. Along these lines "brisk" signifies "as fast as feasible for someone in particular." Similarly, the tantrikas at times talk about their way as "simple," yet this too is a relative term. It is simple just to the extent that different ways are regarded unacceptable for the Dark Age (kali-yuga) and in this way require a greater amount of their professionals. Tantra, as I have clarified in the presentation, was from the start explicitly intended for the requirements of spiritual searchers in the present Dark Age. In light of the general deep and good decadence of the kali-yuga, those naturally introduced to it are now off guard; henceforth, as the Tantras encourage, they should depend on the most intense lessons: the Tantric legacy.

In evaluating the wellness (jogayata) of their devotees, the Tantric adepts recognize the accompanying three dispositional types, or demeanors (bhava):

1. The pashu-bhava (brutal character) is the aftereffect of the solid exchange of rajas and tamas (the dynamic and inertial characteristics of nature), with very nearly a total nonappearance of sattva (clarity factor). This game changing mix creates such unwanted

characteristics as daydream (bhranti), enervation (tandra), and sluggishness (alasya). However only one out of every odd individual of this sort will fundamentally show these inclinations. As indicated by the Kula-Arnava-Tantra, the pasbu is bound by eight bonds (pasha), to be specific, disdain, question, dread, hesitance (lajja), disturb, family, custom, and station. It would not be hard to apply these to a contemporary Western setting.

The mental youthfulness liable for these attributes precludes specialists of the "brutal" demeanor from specific customs and practices. They are required to embrace an increasingly ordinary way to deal with spiritual life and are especially avoided from the custom of the "five substances" (panca-tattva). As indicated by the Kaula-Avali-Nirnaya, they ought to not even intellectually partake right now. Rather they should bend over backward to serve the master so as to filter their foreboding characteristics. The "brutal" disposition isn't consistently clarified in the Tantras, apparently on the grounds that many, if not most, specialists fall into this classification. Frequently the term pashu indicates professionals who practice Tantra in an increasingly ordinary manner, which is, treating the "five substances" - meat, fish, wine, grain, and sex - truly instead of allegorically. Quite, instead of real sacrosanct intercourse with ladies starts, male specialists make a contribution of two sorts of blossoms speaking to the male and female sexual organ individually.

2. The vira-bhava (brave character) is the result of the

interchange of prevalently rajas and sattva, with insignificant obstruction from tamas. As indicated by the Mahanirvana-Tantra, specialists of this demeanor alone are reasonable for the act of Tantra. This sacred writing even prevents the presence from securing the other two dispositions in obscurity age, yet this looks bad, since the attributes of the "savage" personality seem across the board.

3. The divya-bhava (divine character) is likewise the result of the interchange of rajas and sattva, however with the last quality prevailing. Specialists who have this exceptional character are uncommon, particularly in the kali-yuga. The distinction of this character from the gallant demeanor is by all accounts one of degree, with the last being increasingly unique, which suits the Tantric methodology well.

Tantra is the way of the spiritual legend (vira), who is characterized as follows:

Since he is liberated from energy, pride, pain, outrage, jealousy, and hallucination, and because he is far expelled from rajas and tamas [i.e., the characteristics of unsettling and inertia], he is known as a "hero."

As per the Kaula-Avali-Nirnaya, the brave expert has gone past the play of alternate extremes in the psyche. This is a significant necessity, taking into account that Tantra regularly utilizes unpredictable implies that may some way or another entangle the specialist in sentiments of blame or clumsiness. The Tantric hero must be invulnerable to social dissatisfaction or exclusion and solidly remain on the way paying little heed to any resistance or difficulty. In obscurity age, pronounces the Mahanirvana-Tantra, just the chivalrous control (vira-sadhana) bear's unmistakable organic product. For this sacred text, the courageous order is that of the unmistakable Kaula School, which I will present in the following part.

Chapter Nine:

The Tantric Path

The Tantric way unfurls as a play between liquid responsiveness to the regular difficulties of sadhana, or spiritual control, and adherence to the customary types of one's specific school or heredity. The circumstance is equivalent to playing a virtuoso bit of traditional music, where imaginative self-articulation happens inside the general form of the melodic score. Most schools of Tantra are exceptionally formal, however it is comprehended this must not slaughter the pupil's suddenness, without which internal development couldn't occur. The various observances and customs that are vital to the Tantric way are expected to balance out the professional's mind and strengthen their will.

In the past part I have portrayed the capabilities of a supporter, which are significant. Not exclusively should the Tantric start have incredible quality of will and character, however the person should likewise exceed expectations in faith (shraddha). When commencement has been in truth, one ought not to question the viability of master and instructing, nor is the truth of freedom and one own deep potential. Faith, which is no insignificant visually impaired conviction, is a deep level, high-energy perspective. The Bhagavad-Gita expresses that faith is as per the very embodarkent of an individual. "Whatever his faith is," this sacred text announces, "that verily is he." The Yoga-

Bhashya compares faith to a mindful mother, since it secures the jogin and yogini. Vacaspati Mishra, creator of the Tattva-y Vaisharadi, talks about faith as "the base of Yoga." The Shiva-Samhita watches:

Success goes to an individual of faith and fearlessness, yet there is no accomplishment for other people. Henceforth practice hard.

The main indication of progress is certainty that [one's efforts] will prove to be fruitful. The second is by and large firm in that faith; the third is love of the master;

The fourth is poise (samata-bhava); the fifth authority over the faculties; the 6th is moderate eating; there is no seventh.

After faith, dedication to the instructor (master bhakti) is the absolute most significant practice and uprightness. The explanation behind this necessity ought to have gotten evident at this point. Without such dedication, the instructor is probably not going to move cognizance energy to the follower in the Tantric inception custom or, a short time later, transmit the fundamental lessons and screen the pupil's advancement both on the physical and the unobtrusive levels. The connection among master and follower is obviously not a business game plan but rather a sincere association. Similarly as the teacher is totally devoted to arousing the student, the devotee must be happy to draw in this procedure by developing adoring respect for the instructor. It is through the pipeline of affection and commitment that spiritual transmission streams. This must not be mistaken for love or sentimental fascination. Dedication to the master, most importantly, comprises of deep regard and appreciation.

The third part of sadhana is sincere application to all the controls given by the teacher, anyway troublesome, self-assertive, or muddled they may appear. The teacher has no motivation to trouble the pupil with a pointless program of self-filtration. Likely the gum will prescribe a strategy that has borne natural product in their own case, and the individual in question additionally will consider the devotee's needs and capacities cautiously. Milarepa was given the evidently silly task of building a pinnacle just to have it torn down over and over. This was Marpa's method for helping his supporter to free himself of the unfavorable karma he had procured as a previous dark performer.

Basic faith, commitment to the instructor, and application to the way involve the crucial understanding that the Divine is ubiquitous and that one along these lines must be aware of the Truth in all conditions. It is information, regardless of whether created through self-exertion or beauty or both, that is freeing. Ceremonies, mantras, and the various practices are helper implies. They are intended to expel those variables from the focal point of the psyche that contort Reality. "In the cleaned heart," announces the Mahanirvana-Tantra, "information on the Absolute develops." While the Tantric methods are various, information or insight is solitary, much the same as the Reality that it uncovers.

If information or astuteness is the real freeing specialist, then for what reason would it be a good idea for one to need to focus on some other practices? Tantra itself incorporates a "noninstrumental" (anupaya) approach, a pathless way. Here the plummet of elegance consequently and expeditiously expels the cover of obliviousness. Western understudies are normally attracted to this easy way, however they should understand that this works just for those not very many who have the vital preconditions. All others have generally been encouraged to cleanse themselves properly by methods for whatever regular practices might be endorsed by the teacher. In themselves those assistant controls are not freeing. As per the tenth-century Tantric ace Abhinava Gupta, the appendages of Yoga can, best case scenario lead to the elated say in which the contemplator accomplishes distinguishing proof with the glorified object of thought (e.g., the imagined divinity), however not with the item itself. At the end of the day, they are not finally freeing, since they neglect to stir pure ideation (shuddha-vikalpa), which springs legitimately from one's fundamental nature.

Without a teacher, who has extraordinary knowledge into the supporter's qualities and liabilities, there is the ever-present threat of overestimating one's deep limit. Western understudies, who will in general be eager, effectively fall prey to self-daydream. They may practice the pathless way or "direct methodology" for a considerable length of time, maybe subsequent to reading a book or going to a discussion or workshop, and become persuaded they have accomplished a high ff **

condition of acknowledgment. In actuality, their fulfillment is as a rule mental. Apprenticeship would rapidly disperse their wrong self-recognition. As one author watches, "much after long stretches of exertion, moderately barely any individuals using the immediate methodology figure out how to get past the rudarkentary phase of stilling the brain for a brief period."

In any event, when one has gotten shakti-pata - and there are these days various teachers offering commencement to everyone - there still stays a lot of work to be done by and large. Some imagine that since they have been allowed commencement they can proceed individually, unrestricted by the desires and requests of a master. This in itself shows an absence of status and the requirement for guidance and teaching. During shakti-pata everything may without a doubt be given, however whether a searcher can utilize this enlivening admirably or at all is another issue.

Information on the Truth itself is the path however, as the Kula-Arnava-Tantra confirms, along these lines must be uncovered by a certified instructor. This sacred text additionally says:

The shrewdness of kula sparkles forward, O Goddess, in an individual whose contaminations have dwindled through past severities, good cause, penances, journeys, recitation, and promises.

The shrewdness of kula sparkles forward, O excellent Goddess, in one who satisfies both you and me in light of his commitment to god and teacher.

The shrewdness of kula sparkles forward in one who is

pure disapproved, serene, drew in, committed to the teacher, extremely reverential, and covered up [i.e., fit for practicing without causing to notice oneself).

THE TANTRIC PATH IN OUTLINE

The Tantric way changes from school to class. Throughout the hundreds of years the Tantric experts have built up various sadhanas, all of which have driven specialists to higher acknowledge and perhaps even freedom. For example, the Buddhist Sadhana-Mala depicts 312 particular sadhanas, or projects of love, total with perceptions, mantras, and customs. It has been evaluated that 80 percent of the topic in the Tantras manages custom, and this gives one a decent feeling of the common Tantric methodology. The customs include both outer ceremonies and what is known as the "internal penance" (antar-yaga), which is oneself rising above disposition to be kept up in all regards. Together these two sorts form an exhaustive Yoga of self-change. A few Tantras benefit themselves of the notable model detailed in the Yoga-Sutra of Patanjali, who outlined in concise axioms the accompanying eight "appendages" (anga):

1. Yama - moral restriction comprising of nonharming, honesty, nonstealing, modesty, and greedlessness, which are said to be substantial on all levels, consistently, and all over

2. Niyama - patience through immaculateness, satisfaction, starkness, study, and dedication to the Lord

3. Asana - act, which makes the professional insusceptible against the attack from the sets of alternate extremes (dvandva, for example, warmth

and cold or dry and wet

4. Pranayama - lit. "Expansion of the existence energy" by methods for breath control

5. Pratyahara - tactile restraint

6. Dharana - focus, or fixing one's consideration upon a chose object, be it a mantra or the realistic portrayal of a divinity

7. Dhyana - reflection, which is an extending of focus set apart by a dynamic unification of cognizance

8. Samadhi - lit. "Assembling," or joy, which comprises in one's finished converging with the object of meditation.

The Sharada-Tilaka-Tantra, an up to this point untranslated Sanskrit content, gives an extended understanding of the eight appendages that contrasts from the definitions proffered by Patanjali in noteworthy regards. For example, it remembers for the class of good restriction five extra prudent practices, in particular, empathy, integrity, tolerance, strength, and moderate eating, and rather than greedlessness names tidiness (shauca). Raghava, the fifteenth-century analyst on this Tantra, has fascinating citations that show how these ideals are applied. Consequently want is aced by methods for nonharming and modesty; outrage by methods for empathy and persistence; insatiability by methods for nonstealing, honesty, and integrity; hallucination by methods for moderate eating and tidiness; pride by methods for tolerance and integrity; desire (or jealousy) by methods for nonharming, sympathy, integrity, and tolerance.

The classification of patience, once more, is extended to remember conviction for the hallowed custom, good cause, love of the gods, tuning in to the lessons, unobtrusiveness, acumen, recitation of mantras, and ceremonial contributions.

Besides, while Patanjali recommends no specific stance, the Sharada-Tilaka-Tantra singles out the accompanying five to delineate the class of asana: lotus act, svastika act, jolt act, promising stance, and saint's stance.

Pranayama and pratyahara are clarified along progressively regular lines. The previous is characterized as inward breath through the left channel (ida) for sixteen units, maintenance for sixty-four units while managing the existence power into the focal channel (sushumna), and exhalation through the correct channel (pingala) for thirty-two units. Breath control can be with seed (sagarbha) or without seed (vigarbha), that is, with or without going with mantric recitation.

Withdrawal of the faculties, once more, is clarified as the powerful pulling back of the wandering faculties from their individual articles.

This Tantra, besides, clarifies dharana as one's holding the indispensable air (prana-marut) in different areas of the body, for example, the toes, lower legs, knees, thighs, perineum (sivani, lit. "Suture"), penis, navel, heart, neck, throat, uvula, nose, between the eyebrows, temple, top of the head, and the mysterious spot twelve digits over the head. This procedure evacuates deterrents in the unobtrusive channels (nadi) and upgrades the progression of the crucial power, which thus centers the brain and along these lines allows a developing distinguishing proof with one's meditational god.

Dhyana, once more, is characterized as consideration of one's picked god as the extremely Self. In Tantra, this training commonly represents thoughtful representation in which one's god accept a similar distinctiveness.

As a distinct difference to Patanjali, the Sharada-Tilaka-Tantra clarifies the term samadhi as implying the steady examination of the equality between the individual mind (jiva) and a definitive Self. This definition outlines the nondualistic transcendentalism of this Tantra and is a significant purpose of contrast with Patanjali's Yoga, which is customarily held to be evidently dualistic.

In no way, shape or form do all Tantras buy in to the sort of exacting nondualism that, for example, denotes the Mahanirvana-Tantra. Truth be told, the more firm nondualistic transcendentalism is a genuinely late advancement inside Tantra. For instance, the Agamas of South India favor a to some degree progressively dualistic mysticism, making an understood qualification between the Lord and his creation. Early Tantra seems to have slanted toward the sort of qualified nondualism that additionally portrays the lessons of numerous Upanishads. In the Kula-Arnava-Tantra Shiva himself advises us that eventually such differentiations have a place with the limited domain and involve sentiment:

Some pick nondualism, others pick dualism. In any case, they realize my Reality as rising above dualism and nondualism.

On the degree of training, these philosophical

differentiations are generally very unimportant. While the applicant is occupied with the way toward getting edified, there consistently is a pretty much articulated feeling of duality or extremity, with the professional taking a gander at the Divine, or the Self, as the object of love and yearning. Before illumination, the human heart appears to require an adjust conscience for its outpourings of adoration and a target establishment for its expectation and longing. Indeed, even propelled experts, who mentally comprehend and furthermore have a solid instinct of the Divine as their own fundamental nature, may at present decide to rehearse dualistic love. Indeed, even such an extreme nondualist and dynamic rationalist as Shankara, who is likewise recognized as a quintessential Tantric skilled, made excellent songs to the Divine as God and Goddess, however a few researchers have challenged his initiation of these works.

While Patanjali's eightfold way compliments itself as a general composition, it doesn't represent various remarkably Tantric highlights. Supposedly, these have never been exhibited in an organized manner in the Tantras, thus it appears to be helpful to give an unpleasant form here. The accompanying practices, which are not really found in all schools, are to be comprehended as supplementing the eight appendages of Yoga:

1. Preliminary filtration: (a) cleaning of oneself mostly by methods for the cleansing of the components (bhuta-shuddhi); (b) filtration of the spot of custom or spiritual practice by cleansing until it resembles a flawless mirror and by brightening it with blossoms, festoons, incense, camphor, and lights; (c) filtration of the primary mantra by connecting the mantra to

the letters of the letter set both in forward and turn around request; (d) cleaning of the ceremonial substances by sprinkling water on them while discussing a purificatory mantra and making suitable representative hand motions (outstandingly the dhenu-mudra); (e) decontamination of the picture of the god by sprinkling water and recounting the foremost mantra (which is the quintessence of the divinity).

2. Primer practice (purashcarana) is embraced so as to fit the bill for full sanctification (purna-abhisheka) and comprises in broad reiteration of mantras to evacuate checks and develop energy for representation (dhyana) and custom. In the Kula-Arnava-Tantra, notwithstanding, this training is described as follows: "Th e adore at the multiple times [i.e., sunrise, early afternoon, dusk], day by day recitation, water offering (tarpana), penance, and encouraging of brahmins are called preparation."5 This sacred text likewise considers starter practice the five-limbed love (panca-anga-upasana), which should be possible in pure areas, on riverbanks, caverns, mountain tops, journey centers, intersections of waterways, sacrosanct forests, betrayed gardens, the foot of bilva trees, mountain inclines, sanctuaries, the coastline, and one's own home.

3. Purashcarana can likewise be drilled to turn away threat or battle sick wellbeing. For each situation, the mantra is presented a thousand times or more. An occasion of this in Buddhist Tantra is the recitation

of the mantra of Vajrasattva, which amateurs are approached to perform multiple times. The Mahanirvana-Tantra sanctions 32,000 reiterations of a mantra. The Kan-kala-Malini-Tantra prescribes the starter mantric practice on certain promising days, when it ought to be done from first light to sunset. Then again, it proposes that one should pick quickly and rehash the mantra an aggregate of multiple times. The Vma-Shikha-Tantra prescribes 1,008 redundancies to render a mantra "incomparable," that is, to fortify it. This kind of mantric practice, which potentiates the mantra and readies the psyche for the rigors of full apprenticeship, covers with the classification of preliminary filtration.

4. Mantra recitation is the general methods for Tantra.

5. Development of a mandala (or yantra) filling in as the divinity's seat is a significant part of the Tantric ceremony. The development makes sacrosanct space that is appropriately ensured against unwelcome elements and negative energies.

6. Nyasa is the custom imbuement of life power into an item, including one's own body, by which it is divinized.

7. Mudra likewise is a significant part of sadhana in numerous schools. It alludes to hand motions used during ceremonies.

8. Devata-puja is the love of one's picked divinity. This includes the accompanying methods: setting up a seat (asana) for the god; inviting the person in question; washing the feet; offering unboiled rice, water, milk,

nectar, blossoms, shoe glue, durva grass (a sort of millet grass), fabric, gems, scented things, incense sticks, nourishment, and different substances; introducing water for washing; waving lights; and supplication. Love additionally incorporates the fire penance (homa), which returns to Vedic occasions.

Substances are offered into the fire, which then conveys them to the divinity in purged form.

9. Master puja is the custom love of the instructor, who is treated as an exemplification of the Divine. This distinctions the instructor as well as reinforces the spiritual connection among master and devotee. Without the instructor, their shoes (paduka) are used as a substitute during this custom.

10. Dakshina is the sayly present for the instructor. The blessing is representative of the correspondence without which deep transmission can't happen. It is an indication of the devotee's willful accommodation to the spiritual procedure as started and kept up by the master.

11. Yatra alludes to journey to sacrosanct places or force spots where the professional can encourage their sadhana. For Tantric specialists the most significant sacred destinations are those that were blessed by a body some portion of the Goddess. As per Tantric folklore, as told in the Kalika-Purana, Shiva's better half, Sati (i.e., Devi), immolated herself subsequent to being offended by her dad, Daksha. Shiva was so melancholy at her demise that he meandered capricious around the earth conveying her dead body on his shoulders. The gods entered the body and

discarded it piece by piece. Any place a body part would fall, the ground got consecrated. These locales are classified "seats" (pitha), and the writings notice from 4 to 108 such hallowed spots. The most regarded are commonly acknowledged to be Oddiyana in northwestern India, Jalandhara in the Punjab, and Kamarupa (or Kamakhya) in Assam. The last-referenced is believed to be particularly ground-breaking since it is the resting spot of Devi's privates (yoni). However, since the body reflects the cosmos, all journey communities can be found inside it also, and henceforth a few Tantras suggest the internal journey along the hallowed stream SarasvatI (i.e., the focal channel) to the sacrosanct conversion of the two waterways Ganges (Ganga) and Yamuna (i.e., ida and pingala) at the spot of the ajna-cakra.

12. Vrata signifies "promise" and comprises in different observances, notably the durga-puja, or day by day love of the goddess Durga, which is known as the "incredible pledge" (maha-vrata). In addition, the professional may make certain promises (samaya, for example, fasting or remaining conscious for a specific timeframe so as to strengthen their sadhana.

13. Lata-sadhana, or "order of the creeper," is an uncommon aspect of left-hand Tantra and the Kaula custom.

14. Protective special necklaces or spells (the two of which are called kavaca, "defensive layer") assume a significant job in certain schools of Tantra. Here and there these are related with the planets, which are comprehended to be unmistakable types of energy in

cozy relationship to explicit gods. The Kirana-Tantra contains directions for penances to the nine planets (nava-graha). Every divinity is requested of to secure a specific piece of the body, a training referenced in the Varada-Tantra. The Sadhu-Sam-kalinT-Tantra (refered to in the Prana-Toshani) specifies kavacas for every day of the week. These ornaments are associated with their own planets and gods and are to be affixed on the neck or the correct arm (for men) or left arm (for ladies).

15. Alphabetic outlines (cakra) are used to figure out which mantra is appropriate for a professional. The Kula-Arnava-Tantra specifies six such charts: akathaha-cakra, otherwise known as dama-cakra, nakshatra-cakra, rashi-cakra, rini-dhana-cakra, and kula-akula-cakra.

16. The obtaining and exercise of paranormal forces (siddhi) for white and dark enchantment is practically all inclusive in Tantra.

17. The start's day by day plan regularly involves the accompanying practices: cleansing of the components; mixture of the existence power (nyasa), by which the body is changed into a celestial body; mental and physical love of one's picked divinity, complete with a fire penance (homa); and mantra recitation. Whatever outer customs might be played out, the psychological segment (through serious representation) is rarely missing and is the urgent factor. Ceremonial requires a high level of fixation and unprecedented meticulousness, and consequently the people of certain schools respect a

sadhaka with nearly a similar wonderment as an illuminated ace.

Custom love (puja) is commonly isolated into four kinds. The most minimal sort is held to be what comprises in outside acts including either a statue or image of a divinity or its theoretical portrayal as a yantra or mandala. Fairly higher is revere including mantric recitation and the singing of songs of recognition (stava). The following higher class is yogic thought of one's picked god, and the most noteworthy form is recognizable proof with the Divine in which there is no otherness. A popular stava is the Mahimna-Stava, whose creation is credited to Pushpadanta (Flower-Toothed), the pioneer of the melodic spirits (gandharva). It is a wonderful tribute to the enormity (mahimna) of Shiva, who is summoned as the supplier of enduring satisfaction and the master all things considered. Another well-known Tantric psalm, attributed to Shankara, is the Ananda-Lahari, a tribute to the Goddess whose influxes of ecstasy wash over the dedicated specialist, evacuating each hint of transgression. Fundamentally associated with this work and furthermore credited to Shankara is the Saundarya-Lahari, which is the most adored content of the Shrl-Vidya convention. Of specific intrigue additionally is the Kashmiri song Panca-Stavi (c. 900 CE), routed to the Goddess as Tripura, who is lauded as the "mother of the universe."

One last feature of custom love should be referenced. When an expert submits a custom tactless act, the person should instantly address the blunder by a suitable appeasement ritual known as prayashcitta. Contingent upon the gravity of the error, this kind of therapeutic activity can comprise in the recitation of a mantra or a mind boggling custom.

As can be seen, Tantra embraces an exceptionally ritualized way of life. Its motivation is to center the specialist's consideration as solely as conceivable on their sadhana, leaving next to zero space for preoccupation. However, as I noted toward the start of this section, this form must not squelch the unconstrained unfurling of the deep procedure, which is remarkable to every person. The specialist must realize when to push more enthusiastically and when to dial down and furthermore when to stick carefully to the conventional guidelines and when to follow the promptings of the inward intelligence. When edification is achieved, every customary thought and rules are risen above and life is lived suddenly out of the completion of Being.

THE RULE OF SECRECY

Mystery is a significant part of Tantra and numerous other spiritual conventions. The Kaula-Avali-Nirnaya, for example, requests that the lessons are kept as deliberately disguised as a mother would sex. The elusive explanation behind this necessity is that by discussing the initiatory procedure or one's deep encounters one disperses energy. Aside from this, by uncovering Tantric mysteries to the unenlightened one is probably going to welcome objection and hostility, especially concerning the left-hand rehearses. Also, the Tantric information will simply bring calamity upon the individuals who are not prepared for it. A few Tantras ensure serious karmic ramifications for starts who uncover the privileged insights of their custom to contemptible beneficiaries.

This standard of mystery appears to remain as opposed to an astonishing proclamation discovered twice in the Mahdnirvana-Tantra, which expressly proclaims that when the kali-yuga has become solid, the Tantric way ought to be drilled straightforwardly, without disguise. This presumes, however, a great domain for the act of Tantra. In its announced liberal soul, the Mahanirvana-Tantra does without a doubt uncover numerous beforehand mystery ceremonies, which can now promptly be contemplated by anybody. However it is guileless to imagine that the content that today is broadly accessible in interpretation contains all the insider facts of sadhana. In addition, without inception none of the ceremonies are compelling. This bears some assurance to those searchers who need to take in Tantra from books.

Aside from the trouble of appreciating the importance of the Tantric writings without access to the living custom, there is an additional obstruction for noninitiates digging into the Tantras. This is the "nightfall language" (sandhya-bhasha). A secretive time of day, nightfall is particularly accused of intensity - both for good and for abhorrent - and hence starts have since antiquated occasions performed uncommon customs at day break and sunset (just as the progress point around early afternoon). The nightfall language is consequently a language of intensity that at the same time lights up and darkens. Its similitudes make a rich setting while simultaneously disguising to the untouchable the genuine importance. As Lama Anagarika Govinda, a start of Buddhist Tantra, wrote:

This representative language isn't just an insurance against the profanation of the hallowed through scholarly interest and abuse of yogic techniques and clairvoyant powers by the oblivious or unenlightened, yet has its starting point for the most part in the way that regular language is unequipped for communicating the most noteworthy encounters of the soul. The indefinable that must be comprehended by the start or the experiencer must be alluded to through analogies and mysteries.

Instances of sandhya-bhasha are:

Vajra (lit. "Jolt") = linga (lit. "Mark," phallus) =

Shunya (void)

Surya (sun) = rajas (menstrual blood) - pingala (right channel) = right nostril

Avadhuti (female renouncer) = sushumna (focal channel) = prajna (intelligence)

Samarasa (lit."Same taste,"unitive say) = copulation = breath maintenance = mental centering = capture of semen

The expression sandha-bhasha, found in some Tantric writings, has caused some perplexity and an enthusiastic discussion in academic circles. A few specialists comprehend it as an abbreviated type of sandhaya-bhasha, signifying "purposeful language." Since the sacred writings utilize both sandha-and sandhya-bhasha, we may accept that if their significance isn't ientical, it is in any event not totally unrelated either. Regardless, the two terms allude to something very similar, which, in Mircea Eliade's words, is "a mystery, dull, equivocal language in which a condition of cognizance is communicated by a sensual term and the jargon of folklore or cosmology is accused of Hatha-yogic or sexual implications."

RIGHT, LEFT, AND BEYOND

Since Tantra is such a perplexing custom, its instructors have from the get-go searched for approaches to arrange it so as to make it all the more effectively fathomable. Along these lines they developed the possibility of heredity conventions (amnaya), seats (pitha), and flows (srota). The most popular division of the Tantric legacy is into the three classes of right-hand way, left-hand way, and Kaula way. These generally relate to a specific mode or style where Tantra is polished.

The right-hand way (dakshina-marga) is the thing that can be called traditional (samaya) Tantra. Specifically, this methodology comprehends the Tantric center custom of the "five substances" (panca-tattva) in an emblematic instead of strict way. The word dakshina implies both "right" and "south." This double importance is promptly clarified by the way that when confronting east (the cardinal custom heading), south is to one's right side. As indicated by one convention, all lessons gave from the five essences of Shiva, and some traditional specialists attempted to relegate certain Tantras to each face. Every one of these blueprints, in any case, are woefully insufficient when we take a gander at the tangled chronicled truth of Tantra.

The purported left-hand way (vama-marga), associated with the north, is much of the time described as spinning around the obtaining of siddhi in the double feeling of "flawlessness" (i.e., freedom) and "force" (i.e., paranormal function). There is an especially solid enchanted current going through the schools of the left-hand way. Practically all the Tantras of this branch have been lost, and we know some of them just by name. The left-hand schools are those that are most remote expelled from standard (Vedic) Hinduism, involving the edges of Hindu culture and society.

The right-hand way (dakshina-marga), emblematically connected with the south, has from numerous points of view remained nearby to the Hindu universality. It stays away from fanatic practices and looks to maintain the Vedic social request. It is otherwise called dakshina-acara or "right-hand lead." According to the Prana-Toshani, everybody has a place with this way by birth and can enter the left-hand way just through appropriate commencement, however this thought isn't generally acknowledged. For example, the Kula-Arnava-Tantra recognizes seven sorts of "direct":

1. veda-acara - the Vedic lifestyle (customary Brahmanism)
2. vaishnava-acara - the lifestyle of the Vishnu admirers
3. shaiva-acara - the lifestyle of the Shiva admirers
4. dakshina-dcdra - the right-hand approach
5. vdma-acara - the left-hand approach, which particularly in• volves sacrosanct intercourse with a sanctified lady (vama)
6. siddhanta-acara - the Siddhanta lifestyle, which is characterized as a higher type of the left-hand way, stressing internal love
7. kaula-acara - the Kaula approach, which is presented as the most noteworthy type of spiritual practice and

as an amalgamation of the left-hand and right-hand schools of Tantra.

These seven kinds form a stepping stool of spiritual fitness, with the Kula or Kaula approach at the zenith. "There is nothing better than kaula," proclaims the Kula-Arnava-Tantra. The content proceeds:

O Goddess! The kula is the most mystery of privileged insights, the pith of substance, the most noteworthy of high, given straightforwardly by Shiva, and transmitted from ear to ear [i.e., orally]

The Kaula part of Tantra started maybe in the fifth century CE and accomplished incredible unmistakable quality three or after four centuries. It speaks to a blend of the dakshina-and vama-marga and created a noteworthy number of adepts and various sacred texts, a significant number of which, in any case, have been lost. This genealogy of transmission (santati) is comprised of numerous schools and subschools, which are still deficiently comprehended.

A significant early Kaula school, that rotating around the love of the goddess Kubjika, has delivered numerous Tantras, of which more than eighty are known by name. The name originates from the Sanskrit word kubja, signifying "warped," a reference to the serpentd energy of the kundalini in its latent function say, preceding arousing.

Kaula, or Kaulism, as this Tantric stream is at times called, immediately turned out to be practically synonymous with Tantra in the north of the subcontinent. By the thirteenth century, the incredibly persuasive Kaula convention had likewise infiltrated numerous schools of

South India's Siddhanta custom.

What denotes the Kaula part of Tantra is a solid nearness of the shakti component in both hypothesis and practice. One appearance of this is the lessons about the serpent power (kundalini-shakti); another is the way that ladies have constantly assumed a critical job in Kaula hovers both as Tantric consorts and, all the more essentially, as initiators. As per one grouping, the Kaula convention is partitioned into Yogini Kaula and Siddha Kaula schools; the previous is transmitted by female adepts (jogini) and the last by male adepts (siddha). Kaula highlights can likewise be found in numerous other Tantric customs, outstandingly the Shri-Vidya convention of South India and the Krama convention of Kashmir.

A significant Tantric religion is that of the sixty-four Yoginis, to whom a few roundabout sanctuaries are committed. The most popular sanctuary is the one situated at Khajuraho, where it is the most established form, going back to 600 - 800 CE. Khajuraho is a famous vacation destination as a result of the unequivocal sexual stone carvings on the dividers of various forms of this complex in Madhya Pradesh. Of the numerous clarifications offered for what some have named "lustful iconography," Michael Rabe's is the most persuading. He finds in these realistic delineations depictions of the paradisaic joys anticipating the rulers who requested and supported the development of such sanctuaries. The sanctuaries themselves are natural models of heaven (svarga).

The Yoginis, loved as gods, were initially most likely female adepts and initiators into the insider facts of Tantra. Their number is as deeply representative as the sixty-four

Tantras said to exist as indicated by certain writings. The figures of the Yoginis are masterminded around the focal picture of Shiva (either as a human statue or in theory type of a linga).

A few sacred writings additionally notice sixty-four Bhairavas (types of Shiva) and sixty-four Kalas (parts of the incomparable Goddess). In this manner the number 64 is as significant and hallowed to Tantra as the number 108 is to other Hindu customs.

One of the extraordinary bosses of Kaula Tantra was Matsyendra Natha, who is credited with establishing the Yogini Kaula branch. He likewise is customarily held to be the instructor of Goraksha Natha, the maker of unique Hatha Yoga. However, the two experts seem to have been isolated in time by a few centuries. Except if we expect the presence of another adroit by the name of Matsyendra who lived in Goraksha's period, we are left with the yogic accomplishment of brain to-mind transmission as the main other clarification.

The term kula has twenty or so unmistakable lexicographical implications, the essential ones being "gathering," "family," or "large number." Technically, kula alludes to a definitive Reality, which is past the supernatural standards of Shiva and Shakti. In any case, numerous schools and messages utilize the term kula to mean the "astronomical family," that is the show universe and the force natural in it, in particular, Shakti. As the Mahanirvana-Tantra says:

The individual mind (jiva), the standard of nature,

space, time, ether, earth, water, fire, and air are called kula.

O Primordial one! Kula-acara is rehearsing shapelessness (nirvikalpa) by perceiving the Absolute {brahman) in them, which produces excellence, riches, joy, and freedom.

So also, akula, signifying "what isn't the kula" is now and then used to allude to the Shiva guideline, rather than the preeminent Being.

The word kula can likewise represent the condition of joining among Shiva and Shakti and, by coherent augmentation, to the delight emerging from this association. Finally, the exclusive gathering where the Kaula lessons are polished additionally bears the name kula.

The individuals who seek to the acknowledgment of a definitive kula are called kaulas or kaulikas. Thus the name of this Tantric branch is either Kula or Kaula. The last word is clarified obscurely in the Kula-Arnava-Tantra in this manner:

It is called kaula because it confines youth (kaumara, etc, on the grounds that it disperses birth, passing (laya, etc, and on the grounds that it is associated with the entire kula.

As indicated by Abhinava Gupta's Tantra-Aloka, the author of Kaula Tantra was the proficient Macchanda (assumed name Mina). He may have been an Assamese ruler related with the Tryambaka part of early Tantra and is here and there related to Matsyendra.

Chapter Ten

The Subtle Body And Its Environment

Wedged between our recognizable material universe and a definitive Reality are the various layers of unpretentious (sukshma) presence. In their undertaking to arrive at the One, the Tantric specialists unavoidably should navigate those middle of the road domains, which are imperceptible to customary sight yet in any case as genuine (or stunning) as the material world. The possibility of an unpretentious element of presence can be discovered as of now in the antiquated Vedas and is shared by many, if not most, other spiritual and strict conventions. These inconspicuous domains are viewed as the home of divinities, familial spirits, and different elements, including different sorts of terrestrial wicked creatures (called bhutas, or "elementals").

We consistently take an interest in the unpretentious component of presence, however we by and large stay unconscious of it. Numerous adepts, in India and somewhere else, have underlined that our unmistakable universe is extraordinarily impacted by the powers present in the unpretentious universes. Inasmuch as we are not aware of these powers, we are at their kindness. In this manner Tantric professionals are asked to ensure themselves against unfortunate obstruction consistently, and particularly during the presentation of customs. One method for achieving this is by developing the companionship and help of creatures in the inconspicuous domains, who then expect the job of defender. This is done through supplication as ordinary ceremonial contributions and, at a further developed degree of training, through brain to-mind correspondence. A part of this security against undesirable impact from the soul world is the creation - both intellectually and graphically - of a blazing encompass enclosing the holy space, or mandala, in which the Tantric ceremonies are performed.

Extraordinary Tantric adepts (maha-siddha) regularly have an entire entourage of defenders, who have a place with different degrees of the unpretentious measurement. Since defenders can be viable just in their own unobtrusive condition, everyone has a particular job and function. Insurance is especially vital at the most reduced degrees of inconspicuous presence, to which defenders of higher unobtrusive domains by and large don't approach, however they may have their own chain of importance of subprotectors for assignments to be done on those levels. Yet, this subject is only occasionally examined straightforwardly and requires inception.

THE SUBTLE VEHICLE

Let's take an interest in the unpretentious component of presence. The appropriate response is straightforward: through our own unobtrusive energy field and the psyche. These are regularly treated as independent "bodies" (deha, sharira) or "sheaths/holders" (kosha), yet a few schools see them as establishing a solitary form named ativahika-deha (superconductive body), antah-karana (inward instrument), or puryashtaka (eightfold city).

The possibility of at the same time existing various bodies having a place with a solitary individual returns to the Taittinya-Upanishad, which was created 3,000 years back. This sacred writing recognizes five "sheaths," or envelopes, covering and logically disguising a definitive Reality:

1. Anna-maya-kosha, or "sheath made out of nourishment," is our recognizable physical body, by which we explore in the material world.

2. Prana-maya-kosha, or "sheath made out of life power," is the energy field related with and supporting the physical body. It is the associating join between the physical body and the psyche.

3. Mano-maya-kosha, or "sheath made out of the psyche," alludes to the brain in its lower work as a processor of tactile information. Manas is driven by uncertainty and volition (or want) and sways between externalizing our awareness and pulling back it into the domain of creative mind. This part of the brain is represented basically by the components of latency (tamas) and dynamism (rajas).

4. Vijndna-maya-kosha, or "sheath made out of insight," alludes to the psyche in its higher function as an organ of acumen between what is genuine and stunning, that is, as the seat of knowledge. Where the lower mind causes uncertainty and vulnerability, the higher brain

(frequently called buddhi) additionally brings conviction and faith, just as a feeling of stillness, although the clarity factor (sattva-guna) is prevalent in it.

5. Ananda-maya-kosha, or "sheath made out of euphoria," is compared in the Taittinya-Upanishad with the supernatural Self (atman) itself, however resulting Vedanta schools believe it to be the last cloak encompassing a definitive Reality, or Self. Regardless, ananda (ecstasy) must not be confused with an enthusiastic say, which is progressively higher than intellection or insight (vijnana). Feelings have a place with the anna-maya-and prana-maya-koshas.

1. While this age-old quintuple model isn't regular of Tantra, Tantric starts completely receive its utilitarian qualifications of body, mind, life power, higher knowledge (vijnana or buddhi), and ecstasy.

The thoughtfully very much created Trika school of Tantra recognizes the physical body, the unobtrusive body, and the causal body. The unobtrusive body, regularly assigned as puryashtaka, relates to what we would call the mind or brain. It is joined to a person all through their encapsulations in the physical domain.

The causal body (karana-shanra), as the name recommends, contains the karmic seeds that offer ascent to different vehicles through which we experience the world and make new karma, in this way propping cyclic presence up interminably. It is the substratum for the unobtrusive body. The causal vehicle is otherwise called the "higher body" (para-sharira) and, as per the Trika thinkers, is made out of the ontic rule of maya together with its five "covers" (kancuka), as depicted in section 4. It ensures that there is a congruity from life to life as well as even starting with one grandiose creation then onto the next. In contrast to the unobtrusive body, the causal body isn't devasayd right now of inestimable disintegration (pralaya) yet fills in as the layout for the formation of the following semipermanent unpretentious body. It is disposed of just upon full freedom, when the individual drops all bodies and is available simply as the supernatural Reality, or Self. Probably, the joined karmic seeds of all unliberated creatures are liable for the recharged growing of the tree of molded presence toward the finish of a time of grandiose rest, or torpidity. In this way, working together with every other being, we ourselves are liable for the world we occupy. Together we make and look after it.

The Siddha-Siddhanta-Paddhati (section 1), to give one more model in outline of the supernatural decent variety of Tantra, recognizes six bodies, which are called pinda (bump, ball, circle). These, again, compare to perpetually unpretentious degrees of presence, starting with the "early stage body" (adya-pinda) down to the "undeveloped body" (garbha-pinda). In any case, once more, these are comprehended not as carefully separate vehicles yet as a progressive system of interlocking and reliant forms. They are generally appearances of the particular celestial Power (shakti), which is refracted in different courses in the multidarkensional universe. Most importantly, these forms identify with levels of cognizance and experience.

In their deep climb to a definitive One, Tantric yogins and yoginis continuously escalate their mindfulness, in this way empowering them to encounter perpetually unobtrusive domains of presence. At the material level, we experience the body as discrete from its condition. In the more significant levels of presence, however, the limits among body and condition become progressively obscured, and the early stage body is coextensive with the universe itself. At the end of the day, at the most elevated level of corporeality, we actually are the world. At that level we are really ubiquitous just as omniscient. The further down we step in the stepping stool of psychocosmic advancement, the more articulated the split between cognizance, body, and condition becomes.

Finally, at the material level, we not just experience our body as discrete from its condition however even cut off our brain from the body. This last split is currently demonstrating lethal for the human species in general, since it has distanced us from our sentiments. We can never again read the signs from our body, which is our essential wellspring of correspondence with each other. Along these lines we have gotten irritated from ourselves, from our physical condition, and from one another. Thusly we are encountering a high level of contention on these different degrees of being on the planet, which causes us disarray, uncertainly, and a lot of misery.

For quite a while clinicians looked to cure this circumstance by mindfulness improving strategies. All the more as of late, they have come to perceive that something more is required, although more noteworthy mindfulness doesn't consequently engage an individual to make the important changes. In this way they have started to concentrate on the body as a vehicle of social change. The "Physical Yoga" created by Eleanor Criswell, a teacher of brain research, is an enlivened endeavor to consolidate the information on body-arranged treatment and biofeedback with the insight of conventional Yoga. By encouraging the combination among body and psyche, Somatic Yoga attempts to take advantage of our potential for more deep reflective experience and spiritual development. Tantra, as well, works intimately with the body, however it centers on the body's unpretentious lively format. Since the unobtrusive body is higher ranking than the physical body, the Tantric methodology would appear to be more straightforward and furthermore considers the still increasingly crucial karmic factors answerable for our vigorous and physical examples.

HEALING THE SPLIT: Tantric Medicine

The inconspicuous body is the enthusiastic shape of the physical body. It is increasingly open to the psyche and cognizant control. On the unpretentious level, change is immediate yet additionally to some degree delicate, requesting incredible expectation. When change on the unobtrusive level has separated down to the physical level, however, it will in general become increasingly steady. On the other hand, it is hard to make and keep up change simply on the physical level. This is best found in the territory of wellbeing upkeep. An individual may eat the correct eating routine and exercise normally yet be debilitated by sick wellbeing.

By analyzing that individual's karmic conditions and making modifications in the unpretentious energy field, a Tantric adroit can realize mending efficiendy and at times rapidly, if not in a split second. All the more critically, this sort of mediation can put an individual immovably on the spiritual way by expelling blockages in the unpretentious body that recently caused perplexity, question, absence of will, and eagerness.

Tantra has developed its own type of treatment, which is minimal known in the West. It depends on the possibility of self-refinement at the physical and mental level as well as on the vivacious (or inconspicuous) level. Physical decontamination has been extraordinarily expounded in Hatha Yoga, which is a Tantric Yoga. Mental filtration comprises basically in reflection and representation, particularly picturing oneself as one's picked divinity (ishta-devata). Lively refinement, which is the strong point of Tantra, continues by methods for perception and breath control or, carefully talk ing, prana stimulation and harmonization. Prana is on the unobtrusive level what the breath is on the physical plane. Physical disease is foreshadowed by deterrents in the progression of life energy in the unpretentious body. On the other hand, harm to the physical body has its inconspicuous vigorous results. These, thusly, influence the working of the brain. Since the psyche is the chief instrument by which Tantric professionals endeavor to understand their objective, it must be tirelessly kept in a condition of composure that takes into consideration the deep procedure to turn out to be progressively inconspicuous.

By expelling fiery blockages and amending harm on the degree of the unpretentious body, Tantric specialists forestall physical illness and mental lopsidedness. They see, in any case, that wellbeing is certainly not a lasting accomplishment. Both the unobtrusive vehicle and the physical body are continually affected by their separate surroundings. Also, the karmic seeds planted through our past and present volitions are constantly maturing and looking for sign. Disease may likewise be brought about via recklessness in the execution of the yogic practices, as Cidghanananda Natha calls attention to in his Sat-Karma-Sam-graha. This sacred writing recommends different cleansing practices in situations where common yogic methods and restorative substances neglect to address the issue.

In the typified say, there can be no ideal harmony. Everything, including our wellbeing, is in a ceaseless condition of motion. We can't know how our karma or our condition will influence us. However from the Tantric perspective, a solid, sound body is a clear resource, in light of the fact that the spiritual procedure is requesting, and an incapacitated body will be unable to withstand the fire of deep self-change. Along these lines Tantric specialists are quick to keep up their physical prosperity.

To this end, they benefit themselves of the strategies of Hatha Yoga and the numerous naturopathic cures of Ayurveda (Life Science) - from herbs to slimming down to fasting. They even utilize catalytic inventions said to advance wellbeing and life span. From soonest times, there has been a nearby connection between Tantra, medication, and speculative chemistry. Every one of the three were created through experimentation and individual experience over numerous hundreds of years. Various adepts have created messages on Yoga and on medication. In this manner Patanjali, the arranger of the Yoga-Sutra, is credited with the initiation of deals with medication and language structure also.

In South India the Tantric cittars built up their own particular image of medication, which utilizes inorganic substances (prominently salts, metals, and even harmful mixes). They guarantee to have built up their framework freely of Ayurveda, the naturopathic convention of the North. Yet, similar to their Northern partners, the Tantric adepts of the South likewise have underscored the superlative significance of the brain and prana in the healing procedure.

Cittar medication - known as citta-vaittiyam or "study of the brain" - is customarily followed back to the incredible ace Agastya (Tamil: Akattiyar). Agastya, whose date is questionable, was an edified ace as well as a healer and marvel specialist. A diviner (rishi) by that name made a few songs out of the antiquated Rig-Veda and was hitched to Lopamudra, the girl of the leader of the Videha clan. The Rig-Veda has protected an entrancing discussion between them, which is important here. Lopamudra, aware of maturing, became exhausted of sexual forbearance. Her better half had taken to parsimony and celibacy to incite energy for the spiritual procedure. She admitted her staggering sexual want for him, and Agastya advised her that parsimonious enthusiasm is satisfying to the gods and that this undertaking is never futile. However, then he included, "We will conquer a hundred misfortunes if we join as a team (mithuna)." This appears to allude to sex as an open door for higher association through self-amazing quality. However, as the psalm proceeds, after Agastya had yielded to sexual congress, Lopamudra just "sucked dry the gasping sage." as such, rather than saddling the additional energy delivered during sexual congress, the diviner lost his concentrate quickly and spilled his semen. However, the story has a glad closure, for we are informed that Agastya "discovered satisfaction of his genuine expectations among the divinities."

As per Indian convention, Agastya carried the Vedic legacy toward the south of the subcontinent. It is conceivable that he is in fact the Agastya recalled in the Tantric sacred texts of the Tamil-speaking South, yet there may likewise have been other incredible adepts bearing this name, which is frequently referenced in numerous writings and sorts of Hindu writing.

Tantric medication, regardless of whether of North or South India, was created with regards to spiritual practice and was intended to help the individuals who tried to scale the Himalayas of their own mind. Its disclosures about the exchange among body and psyche through the vehicle of unpretentious energy flows are substantial even today. A couple of Western doctors have begun to investigate this concealed component of substantial presence and are affirming a portion of the discoveries of the Tantric adepts and healers. Without a doubt, the contemporary pioneers of "energy medication," or "vibrational medication," would profit incredibly from a more deep viable investigation of Tantric medication, which has a long history.

OF LOTUSES AD SUBTLE TENDRILS

The energy of the unpretentious body is called prana signifying "life" or "life power." This is an exceptionally old Sanskrit term discovered as of now in the Vedas. In the Rig-Veda it represents the "breath" of the macranthropos, or Cosmic Person, and somewhere else is utilized for the breath of life when all is said in done. As per the Atharva-Veda, the existence power garments an individual as a dad would dress his dear child. This sacred writing additionally alludes to seven pranas (in-breaths), seven apanas (out-breaths), and seven vyanas (through-breaths), along these lines foreseeing the pneumatological theories of the later Upanishads and Tantras. We can see from this that the sages of India from the earliest starting point have corresponded the breath with the fundamental energy itself, which is thought to spread all through the universe, breathing life into everything. In its more deep significance, then, the Sanskrit word prana communicates a similar reality that is likewise caught in the Latin expression spiritus, which is contained in breath-related words like motivation and lapse. The association among soul and breath is comparatively protected in the Greek word pneuma and the Hebrew word ruah. This association is of extraordinary importance and recommends an early comprehension of the capacity of the breath in deep experience.

Prana is intermittent indispensable energy, which pools to frame flows (nadi) and vortices (cakra). In some cases these flows are comprehended as "courses" closely resembling veins, while the cakras are mistaken for nerve plexuses. One of the primary Westerners to expound on the serpent force and its climb through the cakra framework was

Vasant G. Rele. He direct likened the cakras with the significant nerve plexuses, contending that the forces (shakti) related with the psychoenergetic centers of the unpretentious body are equivalent to the efferent driving forces that restrain apprehensive movement. He ignored the way that these forces are described in the Sanskrit sacred writings as heavenly energies of awareness as opposed to oblivious neurophysiological powers. Some Western clinical specialists even ventured to such an extreme as to recommend that the cakra framework is only a misguided anatomical model.

The facts demonstrate that there are sure correspondences between the forms of the unpretentious body and the anatomical organs and endocrine arrangement of the physical body, however these are equal or similar to instead of indistinguishable. Most fundamentally, while the nerve plexuses are situated outside the spinal segment, the cakras are depicted as being inside the focal channel, which is arranged inside what on the physical level would be the spinal segment. Clearly, the cakras can't be found by analyzing the body however by entering a thoughtful say and encountering the energy field from inside or by modifying one's outer recognition to a higher recurrence (to be specific, that of perceptiveness).

To perceptive vision, the unpretentious body shows up as a brilliant, sparkling energy field that is in steady interior movement and is bungled by radiant fibers, or ringlets. In contrast to the physical body, which seems strong and stable, it is neither minimized nor inflexible. Despite the fact that it contains areas of relative soundness, the inconspicuous body is exceptionally receptive to the psyche and mirrors an individual's changing mental says loyally.

The steadiest forms of the inconspicuous body are known as "wheels" (cakras) or "lotuses" (padma) in light of their roundabout structure and spinning movement and furthermore due to the manner by which the prana flows end at or issue from them. These significant setups of our "unobtrusive life forms" are particularly receptive to mental control and hence are regularly made the central purposes of contemplation and perception. Numerous Tantric teachers talk about seven head psychoenergetic centers, however a few schools list five, and others name nine, ten, eleven, or a lot of something else. A few essayists have deciphered this dissimilarity as a sign that the cakras are simply nonexistent. This is negated by most Tantric writings themselves, very separated from the way that Eastern and Western clairvoyants have freely given comparative depictions of these unobtrusive "organs." Furthermore, the Japanese ace and scientist Hiroshi Motoyama has had the option to dispassionately show the presence of cakras by methods for a contraption estimating the body's bioenergetic flows.

Rather than this, some Tantric works treat the cakras as manifestations of extreme yogic representation; one such work is the Ananda-Lahari, attributed to Shankara. In any case, it is conceivable to accommodate the two understandings to the extent that fixation on the cakras empowers them, making them increasingly radiant and consequently likewise progressively noticeable to visionary sight. In the conventional individual, as most Tantric specialists would concur, the cakras are working at a negligible level and along these lines have been contrasted with hanging, shut lotus blossoms. From a yogic perspective, they can be said scarcely to exist. Through internal work, in any case, they naturally become progressively dynamic, opening like lotuses in full blossom and broadening upward toward the Light (which is extremely inescapable).

Besides, in the normal individual, the cakras work less than impressive and are not fit with one another. Over the span of spiritual practice, they are progressively blended until they vibrate as one. It is then that the unobtrusive sound om, which is resounding all through the universe, can be heard in the condition of joy. This likewise concurs with the decent working of the body-mind.

The way that various specialists have referenced different quantities of cakras need not be taken as an indication of difference between them. The cakra models are only that: models of reality that are intended to help the Tantric specialists in their internal odyssey from the Many to the One. As will have gotten apparent at this point, this topic is amazingly complicated. In their fantastic book Yoga and Psychotherapy, Swami Rama and two of his understudies and associates appropriately noted:

The chakras give a kind of main issue, a hidden structure, wherein a huge number of components cross and cooperate. It ought to be certain that the experience of these centers is a deeply unpredictable and complex undertaking. Any endeavor to communicate it in words is sure to end up being just somewhat fruitful.

The most widely recognized cakra model perceives the accompanying seven psychoenergetic centers in diving request:

1. Sahasrara-cakra10 (thousand-spoked wheel), which is situated at the crown of the head, is otherwise called the "brahmic crevice" (brahma-randhra) in light of the fact that right now of freedom, while still exemplified, cognizance leaves the body through this leave point to converge with the Absolute (brahman). This psychoenergetic focus is an iridescent structure made out of an apparently perpetual number of fibers that stretch out from the head upward into limitlessness. It relates to the degree of extreme Reality from one perspective and to the mind on the other. Emblematically, it is the pinnacle of Mount Meru (relating to the spinal segment), which is Shiva's perfect seat. The Tantric professionals target rejoining the Goddess Power (Shakti) with Shiva, therefore achieving the illuminated say flooding with rapture. This unification, showing in bliss and eventually edification, relies upon the excitement of the serpent power (kundalim-shakti) lethargic in the most minimal psychoenergetic focus. In the common individual, the sahasrara-cakra is answerable for the higher mental capacities, particularly acumen (buddhi). In the yogin and yogini, its maximum capacity shows as supernatural experience and brightening.

2. Ajna-cakra (direction wheel), which is arranged in the head, is normally demonstrated by the dab (bindu) worn on the brow by Hindu ladies. This is the inconspicuous organ that goes about as a transmitter and collector of clairvoyant communi cations, particularly those between the master and the supporter. Prevalently called the "third eye," it is

regularly delineated thusly on the temples of divinities (strikingly Shiva) and Yoga aces. This centers to its capacity as an "organ" of special insight, remote survey (dura-darshana), and other comparative paranormal capacities. It is commonly delineated as a two-petaled lotus, the two petals being identified with the normal polarization of the human psyche (and mind), which is sorted out as an on/off PC. The lower mind, called manas in Sanskrit, has generally been characterized as that capacity of awareness which sways between yes/no, either/or. Most fundamentally, the ajna-cakra can be utilized to either serve the lower elements of the body-mind (the exercises of the initial three cakras) or the higher elements of the crown community, which encourages self-amazing quality, intelligence, and illumination. Since the ajna-cakra is the gathering spot of the three chief channels (i.e., ida, pingala, and sushumna), it is additionally called "triple conversion" (tri-veni).

3. Vishuddha-cakra (pure wheel), or vishuddhi-cakra (wheel of purity), is found at the throat and henceforth is additionally called "throat wheel" (kantha-cakra). It is particularly associated with the fifth component, ether (akasha), and in this way with sound and hearing. Its name apparently alludes to the virtue of the ether, which is the wellspring of the other five components (air, fire, water, and earth). As indicated by Kalicarana's discourse on the Shat-Cakra-Nirupana, this psychoenergetic focus is esteemed pure on the grounds that one accomplishes virtue after observing the hamsa while thinking about this cakra. Here hamsa alludes to the celestial

digestion of Shiva-Shakti, which on the physical level shows as the mood of inward breath and exhalation. The concealed noteworthiness of this cakra is by all accounts that of equalization (which would clarify its relationship with hearing), particularly the harmony among giving and accepting, as showed in inward breath and exhalation, discourse and quietness, just as digestion. This middle stands halfway between the essential (material) body and the irrelevant brain. Its sixteen petals are connected with Sanskrit vowel sounds just, which alludes to the status of this cakra as a lattice for discourse, the vowels being cruder than the consonants.

4. Anahata-cakra (wheel of the unstruck [sound]), situated at the heart, is additionally broadly known as the "heart lotus" (hrit-padma or hhdaya-kamala). Since the time the hour of the Rig-Veda, the heart as opposed to the head has been viewed as the genuine scaffold among cognizance and the body. Later sacred texts like the Dhyana-Bindu-Upanishad portray the individuated awareness as spinning all around in the twelve-spoked wheel of the heart, induced by its great and awful karma. This unending movement of awareness (or consideration) is halted distinctly with the acknowledgment of the Self as one's actual personality.

Numerous teachers want to work with this cakra, as its stimulation is suspected to prompt the amicable advancement of the various psychoenergetic centers. Without the enlivening of the heart community, enactment of any of different centers can cause physical and enthusiastic issues. The Tantrie adepts look to raise the serpent power (kundalini-shakti) from the most minimal focus as fast as conceivable to the heart community so as to sidestep the perils in initiating the initial three habitats (in rising request). These centers are identified with lower substantial capacities (strikingly disposal, sexuality, and assimilation) and their relating passionate mental driving forces as wants, if not fixations.

The centers over the heart are nearly sheltered, yet without earlier actuation of the heart community, they also can cause issues, for example, mental lopsidedness, clairvoyant excessive touchiness, or extraordinary helplessness to spiritual says (instead of veritable illumination) or even to visualization. The heart community can be opened in a roundabout way by developing thoughtfulness, empathy, dispassion, serenity, and other comparative ideals, which are central to the deep way. Being immovably grounded in them maintains a strategic distance from or if nothing else limit the negative reactions of actuating the three lower cakras.

When the heart place is actuated, it is conceivable to hear the unpretentious inward stable called nothing, which is "unstruck" in light of the fact that it isn't created by any mechanical methods and isn't pushed through space however is a central inescapable vibration - the sound om. This thought has its equal in the Gnostic idea of the "music of the circles," first referenced by Pythagoras.

5. Manipura-cakra (wheel of the gem city) is otherwise

called the nabhi-cakra (navel wheel), which demonstrates its area in the body. It compares on the physical level to the sun powered plexus, which has been called our "second cerebrum" since it speaks to such a very much created structure of the sensory system. This ten-petaled lotus is related with the fire component. As indicated by the Shat-Cakra-Nirupana of the sixteenth century Bengali ace Purnananda, by mulling over this cakra one gets the paranormal capacity to crush and make the essential world. Each psychoenergetic focus is related with a particular directing ladylike god, and on account of the manipura-cakra this is Lakini, who is said to be attached to meat and blood. This centers to the cakra's association, on the physical level, with the stomach related procedure. It gets its inquisitive name from the way that it is "brilliant like a jewel."

6. Svadhishthana-cakra11 (wheel of oneself base), situated at the private parts, is related with the water component and the feeling of taste. As Swami Sivananda Radha has brought up in her spearheading book Kundalini Yoga for the West, taste here includes our gustatory sense as well as taste in the allegorical sense also: our craving for specific encounters and our fundamental way to deal with life (which might be thoughtful or dull). More than some other focus, this cakra identifies with want, particularly the sexual desire. As indicated by the Rudra-Yamala, this middle gets its name from the way that it is the spot of the para-linga (preeminent image) - communicated in the word sva (possess). It is delineated as a six-petaled lotus whose petals are

associated with the six afflictive feelings of desire (kdma), outrage (krodha), covetousness (lobha), dream (moha), pride (mada), and envy (matsarya). These elements, which all emerge from the personality sense (ahamkara), can be overwhelmed by examining this psychoenergetic lattice.

7. Muladhara-cakra (root-prop wheel), situated at the base of the spine, is the counterpole to the crown place. If the sahasrara-cakra speaks to amazing quality, divine ubiquity (paradise), and opportunity, the muladhara-cakra symbolizes innateness, physical restriction, and subjugation. It has in certainty been customarily associated with the earth component, as is emblematically caught in its four petals (speaking to the four headings of room). It is the root (mula) and support (adhara) of the different cakras, on the grounds that it fills in as the resting spot of the celestial energy in the human body, called kundalini-shakti. Despite the fact that this is the least community - both spatially and practically - without it freedom would not be conceivable. Here we have again an away from of the high worth put in Tantric way of thinking on material epitome, the lower domains of presence, and the shadow side of life. A long way from being repetitive or only polluted or "shrewdness," the earth component (and all that it represents) is instrumental in our self-improvement and extreme illumination. Hence we should not disregard however grasp it, however without getting appended to it.

The enlivening of a given cakra compares to a specific

condition of energy and cognizance, with the crown place as the summit of the whole arrangement. When the celestial energy is raised from the least place to the thousand-petaled lotus at the highest point of the head, an extreme move in cognizance happens: the boundary among subject and item is lifted and the skilled encounters a condition of immaculate solidarity and whole• ness. The heavenly or serpent power is directed to the crown community along the pivotal pathway that interfaces all cakras, as certain sacred writings put it, similar to globules on a string. This pivotal pathway, or sushumna-nadi, is one of various such fibers of fundamental energy that make the woven artwork out of the inconspicuous field, or unobtrusive body (sukshma-sharira). This system is called nadi-cakra.

A few Tantras talk about 72,000 conductors (nadi), however the Shiva-Samhita gives the figure 350,000, while the Tri-Shikhi-Brahmana-Upanishad demands that they are extremely innumerable. The Shiva-Svaro-daya pronounces:

In the body exist numerous sorts of channels, which are extremely broad. The sage must comprehend them so as to under• stand his own body.

Running transversely, up, and down, they all exist in the body combined like a wheel, subject to the existence power and connected to the breath of the body.

Indeed, even in the Sanskrit writing, the nadis are now and then treated - with lost solidness - as paths through which the existence power flows. All the more precisely, they are flows of crucial energy. For comfort, I will switch unreservedly between these two analogies, requesting that the readr remember the favored translation. The most established convention, as recorded for example in the Brihad-Arany- otherwise known as Upanishad, is aware of 101 such flows of psychoenergy, of which just one is said to pass right to the crown of the head, where it prompts eternality. This extraordinary current is none other than the hub pathway, which holds unique importance in all schools of Tantra Yoga, as is evident from such elective specialized terms for it as moksha-marga (approach to freedom) or "unsupported inside" (niralam hana-antara). Essentially, its most basic name, sushumna-nadi, signifies "most thoughtful current" - benevolent in light of the fact that it is the imperial street to opportunity.

As indicated by the Shat-Cakra-Nirupana, the pivotal pathway is made out of a few layers, each consequent layer being more unobtrusive than the past one. The deepest current is called citra-or citrim-nadi, and among it and the sushumna-nadi is the firm current (vajra-nadi). The deepest current, otherwise called the brahmic current (brahma-nadi), is the conductor for the stirred serpent power. All these glowing fibers of imperative energy start at the egg-molded "bulb" (kanda), which is arranged at the perineum. Its size is frequently indicated as being nine or twelve digits in length and four digits wide, which would make it arrive at just beneath the navel. This position generally relates to the hara discussed in the Japanese Zen sacred texts.

The more significant flows of the existence power end at the "direction wheel" in the midbrain, however just the focal pathway stretches out right to the middle at the crown of the head and from that point opens into endlessness. Numerous Tantric sacred writings list the accompanying fourteen head flows: sushumna, ida (comfort), pingala (brownish), sarasvati (she who streams), pusha (nourisher), varuna (including), hasti-jihva (elephant tongue), jashasvini (awe inspiring), alambusa (or alam-busha, both signifying "plenteously hazy"), kuhu (new moon), vishva-udara ("world paunch," wrote vishvodara), payasvinfi(watery), shankhim (mother-of-pearl), and gandhara (or gandhan, "princesslike" or "fragrant"). These names are normal yet not constant. A few sacred writings discuss just ten head conductors, which they connect to the ten openings or "doors" (dvara) of the body: eyes, ears, nostrils, mouth, urethral opening, rear-end, and either the navel or the "brahmic gap" (brahma-randhra) at the crown of the head.

Turning around the focal pathway in helical design and intersection at each cakra are the ida-nadi and the pingala-nadi. The previous is said to be on the left half of the sushumna-nadi, and the last on the correct side. On the physical level, they are identified with the left and right nostril and to the parasympathetic and thoughtful sensory system separately. Emblematically, the previous is related with the cooling moon and the last with the warming sun. Here we should again recall that in Tantric transcendentalism, the cosmos is dependably reflected in the microcosm of the individual body-mind. Along these lines sun and moon represent significant wonders in the psychoenergetic framework. Through the exercises of the lunar and sun powered channels and the elements between them, cognizance (mindfulness) is kept in consistent cyclic movement, causing rest and waking, just as internal directedness and external directedness. They are answerable for the essential strain inborn in the conventional psyche.

The lunar and sun powered channels, however, are not

quite the same as the microcosmic sun and the moon. The previous is believed to be set in the stomach, where it expends the nectar (amrita) overflowing from the moon positioned in the head. The yogin or yogini must oversee this normal procedure and increase it, with the goal that the ambrosial liquid is disseminated over the whole body as opposed to squandered in the stomach. This is said to prompt energy, wellbeing, and life span. In Hatha Yoga the altered stances, for example, shoulder stand and headstand are intentionally utilized to turn around the situation of the microcosmic sun and moon, to forestall the wastage of the lunar nectar.

As David Gordon White has appeared in some detail, the microcosmic lights additionally assume a focal job in speculative chemistry, which at any rate is firmly identified with both Yoga and Ayurveda. The microcosmic moon is portrayed as having sixteen digits or units (kala), which compare to the lunar stages. The sixteenth digit, which makes the macrocosmic moon into a full moon, is related with eternality and the way of discontinuance (nivritti-marga), that is, the yogic procedure of inversion, thoughtfulness, renunciation, and recuperation of one's actual nature. Just when the existence energy moves through the middle pathway, which it does intermittently for brief timeframes for the duration of the day, is there relative parity in our body-mind. The progression of psychoenergy in the sushumna is the best approach to everlasting status, which is, to the full utilization of the transformative ambrosial nectar dribbling from the microcosmic moon situated in the head. By and large, however, the course through the hub pathway is a minor stream and hence doesn't show its beneficial outcomes completely. A few people are ida prevailing; others are pingala predominant. Just adepts are sushumna focused, which communicates in internal harmony, congruity, and clarity. Custom relates these three head pathways and their reaction frameworks to the three essential characteristics of nature: tamas (guideline of idleness), rajas (standard of dynamism), and sattva (rule of clearness).

Before the serpent force can climb the hub pathway all polluting influences must be expelled from the system of nadis. In the normal individual the flows exist in a contaminated say, forestalling the free progression of fundamental energy and in this way causing physical and mental irregularity, just as spiritual visual deficiency. This is one more method for understanding the human condition, and it uncovers the exclusive part of the yogic procedure of self-decontamination. I will say all the more regarding this in the following part.

Chapter Eleven

Awakening The Serpent Power

The manner in which we see the world relies upon what our identity is. On the easiest level, a kid strolling down the road will promptly detect all the toy stores; a pennywise customer will see all the deals showed in shop windows; a planner will see surprising structures; and a cabbie will rush to find house numbers. For each situation, recognition is particular, contingent upon the individual's advantage and consideration. This stretches out to increasingly huge parts of life too, for example, our disposition toward connections, ethical quality, work, recreation, wellbeing, ailment, agony, passing, and the incredible past. These perspectives are formed by a wide range of components, of which karmic molding, as the Tantric sacred texts would demand, is the most persuasive one.

We are molded by our past decisions, which is equivalent to stating that we are animals of propensity. In yogic terms, our considerations and activities generally follow the easiest course of action. In other words, they are overdetermined by the lively format of the unpretentious body. This clarifies why it is so hard to change our conduct in any event, when we have understood that our old examples aren't right, useless, or harming. Consequently notwithstanding conduct change, Tantric specialists endeavor to alter the pathways of the existence power straightforwardly. This change involves cleansing the nadis, a training called nadi-shodhana.

As noted in the past part, in the standard individual the energy flows exist in a condition of relative pollution. They are not completely utilitarian and subsequently hinder physical prosperity and deep development. The Tantric skilled's particular objective is to open the focal channel so the existence power can stream uninhibitedly through it and, at the appointed time, allure the far more prominent energy of the kundalini to stick to this same pattern.

Without earlier cleansing of the nadi framework, raising the serpent power (kundalim-shakti) along the hub pathway isn't just outlandish yet additionally extremely perilous to endeavor, for as opposed to entering the focal channel (sushumna-nadi) it is probably going to constrain itself into the ida-or the pingala-nadi, on either side of the focal channel, causing monstrous devastation in the body and brain. This is the thing that happened to Gopi Krishna during his unconstrained kundalini arousing, and his holding record of the physical agony and mental anguish coming about because of it remains as an immortal notice to all beginners fiddling with the serpent force, or shakti. He wrote:

My face turned out to be very pale and my body slender and frail. I felt an abhorrence for nourishment and discovered dread gripping my heart the minute I gulped anything My anxiety had expected such an express, that I was unable to sit unobtrusively for even 30 minutes. When I did as such, my consideration was drawn powerfully towards the bizarre conduct of my psyche. Promptly the ever-present feeling of dread was escalated, and my heart pounded fiercely.

He further depicted how the kundalini produced gigantic warmth in his body, "causing such insufferable torment that I squirmed and turned from side to side while floods of cold sweat poured down my face and appendages." He proceeded:

There were awful unsettling influences in all the organs, each so disturbing and difficult that I wonder how I figured out how to hold my presence of mind under the assault. The entire sensitive creature was consuming, wilting endlessly totally under the blazing shoot dashing through its inside.

I realized I was biting the dust and that my heart couldn't stand the huge strain lor long. My throat was seared and all aspects of my body blazing and consuming, however I could do nothing to reduce the terrifying affliction. On the off chance that a well or stream had been close to I would have hopped into its cool profundities, inclining toward death to what I was experiencing. I racked my occupied mind for a method for escape, just to meet clear gloom on each side. The exertion depleted me and I felt myself sinking, slowly aware of the burning ocean of torment in which I was suffocating.

Other comparative cases have been accounted for in the writing. The American therapist Lee Sannella, one of the main individuals from the clinical foundation to try to comprehend the kundalini marvel, has proposed that the blockages in the vigorous field are "emphasize focuses." As he clarified in his generally readd book The Kundalini Experience:

Over the span of its upward movement, the kundalini is held to experience a wide range of contaminations that are singed off by its dynamic action. Specifically, the Sanskrit sacred writings notice three significant auxiliary blockages, known as "ties." We can view these blockages as emphasize focuses. In this manner, in its rising, the kundalini makes the focal sensory system lose pressure. This is generally connected with the experience of agony. When the kundalini experiences these squares, it works away at them until they are broken up.

Sannella's announcement remains constant just in situations where the kundalini has been rashly or wrongly stimulated, that is, without satisfactory arrangement. The Tantric sacred texts stress the requirement for careful foundation before embracing any practices that focus on awak• ening the serpent power straightforwardly. As the fourteenth-century ace Svatmarama says, the kundalini "gives freedom on yogins and subjugation on the ignorant."5 A sharp blade in the hands of a talented doctor can spare an actual existence however in the hands of a blockhead can do unavoidable damage. The kundalini in itself is neither acceptable nor terrible. It basically is the Goddess energy as it shows in the human body. Except if we consciously work together with it, it stays on the most unobtrusive degree of presence, supporting us through the organization of the existence power (prana) however never entering our field of mindfulness. Through self-cleansing and a suitable course of controls, we can profit by it all the more quickly by welcoming it into our life as a ground-breaking transformative power. In its shrouded express, the kundalini is said to be sheer possibility. This is just generally right, for the Goddess energy is constantly dynamic for our benefit, keeping up all the unobtrusive vigorous procedures that underlie our physical and mental structures and capacities. In its stirred say, however, the kundalini is an unfathomable organization of change, spiritual development, and finally edification. As the Rudra-Yamala insists: "The kundalini is ever the ace of Yoga." In a similar sacred writing the serpent power is known as the "mother of Yoga" and the "bestower of Yoga."

Different stances (asana) are said to impact the cleansing of the conductors or channels (nadi). The Hatha-Yoga-Pradipika singles out the adroit's stance (siddha-asana, wrote siddhasand) as being especially appropriate for this reason, yet different sacred texts favor various stances. The adroit's stance is drilled by setting the left heel at the rectum and the correct heel over the privates, while laying the jaw on the chest and looking at the spot between the eyebrows. Once in a while the situation of the legs is turned around. The strength of this mainstream act gets from the way that it adjusts the inconspicuous energies and along these lines stirs the serpent power.

While stances like the siddha-asana are significant, the chief methods for cleansing the channels is controlled breathing, as has been expounded in extraordinary detail in the sacred writings of Hatha Yoga. The Gher-anda-Samhita recognizes two fundamental kinds of decontamination rehearses: samanu and nirmanu, which indicate "mental" and "nonmental" separately. As the content clarifies, the last comprises in physical cleansing procedures called dhauti, including the accompanying strategies:

1. Antar-dhauti (internal cleansing) comprising of the accompanying four methods:

    a. vata-sara (air process), breathing in through the mouth and ousting the air through the lower section

    b. vari-sara (water process), tasting water until the stomach is totally filled and ousting it through the lower section

    c. vahni-sara (fire process), pushing the navel one hundred times back toward the spine, which builds the "gastric fire"

    d. bahish-krita (outer activity), sucking in air through the mouth until the stomach is filled, holding it for an hour and a half, and afterward ousting it through the lower entry; this is trailed by remaining in navel-deep water and pushing out the lower intestinal tract for cleansing

2. danta-dhauti (dental cleansing), which incorporates cleaning the teeth and the tongue, just as the ears and frontal sinuses

3. hrid-dhauti (lit. "Heart cleansing"), which comprises of:

    (a) Presenting the stalk of a plantain, turmeric, or stick into the throat to clear it out

    (b) Filling the stomach with water and afterward ousting it through the mouth

    (c) Gulping a long portion of slender fabric and afterward hauling it out once more (a procedure called vaso-dhauti, "material cleansing")

4. mula-shodhana (rectal cleansing), which is finished by methods for turmeric, water, or the center finger

The samanu sort of purificatory practice comprises in breath control "with seed" (sabija), that is, with quiet mantra recitation. As the Gheranda-Samhita clarifies:

Situated on a seat, the yogin ought to accept the lotus act. Next he should put the master, and so on [in his heart], as taught by the master, and initiate with the sanitization of the channels for decontamination through breath control.

Pondering the seed syllable (bija) of the air component, which is enthusiastic and of the shade of smoke, the sage ought to breathe noticeable all around through the lunar [channel, i.e., the left nostril], rehashing the seed syllable multiple times.

Then he ought to hold it for sixty-four reiterations [of the seed syllable] and breathe out the air through the sunlight based channel [i.e., the privilege nostril] more than thirty-two redundancies.

Raising the fire from the base of the navel [i.e., the kanda], he ought to think about the shine related with the earth component. Then, while rehashing the seed syllable of the fire component multiple times, he ought to breathe in through the sun based channel [i.e., the privilege nostril].

Next, he ought to hold the air for sixty-four redundancies and afterward breathe out it through the lunar channel [i.e., the left nostril] more than thirty-two reiterations.

Pondering the glowing impression of the moon at the tip of the nose, he ought to breathe noticeable all around through the ida [i.e., left nostril] for sixteen reiterations of the seed syllable tham.

Then, while thinking about the nectar overflowing [from the moon at the tip of the nose], he ought to hold the air for sixty-four redundancies of the seed syllable vam and along these lines wash down the channels. At long last, he ought to immovably breathe out for thirty-two [repetitions] of the la sound.

The seed syllables referenced in the above entry are the root sounds related with the four components: yam for air, slam for fire, lam for earth, and tham for the pictured moon, which represents the water component in its higher viewpoint as the nectar of everlasting status (am-rita). The regular seed syllable for water is vam. The fifth component, "pith," is ether, whose seed syllable is ham. Despite the fact that this isn't referenced in the cited section, oral transmission considers the ether component too.

Subsequently the eminent contemporary Hatha Yoga ace B. K. S. Iyengar has clarified the association between breath control and the components as follows:

In our body we have five components. The component liable for creation of the remedy of life (prana) is earth. The component of air is utilized as a beating pole, through inward breath and exhalation, and dispersion is through the component of ether. Ether is space, and its quality is that it can contract or extend. When you breathe in, the component of ether grows to take the breath in. In exhalation, the ether agreements to push out poisons.

Two components remain: water and fire. In the event that there is a fire, water is utilized to douse it. This gives us that fire and water are restricting components. With the assistance of the components of earth, air, and ether, a rubbing is made among water and fire, which creates energy as well as discharges it, similarly as water moving turbines in a hydroelectric force station produces power. To produce power, the water needs to stream at a specific speed. A lacking stream won't deliver power. Correspondingly, in our framework, typical breathing doesn't create that extraordinary energy. This is the reason we are on the whole experiencing anxiety, causing poor dissemination, which influences our wellbeing and satisfaction. The current isn't adequate so we are just existing, not living.

In the act of pranayama, we make the breath long. Right now, components of fire and water are united, and this contact of fire and water in the body, with the assistance of the component of air, discharges another energy, called by yogis divine energy, or kundalini sakti, and this is the energy of prana.

Different writings suggest comparable methodology in which the left and the correct pathway of the existence power are on the other hand actuated. As per the Shiva-Samhita, substitute breathing ought to be performed multiple times, four times each day - at day break, noontime, dusk, and 12 PM. Whenever done consistently for a quarter of a year, this methodology, we are told, will scrub the channels. It is at exactly that point that the professional should go to breath control appropriate.

The Shiva-Samhita additionally expresses that when the nadis have been cleansed, certain signs will show: The body gets amicable (sama) and lovely and produces a wonderful fragrance, while the voice gets resounding and the craving increments. Likewise, the yogin whose unobtrusive pathways are completely purged is constantly "full hearted," lively, and solid. The Hatha-Yoga-Pradipika specifies leanness and splendor of the body as signs of a cleaned nadi framework, however there have been adepts with a stirred kundalini who were chunky. The Hatha Yoga messages and Tan-tras additionally notice that the inward stable (nothing) gets perceptible to the expert, showing in dynamically subtler structure.

Presently the sadhaka resembles a finely tuned instrument and prepared to connect with the higher procedures of Tantra, prompting the actuation of the serpent power. As plot in the past part, these procedures go from breath control to complex customs and perceptions. Before portraying the Tantric collection in more detail, we should comprehend the idea of the serpent power, which is at the center of Tantra Yoga.

AWAKENING THE GODDESS ENERGY

As we have seen, the universe is an appearance of the play, or supernatural polarization, among Shiva and Shakti, God and Goddess, Being and Becoming, Consciousness and Energy. In the human body, which microcosmically imitates every single vast guideline and levels of presence, the heavenly Energy communicates in two chief structures - the existence power (prana) and the serpent power (kundalini-shakti).

The existence power is all around present in the universe and accordingly is known as mukhya-prana, or "essential life constrain." It expect the accompanying five practical perspectives regarding the human body, which the old Chdndogya-Upanishad styles the "guards of the eminent world":

1. Prana, in the feeling of the rising imperative energy that is mainly situated in the zone between the navel and the heart, is connected especially with inward breath however can represent both inward breath and exhalation.

2. Apana (down-breath) is the slipping imperative energy related with the lower half of the storage compartment and with exhalation.

3. Vyana (through-breath) is the crucial energy flowing in all the appendages.

4. Diana (up-breath), which is associated with physiological capacities, for example, discourse and eructation, additionally signifies the climb of consideration into higher conditions of awareness.

5. Samana (mid-breath) is limited in the stomach district, where it is associated with the stomach related procedure.

1. Notwithstanding the above chief sorts of life drive, a few sacred writings additionally know about five optional sorts (upaprana), in particular naga (serpent), kurma (tortoise), kri-kara (kri maker), deva-datta (natural), and dhanam-jaya (success of riches), which are individually connected with spewing or eructation, squinting, appetite or sniffling, rest or yawning, and decay of the cadaver.

From a yogic point of view, the two most significant types of the essential energy are prana and apana, on the grounds that they are the inconspicuous real factors fundamental the back and forth movement of relaxing. Breath control legitimately influences the rising and plummeting current of the existence power, which normally exchanges - generally like clockwork - between the channel on the left (called ida) and the one on the right (called pinoccasion) of the focal pathway. A definitive motivation behind breath control is to impact the progression of prana through the focal entry, which then draws the considerably more remarkable energy of the kundalini into it.

What precisely is the kundalini In responding to this inquiry, I will submit my general direction to Sir John Woodroffe, who considered it as some time in the past. As he noticed, the perfect Energy is enraptured into a static or potential structure (called kundalini) and a unique structure (called prana). The last is answerable for keeping up all the existence forms that make epitome conceivable. The previous is the boundless pool of Energy curled into possibility at the base of the focal pathway, in the most minimal psychoenergetic focus. This cakra is the regularly shut attachment opening to the interminable storage facility of Energy (and Consciousness).

In his voluminous work Tantra-Aloka (part 3), the incomparable Tan-tric ace Abhinava Gupta recognizes the purna-kundalini, prana-kundalini, and urdhva-kundalini. The first is the perfect force as the Whole or Plenum (purna); the second is the awesome force in its sign as life energy; the third is the celestial force as the stirred serpent moving upward (urdhva).

By methods for the dynamic energy of prana, which is unreservedly accessible in the body and its condition, the yogin or yogini can take advantage of the lively lattice, the

Goddess Power, itself. The psychoenergetic focus at the base of the hub channel compares to the most reduced degree of appearance. It is the terminal purpose of infinite advancement, as fueled by Shakti. Here the Goddess stops in the earth component. A long way from having depleted itself, this preeminent Power presently basically exists as sheer possibility anticipating its stiring through cognizant activity. The Sanskrit writings talk about the kundalini as being "curled up" three and a half times around the linga, the "sign" of Shiva. The loops have been taken to allude to the ground of nature (prakriti) and its three essential constituents or characteristics - sattva, rajas, and tamas. This thought might be identified with the Vedic instructing of Vishnu's three stages by which he crossed the whole universe. Just a being more prominent than the universe can cross it right now.

On account of the serpent power, this amazing quality is recommended by the additional half curl. The name kundalini signifies "she who is wound" and is identified with the word kundala, stud, maybe as worn by the Pashupatas and later by certain professionals of Hatha Yoga, outstandingly individuals from the Kanphata faction. A few writings abbreviate the word to kundali, while others utilize the term kutilangi (slanted bodied). The curls of the kundalini graphically pass on the thought of probability. For a similar explanation, the Sharada-Tilaka-Tantra alludes to the serpent power as a "bump" (pinda).

We can comprehend the transformative procedure from the supernatural plane to the earth domain through a practically equivalent to show outfitted by current cosmology. At the "time" of the Big Bang, the world existed in an express that can be portrayed as an unbelievably dense bundle of energy, in some cases called "quantum vacuum." Suddenly (and for no known explanation), somewhere in the range of fifteen billion years prior, a chain response happened right now energy soup that prompted the production of hydrogen molecules. This occasion harmonized with the rise of reality and the steady development of our spatiotemporal universe, with its billions of worlds, supernovas, dark gaps, and quasars and the cool dull issue sprinkled between them. Inside this impossible boundlessness are the planet Earth and the human species - the two results of the first glimmer from turmoil to universe or, in yogic terms, of Shiva's euphoric move.

Presently researchers are caught up with investigating methods for opening up the energy put away in issue by crushing high-energy subatomic particles into protons. Yogins and yoginis are occupied with an equal activity in the research facility of their own body-mind. They utilize the fundamental energy to over and over "crush" against the blocked opening of the focal pathway of the nadi framework. The Goraksha-Paddhati depicts this procedure obviously:

The serpent power, shaping an eightfold curl over the "bulb" (kanda), stays there, at the same time covering with its face the opening of the entryway to the Absolute.

Through that entryway the protected way to the Absolute can be come to. Covering that entryway with her face, the incomparable Goddess is snoozing [in the normal individual].

Stirred through buddhi-yoga' together with [the consolidated activity of] psyche and breath, she rises upward through the sushumna like a string through a needle.

Dozing as a serpent, looking like a brilliant rope, she, when stirred by the Yoga of lire [i.e., mental focus and breath control], rises upward through the sushumna.

Similarly as one may coercively open an entryway with a key, so the yogin should tear open the entryway to freedom by methods for the kun-dalini.

Vimalananda, a contemporary ace of the Aghori part of Tantra, likewise commented that to stir the kundalini, one must squeeze it, and it will climb just inasmuch as this weight is maintained.13 Perhaps joking, he censured gravity for its tendency to rest in or, whenever stirred, return as fast as conceivable to the most reduced psychoenergetic focus of the body. In the Hatha-Yoga-Pradipika, we locate the accompanying stanzas:

One ought to stimulate that resting serpent by holding onto its tail. Then that shakti, arousing from her sleep, compellingly rises upward.

One ought to hold onto the leaning back serpent by methods for pari-dhana and, while breathing in through the sunlight based channel, each day cause her to mix for around an hour and a half, both morning and night.

The training referenced here is known as shakti-calana (mixing the force). It is finished by getting the sphincter muscle and by applying the throat lock (jalandhara-bandha) while holding the breath, which causes the prana and apana to blend and "combust," along these lines driving the existence power upward into the focal channel. Manthana (stirring) is another term utilized in the writings to portray the way toward constraining prana and apana to "combust" by methods for breath maintenance (kumbhaka) and most extreme fixation. The Kashmiri yogini Lalla alludes to this procedure in one of her supernatural sonnets:

Shutting the doors and windows of my body, I held onto the hoodlum, prana, and shut him in.

I bound him firmly inside the corner of my heart, and lashed him hard with the whip om.

I pulled the reins of the steed of the brain;

I compacted the existence power circling through the ten channels;

Then, surely, did the lunar molecule (shashi-kala) liquefy and break down, also, the Void converged with the Void.

Focusing on the om-sound,

I made my body like blasting coal. Deserting the six junction, I ventured to every part of the way of Truth.

And afterward I, Lalla, arrived at the Abode of Light.

The previous picture of holding onto the serpent by the tail is characteristic of the mighty (hatha) approach of Hatha Yoga. Some customary specialists may think that its discourteous to talk about the heavenly Shakti right now, others would protest the possibility that one can co• erce the Goddess and get her freeing beauty by mechanical methods.

All are concurred, in any case, that the serpent energy

must climb along the focal pathway, which is additionally called the "extraordinary way" (maha-patha) and "incineration ground" (shmashana) in light of the fact that only it prompts freedom. With regards to this normally Tantric imagery, the Gher-anda-Samhita determines that the yogin occupied with this elusive practice ought to besmear his body with cinders, an outward indication of his inner renunciation of every common thing and wants. The capable who tries to stimulate the kundalini must be set up to bite the dust, since this procedure truly envisions the demise procedure. As the serpent power ascends along the focal entry, the yogin's or jogini's microcosm is bit by bit disintegrated. I will manage this procedure without further ado, however first I need to specify Abhinava Gupta's idea of prana-danda-prayoga, or the "procedure of making the existence power like a pole (danda)."

A cobra is hazardous just when it is serpented, prepared to strike in a moment; when its body is totally erect it is very innocuous. Thus, the kundalini is risky just in its type of the diffuse life energies, which fuel the unillumined individual's craving for tangible and arousing encounters, snaring the person in question perpetually in common karma. When the serpent power is erect, however, it isn't harmful however a wellspring of ambrosia, since it is erect just when it has entered the focal pathway prompting freedom and joy. As Jayaratha clarifies in his analysis on the Tantra-Aloka, when one strikes a serpent it draws itself up and turns out to be firm similar to a pole. Correspondingly, through the way toward "beating," the kundalini extends upward into the opposite pathway of the sushumna, coming to with its head for the highest psychoenergetic focus.

The climb of the Goddess power in the body is related with the dynamic disintegration of the components, a procedure that is called laya-krama (procedure of disintegration) or laya-yoga (order of disintegration). In the present setting, the specialized term laya alludes to the resorption of the components into the pretemporal and prespatial ground of nature (prakriti-pradhana). That this obscure procedure has frequently been misconstrued can be assembled from the accompanying remarks in the Hatha-Yoga-Pradipika:

They say "laya, laya,"" yet what is the idea of laya? Laya is nonremembrance of the sense objects on the grounds that the inclinations (vasana) don't emerge once more.

This stanza from the pen of the adroit Svatmarama shows that the yogic procedure of microcosmic disintegration realizes an emotional change in the psyche, for it cleans off karmic seeds put away in the intuitive. This is the motivation behind every single higher procedure of Yoga, for just when the karmic seeds are scorched totally is their future germination rendered inconceivable and freedom guaranteed. However, Svatmara-mama's remarks don't reveal to us how this Tantric procedure really happens. The Tantras are minimal progressively informative on this point, which is one of the numerous experientially based certainties of Tantra Yoga.

On a fundamental level, laya is affected as the kundalini ascends from focus to focus. Its appearance makes each inside vibrate seriously and to work completely, however as it goes to the following higher psychoenergetic focus, the flight of the Goddess power leaves the past focus or focuses as though void. The purpose behind this is at each inside

Shakti works the marvel of a significant cleaning of the components (called tattva), rendering them amazingly subde. All the more decisively, their vibration is speeded up to the most unpretentious degree of nature (prakriti), and subsequently they are said to have become reabsorbed into the vast grid. The savvy Goddess power from this time forward - or possibly for the time of kundalini excitement - assumes control over their individual capacities.

This exclusive procedure is the reason for the bhuta-shuddhi custom, in which the components are envisioned as being cleansed through their dynamic retention into the heavenly Shakti. This training, which is examined in detail in the Bhuta-Shuddhi-Tantra, is done preceding imagining oneself as one's picked god (ishta-devata) and doing custom love. The earth component oversees the territory between the feet and the thighs; the water component has authority over the zone between the thighs and the navel; the fire component manages the zone between the navel and the heart; the air component rules over the segment between the heart and the temple; the ether component administers the territory over the brow. The expert envisions earth dissolving into water, water into fire, fire into air, air into ether, and afterward ether into the higher standards (tattva), until everything is broken up into the Goddess power itself.

Therefore the yogin or yogini begins as a polluted being (daddy purusha) and through the intensity of representation reproduces oneself as an unadulterated being, a commendable vessel for the awesome Power. Through the kundalini procedure, this imagined unadulterated body-mind then becomes fact, for the rising of the serpent power through the pivotal pathway of the body summarizes the psychological procedure of bhuta-shuddhi, actually changing the body's science. Through rehashed practice of kundalini-yoga, Tantric adepts prevail with regards to accelerating the vibration of their body forever, prompting the production of the much-wanted "divine body" (divya-deha).

The language of vibration is in no way, shape or form present day yet is basic to the jargon of Tantra, especially the Tantric schools of Kashmir. The figure of speech of vibration has been created in incredible detail by the logician yogins of the Spanda School. As indicated by them, everything is vibration - the components, their inconspicuous layouts, the sense protests, the existence power, and the cakras. Indeed, even a definitive Shakti itself is vibratory in nature, however its vibration is, in contemporary terms, "translocal." The Spanda experts talk about this as a "semi vibration." But they demand that we should expect the supernatural Shakti to be dynamic, as in any case there is no conceivable clarification for the presence of the world or the way that it is continually evolving. A comparable to idea, which it may be useful to summon here, is physicist David Bohm's "holomovement," which is basically undefinable and immeasurable. This coinage alludes to a definitive establishment of all "embroil orders," that is, the increase included reality reflected in every one of its parts.

Essentially, the kundalini is a definitive, translocal vibration - Shakti - influencing the space-time continuum all the more straightforwardly as the yogin's or yoginis confined body-mind. Its supervibration deeply transmutes the constituents of the body-mind, at last making a transubstantiated or divinized body (divya-deha) enriched with exceptional limits that rise above the laws of nature as we probably am aware it.

The earth component, which is associated with the most minimal psychoenergetic focus, is disintegrated into its vigorous capability of smell (gandha-tanmatra). This is directed by the rising kundalini to the second psychoenergetic focus, where the Goddess power next disintegrates the water component into its vigorous capability of taste (rasa-tanmatra). This unobtrusive item is raised to the degree of the psychoenergetic focus at the navel. Here the kundalini transmutes the fire component into its vivacious capability of sight (rupa-tanmatra). This distillate is then taken to the degree of the heart place, where the kundalini impacts the transmutation of the breeze component into its lively capability of touch (sparsha-tanmatra). This unobtrusive type of the breeze component is next raised to the degree of the throat place, where the kundalini refines the ether component into its fiery capability of sound (shabda-tanmatra). This result of yogic speculative chemistry is directed to the degree of the ajna-cakra, in the head, and here the lower mind (manas) is disintegrated into the higher psyche (buddhi), which, thus, is broken down into the unpretentious grid of nature (sukshma-prakriti). The last period of disintegration happens when the serpent power comes to the highest psychoenergetic focus, where the unobtrusive grid of nature is broken up into the para-bindu, which is the preeminent purpose of birthplace of the individuated body-mind. Disintegration (laya) is key to Tantra Yoga. Henceforth we can read in the Kula-Arnava-Tantra:

Ten million customs of love equivalent one psalm; ten million songs equivalent one recitation [of a mantra]; ten million recitations equivalent one contemplation; ten million reflections equivalent a solitary [moment of] ingestion (laya).

In this way, in its rising toward the crown place, the kundalini-shakti strengthens the different cakras and afterward makes them shut down once more. In any case, this shutdown contrasts from the previous condition of negligible capacity in the normal individual, for the cakras of the skilled are never again shut down in light of pollutions (or karmic blocks) but since their energy has been transmuted. Henceforth when the kundalini comes back to its resting place at the base of the spine, the cakras continue their individual capacities yet in an undeniably increasingly incorporated or agreeable way.

When the kundalini punctures the inside in the midbrain - the ajna-cakra - it expect another type of presence and becomes cit-kun-dalini, or the "serpent of Consciousness." This occasion is joined by the incredible euphoria of nondual acknowledgment. This joy, emerging from the association of the Shakti with Lord Shiva, reaches out all through the body while yet rising above it.

Along the course, the rising kundalini may create a wide range of physiological and mental marvels, which are for the most part the aftereffect of inadequate recognizable proof with the Goddess power and a specific connection to the body. The Tantras notice starded hopping (udbhava or pluti), trembling (kampana), a spinning sensation (ghurni), tiredness (nidra), just as overjoyed emotions (ananda) that are not, nonetheless, of a similar greatness or importance as the preeminent delight of supernatural acknowledgment. The writings likewise discuss a wide range of sound-related marvels, progressively unpretentious indications of the inward stable (nothing). The rising of the serpent power through the six head "wheels" of the body is actually called pooed cakra-bhedana, or "puncturing the six communities." This inquisitive articulation is clarified by the way that in the customary individual the cakras are lacking and increasingly like bunches (granthi) than lovely lotus blossoms. The stirred kundalini tears them open, unravels their energies, and vitalizes and balances them. Three of the cakras speak to a specific test to the yogin andyogini. Subsequently the Tantric and non-Tantric sacred texts notice three bunches, at the base of the spine, the throat, and the "third eye." They are called brahma-, vishnu-, and rudra-granthi individually, after the gods Brahma, Vishnu, and Rudra (= Shiva).

There are different spots at which the existence power is "hitched," causing tightening influences. Blockages can happen especially at the touchy spots called marmans (intersections), which are disseminated over the entire body. Yoga, Tantra, and Ayurveda for the most part perceive eighteen such spots. The Shandilya-Upanishad makes reference to the accompanying twenty-five areas for them: the feet, enormous toes, lower legs, shanks, knees, thighs, butt, penis, navel, heart, throat, jugular score (called kupa, "well"), the sense of taste, nose, eyes, center of the eyebrows, temple, and head. Hatha Yoga, which is a Tantra based order, incorporates rehearses intended to release blocked energy in these marmans. These include managing the existence power through centered representation to each marman and afterward holding the breath, which actuates them. Upon exhalation, the blocked energy is discharged. This is likewise a great method for supporting the mending procedure where infection is available.

The objective of Tantra is to have the kundalini remain for all time raised to the highest psychoenergetic focus, which state harmonizes with freedom. Toward the start, in any case, the kundalini will in general come back to the cakra at the base of the spine on the grounds that the body-mind isn't yet sufficiently arranged. Along these lines the specialist should over and over welcome the Goddess capacity to join with her perfect companion, Shiva, at the highest point of Mount Kailasa, that is, in the sahasrara-cakra. This will step by step expel the karmic tendency toward relating to the body-mind as opposed to Shiva-Shakti as one's definitive personality. In Kashmiri Tantra, this ever-joyful supernatural personality is called aham ("I") versus the limited inner self (ahamkara, "I-creator"), which is driven by the craving to expand delight and limit torment but then consistently plants the seeds of affliction.

Tantra Yoga targets dissolving the deception of being a different limited substance, and it does as such by methods for the association of the kula-kundalim with the supernatural rule of akula, or Shiva. When this is cultivated there is nothing that isn't understood as completely delighted. Indeed, even the body, recently experienced as a material bump (pinda), apparently is remarkably cognizant and suffused with the strengthening nectar of happiness and at one with every single other body and with the universe itself.

Affected by Shakti, the body's science begins to change

and the specialist looks transfigured to the eyes of outside eyewitnesses. The person in question turns out to be progressively brilliant, showing the preeminent Consciousness-Bliss (cid-ananda). The Tantric adroit actually turns into a reference point of Light on the planet.

Chapter Twelve:

Potency Of Sound

Present day science and antiquated Tantra concur: the universe is an expanse of energy. Where they vary is in how this reality ought to be comprehended. The Tantric methodology attests that this finding has individual ramifications. On the off chance that issue can in reality be set out to energy, then the human body, as a result of the material universe, is moreover energy at a progressively essential level. As the Tantras further demand, energy and awareness are eventually conjoined as the two posts of a similar Reality, Shiva-Shakti. In this manner the human body is, in the last examination, not simply oblivious issue but rather a ventured down form of superconscious Energy. This understanding has broad pragmatic implications for every individual. For if the body isn't only the stone casket of an insignificant soul however a lively, living reality suffused with a similar Consciousness that likewise enlivens the brain, then we should stop to see the body as an outside item drastically unmistakable from our cognizant selves. The ongoing split among body and psyche isn't just baseless however adverse to the completeness which spiritual searchers hope for. To place it in customary terms, the body is a sanctuary of the Divine. It is the establishment for understanding the basic unity of everything; it is the springboard from which we can achieve illumination - an edification that for it to be genuine should fundamentally incorporate every one of the physical body's thirty billion cells.

The Tantric position is clear: presence is One, and we are it. All division and disruptiveness is a consequent mental develop (vikalpa). In any case, the Tantras don't deny separation all things considered. The Many shows up inside the One however while never getting disconnected from it. The Tantric adepts only reject the idea of duality and the going with self image driven demeanor of separativeness. Presence is progression "extending from the Radical Potential to its actualisation as the outside layer of issue."

This is wonderfully contained in the idea of the serpent power (kundalini-shakti), which is a definitive Energy, or Shakti, as it shows at an appropriately ventured down degree in the human body. The kundalini is the intensity of Consciousness (cit-shakti), and thusly is the hyper-savvy power supporting the body and the psyche through the office of the existence energy (prana). Upon full arousing, the kundalinis basic job in the support of our physical and mental structures and capacities is seen straightforwardly. Gopi Krishna has communicated this clearly as follows:

I scanned my cerebrum for a clarification and spun each plausibility in my psyche to represent the astounding create merit as I observed mindfully the inconceivable development of this insightful radiation from hour to hour and everyday. On occasion I was astonished at the uncanny information it showed of the muddled apprehensive system and the excellent manner by which it dashed to a great extent as though mindful of each contort and turn in the body.

That the kundalini is an astronomical - even a

supracosmic - savvy energy is borne out by its conventional name sarasvati, signifying "she who streams." Originally, this was the name of North India's mightiest waterway, which coursed through the heartland of the Vedic human progress, presently lying covered under the sand rises of the Thar Desert. A memory of the previous social enormity of that district has made due in the figure of Sarasvati, the goddess of realizing, who is commonly depicted holding a lute (vina). Shakti is in fact the wellspring of all information and insight, for without the Goddess power, neither the psyche nor the cerebrum would exist.

Besides, in the Tantric sacred texts, nna-danda or "fiddlestick" is an exclusive assignment for the spinal section and, by expansion, the focal channel. When the focal channel is initiated through the climb of the existence power (prana) trailed by the serpent power itself, a wide range of unobtrusive sounds can be heard internally. Associated with this is the possibility that the body of the celestial serpent is made out of the fifty fundamental letters of the Sanskrit letter set, which compares to the fifty skulls worn by the goddess Kali as a wreath (mala). The letters in order is classified "wreath of letters" (varna-mala), proposing the higher reason imagined for human language by the Vedic sages, to be specific, to properly respect and communicate divine Reality.

Sanskrit, as the word itself demonstrates, is an intentionally built (samskrita) language. As indicated by convention, it is the language of the divine beings - deva-vani. The content itself is known as deva-nagan (city of the divine beings), which alludes to the Tantric (and Vedic) thought that each letter of the letter set speaks to a specific sort of central energy, or god power. Together these network energies weave the snare of infinite and thus additionally real presence. Here we have again the thought, quintessential to Tantra, that the microcosm reflects the cosmos. The body and the universe everywhere are delivered by a similar energy equations that the Tantrics have communicated as the fifty chief hints of the Sanskrit letters in order, which was created with regards to deep practice and sacrosanct vision.

As the Sharada-Tilaka-Tantra states, the kundalini is the sonic Absolute (shabda-brahman). The sonic Absolute is the soundless Absolute (ashabda-brahman) ventured down to the degree of enormous sound (shabda), comparing to the hermetic "agreement of the circles" and the gnostic logos: "initially was the Word." The Mantra-Yoga-Samhita offers this clarification:

Any place there is movement, it is definitely associated with vibration. Additionally, any place there is vibration seen on the planet it is constantly connected with [audible or inaudible] sound.

Attributable to the separation happening at the underlying minute, creation is vibratory too. The sound delivered then is the pranava, which has the type of the propitious om-kara.

The Sharada-Tilaka-Tantra portrays the cosmogonic procedure as far as the creation of sound as follows: From the incomparable Shakti - unadulterated Consciousness joined with the factor of clarity (sattva) - comes the most unobtrusive sound (dhvani), which is set apart by a transcendence of the elements of clarity and dynamism (rajas). Out of the dhvani builds up the unobtrusive sound (nothing), described by a blend of the components of clarity, dynamism, and idleness (tamas). This inconspicuous sound, thus, offers ascend to the energy of limitation (nirodhika), which has an overabundance of the factor of idleness. This ontic standard exudes the "half-moon" (ardha-indu, written ardhendu), which at this lower level again shows a transcendence of the factor of clarity. Out of it comes the vibratory source point (bindu), the prompt wellspring everything being equal and words. These structure mantras, which are in this manner indications or vehicles of Shakti. This sacred text further clarifies that the bindu is itself made out of three sections: nothing, bindu, and bija (seed). The initial segment has a prevalence of Consciousness (i.e., Shiva), the second a dominance of Energy (i.e., Shakti), and the third an equivalent nearness of Consciousness and Energy. Such exclusive records of the advancement of sound remain moderately muddled outside of Tantric practice. However, they become progressively important as the expert gains ground on the way of mantra-vidya, or "mantric science."

Dissimilar to the sounds we can hear with our ears, the grandiose sound is uncaused. It is a limitless vibration (spanda) that is coextensive with the universe itself and is feasible just in deep reflection when the faculties and the psyche have been deactivated. The early stage sound is emblematically spoken to by the consecrated syllable om. Even though not referenced legitimately in the Rig-Veda, the om sound - likewise called pranava4 and udgitha - is alluded to in different songs. It is first referenced by name in the Shukla-Yajur-Veda. Later on, in the period of the

Upani-shads, it came to be clarified as comprising of the three constituent sounds a, u, and m. As per the Mandukya-Upanishad, these speak to the three conditions of waking, dreaming, and dozing separately. Past these is the "fourth" (turiya), which is the state of absolute alertness all through all conditions of cognizance. It is simply a definitive Being-Consciousness. Resulting sacred texts have explained on this imagery, including the components of nothing (unobtrusive sound) and bindu (zero-darkensional seed point).

The Tantric hypotheses about sound and amazing quality are very old and were foreshadowed by the Vedic idea of vac, divine discourse. In the Rig-Veda, vac is embodied as the Goddess by that name, who articulates the accompanying hallowed words:

I am the sovereign, gatherer of wealth, the astute one, boss among those deserving of penance. The divinities have put me in numerous spots, thus I live in numerous stations and go into numerous [forms].

Through only me, he who eats nourishment sees, inhales, and hears what is said. Staying in Me, they die [ignorant of this fact]. Listen who can hear, I reveal to you that wherein you ought to have faith.

Verily, I pronounce of myself that which is friendly to gods and people. Whomsoever I want I render him imposing (ugra), a soothsayer, a wise, a brahmin.

Another song of the Rig-Veda expresses that "one who looks doesn't see Vac, and another who listens doesn't hear her." She uncovers herself, the content proceeds, as a caring spouse uncovers her body to her significant other. At the end of the day, Vac is very unpretentious and self-uncovering - a specialist of effortlessness. As the opening stanza pronounces, it was through fondness that Vac originally uncovered herself to the Vedic diviners. Then, proceeds with refrain 3, shrewd minstrels followed Vac's way through their penances and discovered her covered up inside the sages. There can be no doubt that this Vedic goddess represents a similar celestial Power that in later occasions came to be revered as Shakti and evoked as the snake power.

What the different models portraying the advancement of sound or vibration share practically speaking is the possibility that there are in any event three levels at which sound exists. The Tantric sacred texts recognize the accompanying:

1. Pashyanti-vac (unmistakable discourse) - the most unpretentious type of sound noticeable just to instinct
2. Madhyama-vac (middle of the road discourse) - sound at the inconspicuous degree of presence, which is the voice of thought
3. Vaikhan-vdc (show discourse) - perceptible sound transmitted through vibration of the air

Past these three is the supernatural level called para-vac, or "preeminent discourse," which is Shakti in ideal association with Shiva. It is soundless sound, alluded to in the Rig-Veda in the expression "the One inhaled enthusiastically."

The three degrees of sound compare to the three structures or levels of the snake power:

1. Urdhva-kundalini (upper snake), the kundalini essentially dynamic in the ajna-cakra and having a tendency to climb toward the thou-sand-petaled lotus at the crown of the head
2. Madhya-kundalini (center snake), the Goddess power dynamic in the district of the heart and equipped for climbing or plummeting
3. Adhah-kundalini (lower snake), the psychospiritual vitality basically connected with the three lower cakras
1. In its celestial angle, the snake power is known as pard-kundalini, or Shakti as such. From the point of view of Tantric way of thinking, each and every structure or part of the universe is a sign of that extreme Power and an image for it. Considering contemporary quantum material science, the "vitality language" of Tantra bodes well than maybe it did to pariahs at the hour of its creation 2,000 and more years prior.

In its upward section through the body's hub pathway, the Goddess power breaks down the cakras bit by bit. This can likewise be comprehended in sonic terms. As indicated by practically indistinguishable depictions found in different Tantras, when the kundalini leaves the base cakra, it accumulates in the central energies caught in the four letters engraved in the four petals of the muladhdra lotus. It then continues to the second cakra, where it assembles the six letter energies from that point, etc. At long last, the letter energies of the ajnd-cakra are broken down into the supernatural seed point together with the cakra itself. When each of the fifty letters of the letter set, or essential vibrations, are along these lines broken up, edification happens. The Sharadd-Tilaka-Tantra depicts a type of inception (diksha) in which the instructor enters the supporter's body and plays out this procedure oneself. This has been depicted in section 7 as vedha-diksha, or "commencement by entrance."

THE NATURE OF MANTRAS

The fifty letters (varna) of the Sanskrit letters in order, which in a way speak to the body of the kundalini, are designated "frameworks" (matrika), a term that can likewise signify "little moms." They are the bellies of all sounds that make up language and are inserted in the unpretentious sound (nothing). These letters produce common words as well as the holy sounds called mantras. A mantra can comprise of a solitary letter, a syllable, a word, or even a whole expression. In this manner the vowel a, the syllable ah, the word aham ("I"), or the expression shivo'ham ("I am Shiva," comprising of shivah and aham) can serve in a mantric limit. Moreover, the four Vedic hymnodies (Rig-Veda, Yajur-Veda, Sama-Veda, and Atharva-Veda) have generally been held to comprise of mantras just, in light of the fact that the psalms have all been uncovered by soothsayers (rishi).

The word mantra is made out of the verbal root man (to think) and the postfix tra, demonstrating instrumentality. Accordingly a mantra is actually an instrument of thought. In his Vimarshini editorial on the Shiva-Sutra, Kshemaraja clarifies that a mantra is "that by which one covertly considers or internally ponders one's character with the idea of the incomparable Lord." This translation centers around the association among mantra and manana (thinking, considering, reflecting). As indicated by another conventional historical underpinnings, mantra gets its name from giving insurance (trana) for the brain (manas).

A long way from being garbage syllables, as a prior age of researchers has asserted, mantras are imaginative powers that demonstration legitimately upon cognizance. Yet, for a sound to have mantric power it more likely than not been transmitted by a start. At the end of the day, the popular om sound without anyone else is not any more a mantra than the word hound. It procures mantric esteem just when it has been enabled by a skilled and transmitted to a devotee. This is a fundamentally significant point that is commonly obscure to Western searchers. The motivation behind why mantras can be in this manner po-tentized at all is that they have the Goddess power for their embodarkent. "Without Her," announces the Tantra-Sadbhdva, "they are as ineffective as mists in fall." But just an adroit in whom the kundalini is conscious can engage a sound - any stable - so it is transmuted into a mantra. As Shiva tells his celestial life partner in the Mahanirvana-Tantra, "O Beloved, your mantras are innumerable."

Fruitful mantra practice depends on appropriate commencement as well as on understanding the substance behind the sound. This is clarified in the Shri-Kanthvya-Samhita, which states:

Inasmuch as the mantrin8 is particular from the mantra, he can't be effective. Insight alone should be the foundation of this; else he isn't effective.

A mantra must be stirred (prabuddha) so as to release its natural force. This is otherwise called "mantric cognizance" (mantra-caitanya), which goes past the discernible sound to the degree of psychospiritual power itself. As the Western skilled Swami Chetana-nanda clarifies:

At last, our act of any mantra is planned to refine our attention to where we experience that throb going on inside every one of us the time. When we can do that, we disregard the mantra itself since we are currently mindful, rather, of the dynamic occasion going on inside and around us. Subsequently, the absolute vibration of what we are is changed. All the while, we change ourselves.

A mantra ailing in "cognizance" is much the same as some other sound.

As the Kula-Arnava-Tantra states:

Mantras without cognizance are said to be minor letters.

They yield no outcome much after a trillion recitations.

The express that shows quickly when the mantra is discussed [with "consciousness"], that outcome isn't [to be gained] from a hundred, a thousand, a hundred thousand, or ten million recitations.

Kuleshvarl, the bunches at the heart and throat are pierced, all the appendages are stimulated, tears of bliss, gooseflesh, substantial delight, and tremulous discourse out of nowhere happen without a doubt.

When a mantra blessed with awareness is expressed even once. Where such signs are seen, the [mantra] is said to be as indicated by custom.

To energize or "reinforce" a mantra, one should rehash it a huge number of times - a strategy called purashcarana (starter practice). As the ShrT-Tattva-Cintamani states:

Similarly as the body is unequipped for activity without the mind, so likewise is said to be a mantra without the fundamental practice.

Accordingly the preeminent of specialists should initially embrace the fundamental practice. Just through such application can the god [of a mantra] be managed.

The last stanza contains a clarification for the distinction between a mantra and a conventional sound. While all sounds are eventually appearances of the awesome Power, mantras are particularly thought articulations of Shakti. This gives them their specific intensity and helpfulness on the profound way. Bringing a god leveled out may sound peculiar or even hostile to Western ears, however as indicated by Tantra these divinities (devata) are in the last examination essentially higher sorts of psychospiritual vitality. Since they are clever powers and seem to have an individual place, the Tantric specialists are careful to identify with them with proper regard and commitment. They see, be that as it may, that these divinity energies are their own actual nature, the Self. To manage a god intends to have the option to utilize their particular vitality for the spiritual procedure or in any event, for common closures. The Tantric professionals should continually shuffle the twofold acknowledgment that there is just the One and that this Singularity (ekatva) seems separated at the degree of wonderful presence. In this manner they realize that they are both lover and a definitive object of dedication.

The Mantra-Yoga-Samhita contains point by point data about choosing a mantra for a follower, promising and ominous days for granting a mantra, and the different products of mantric practice. Mantras can be utilized both for freedom and other auxiliary purposes, for example, fighting ailment or malevolence impacts, or picking up riches and influence. Most noble professionals are hesitant to utilize mantras for something besides the best human objective (purusha-artha, composed purushartha), which is freedom. In Tantric ceremonies, mantras are utilized to cleanse the special raised area, one's seat, executes, for example, vessels and offering spoons, or the contributions themselves (e.g., blossoms, water, nourishment), or to summon gods and defenders, etc. However the study of sacrosanct sound (mantra-shastra) has since old occasions been generally put to mainstream use too. Right now, expect the character of mysterious spells instead of consecrated vibrations in the administration of self-change and self-amazing quality.

The Kula-Amava-Tantra makes reference to sixty deformities that can render mantra practice useless. To list just a portion of these: a mantra can be "obstructed" (by copying a syllable), "wrongly syllabled," "broken," "inert," "contaminated," "insecure," "dread imparting," "frail," and "betrayed." In request to cure these inadequacies, the Sharada-Tilaka-Tantra prescribes the training ofyjoni-mudra. This system, which is notable from Hatha Yoga sacred writings, is performed by getting the muscles of the perineum, which makes the fundamental vitality rise. Moreover, in any case, the Tantric professional ought to imagine the fifty letters of the letters in order climbing from the psychospiritual focus at the base of the spine to the cakra at the crown of the head. This content likewise gives an option in contrast to this training, which can be found in the Kula-Amava-Tantra too. These are the accompanying ten medicinal practices (samskara):

1. Making (janana) - separating a mantra's constituent syllables from the letter set

2. Animating (jivana) - presenting every syllable independently with the om sound prefixed to it

3. Pounding (tadana) - sprinkling each composed syllable of a mantra with water while presenting the seed syllable yam (for the air component)

4. Arousing (bodhana) - contacting each composed syllable with a red oleander blossom while presenting the seed syllable smash (for the fire component); the quantity of blossoms ought to relate to the quantity of syllables

5. Blessing (abhisheka) - sprinkling each composed syllable with water containing the twigs of the ashvattha tree (the hallowed fig tree); the quantity of twigs ought to relate to the quantity of syllables

6. Purifying (vimali-karana) - picturing a mantra's pollutions being singed by discussing om hraum, which is the mantra for light

7. Reinforcing (apyayana) - sprinkling each composed syllable with water containing kusha grass

8. Offering water (tarpana) - offering water to the mantra while saying, "I satisfy mantra someone or other"

9. Offering light (dipana) - prefixing the seed syllables om hrim shrim to a mantra

10. Hiding gupti) - keeping one's mantra mystery

Mantras of concentrate d potenc y are know n as "see d syllables" (bija). Om is the unique seed syllable, the wellspring of all others. The Mantra-Yoga-Samhita considers it the "best everything being equal," including that all othe r mantras get their capacity from it. Along these lines om is prefixed or suffixed to numerou s mantras:

Om namah shivaya. "Om. Respect to Shiva."

Om namo bhagavate. u0m. Respect to the Lord [Krishna or Vishnu]."

Om namo ganeshaya. "Om. Respect to [the elephant-headed] Ganesha."

Om namo narayanaya. "Om. Respect to Narayana [Vishnu]."

Om bhur bbuvah svah tat savitur varenyam bhargo devasya dhimahi dhiyo jo nah pracodaydt. "Om. Earth. Mid-locale. Paradise. Let us mull over the most astounding quality of Savitri, that he may move our dreams." (This is the well known Vedic gayatri-mantra.)

Om shante prashante sarva-krodha-upashamani svaha. "Om. Settled! Assuaging! All outrage be curbed! Hail!" (Note elocution: sarva-krodhopashamani)

Om sac-cid-ekam brahma. "Om. The particular Being-Consciousness, the Absolute." (The word sac is an euphonic variation of sat, signifying "being.")

The Mahanirvana-Tantra calls the last-referenced brahma-mantra the most brilliant all things considered, which instantly presents freedom as well as prudence, riches, and delight. It is reasonable for all professionals and doesn't require cautious calculations before it is given. "Simply by accepting the mantra," this sacred text asserts, "the individual is loaded up with the Absolute." And, this Tantra proceeds, "watched by the brahma-mantra and encompassed with the wonder of the Absolute, he becomes brilliant like another sun for all the planets, and so on."

Over numerous hundreds of years, the Vedic and Tantric bosses have imagined, or rather imagined, various other essential force sounds other than om. These seed syllables (bija), as they are called, can be utilized without anyone else or, all the more regularly, related to other force sounds, framing a mantric expression. As indicated by the Mantra-Yoga-Sam-hita, there are eight essential bija-mantras, which are useful in a wide range of conditions however which yield their more profound riddle just to the yogin:

1. Point (articulated "I'm") - master bija (seed syllable of the instructor), likewise called vahni-jaya (Agni's significant other)

2. Hnm - shakti-bija (seed syllable of Shakti), likewise called maya-bija

3. Klim - kama-bija (seed syllable of want)

4. Krim - yoga-bija (seed syllable of association), likewise called kali-bija

5. Shirim - rama-bija (seed syllable of joy); since Rama is another name for Lakshmi, the goddess of fortune, this seed syllable is otherwise called lakshmi-bija

6. Trim-teja-bija (seed syllable of fire)

7. Strim - shanti-bija (seed syllable of harmony)

8. Hlim - raksha-blja (seed syllable of security)

Different schools or messages outfit various names for these eight essential bijas or even by and large various constructions. Some other notable seed syllables are lam, vam, smash, yam, ham (all related with the five components and the lower five cakras), murmur, murmur (called varman, or "shield"), and phat (called astra, or "weapon").

THE ART OF RECITATION

At the point when a professional has gotten a mantra from the mouth of a start, the person can be sure of achievement in mantric recitation (japa), giving obviously all the guidelines for legitimate recitation are followed too. Care, consistency, and countless redundancies of the mantra are the three most significant prerequisites. Additionally, there are sure consecrated spots where mantra practice is considered especially promising. As per the Kula-Arnava-Tantra, japa close to one's instructor, a brahmin, a cow, a tree, water, or a holy fire is especially encouraging. This content moreover recommends the act of "imbuement" (nyasa) for mantric recitation.

Japa can be acted in three central manners: verbalized (vacika), murmured (upamshu), and recounted intellectually (manasa). The primary style, perceptible recitation, is viewed as substandard compared to the next two styles. In murmured recitation just the lips move however no discernible sound breaks them. Better than this style is mental recitation, where consideration is fixed solely on the inward significance of the mantra.

Twenty-one, 108, or 1,008 redundancies are viewed as favorable. Be that as it may, for the mantra to open its intensity (virya), a huge number of reiterations might be fundamental. When this has happened, in any case, even a solitary way to express the mantra will make its capacity accessible to the mantrin or japin, the reciter of mantras. By and by, sooner or later the mantra recounts itself unexpectedly, and its inborn force can be felt as a consistent charge of vitality present in one's body. This is ajapa-japa, or "unrecited recitation" - otherwise called the hamsa-mantra - which is more than the psychological "reverberation" that happens when we rehash a word again and again. It isn't just a psychological notch brought about by verbal redundancy yet a brain changing lively condition of being.

It is thought imperative to track the quantity of reiterations. This is commonly done by methods for a rosary (mala). Rosaries may comprise of 15, 24, 27, 30, 50, or most normally, 108 dots, in addition to one "ace dab," speaking to one's master or Mount Meru, an image for the focal channel. The number 108 has been held consecrated and promising in India since antiquated occasions. Different translations have been offered for this exceptionally emblematic number, however the most probable clarification lies in space science. As of now in the Vedic time, the sages knew that the moon's and furthermore the sun's normal good ways from the earth is multiple times their individual distances across. As the American Vedic scientist Subhash Kak has appeared, this number was urgent in the development of the Vedic fire special stepped area. Emblematically, 108 is the number connoting the midregion (antariksha), the space among paradise and earth. In this manner the 108 globules can be taken to speak to an equivalent number of steps from the material world to the iridescent domain of the perfect Reality - India's form of Jacob's stepping stool.

O rosary! O rosary! O extraordinary adding machine! You are the embodarkent of all force.

In You are discovered the four objectives [i.e., material flourishing, joy, ethical quality, and liberation]. Subsequently award me all achievement.

Another customary method for monitoring the quantity of reiterations is by tallying with one's fingers. Different techniques are known, and some are explicit to specific mantras. It is viewed as foreboding to tally just with the tip of one's fingers, and rather one should, as per the Mantra-Yoga-Samhita, utilize the different phalanxes also.

A mantra ought to be presented with the correct sound, as gained from one's instructor, and furthermore at the best possible pace. In the event that, as the Kula-Arnava-Tantra clarifies, it is rehashed excessively quickly, there is the risk of illness. On the off chance that it is discussed too gradually, notwithstanding, it will decrease one's vitality. In either case, japa will be "futile like water in a messed up vessel." This Tantra besides calls attention to the normal polluting influences at the beginning and the end of recitation, which must be canceled by an uncommon mantric practice, in particular, by presenting the mantra 7 or multiple times with om toward the start and the end.

Since mantras must be recounted various occasions over numerous hours consistently before they can manage natural product, it is simple for a professional to get drained. All things considered the sacred writings regularly prescribe moving from japa to contemplation. Of course, when the psyche is depleted from reflection, exchanging back to discussing one's mantra can bring reestablished energy and excitement.

Mantras may not exclusively be spoken or intellectually discussed yet additionally worked out on paper, metal, fabric, or different materials. This procedure is known as likhita-japa, which, in the expressions of Swami Sivananda Radha, "brings harmony, balance and quality inside." The equivalent is obviously valid for different types of japa also. Likewise with every yogic practice, the achievement of mantra recitation depends to an enormous degree on the expert's inspiration and commitment.

Tantric Sex

A Guide in the Tantric Philosophy to discover
Tantric Sex Positions, Tantric Massage and
Tantric Meditation

Avaya Alorveda

Chapter One

Tantra And Tantric Sex

Before beginning with tantric sex, it is pivotal to comprehend the idea of Tantra. The act of Tantra can be followed back to antiquated India, where a few holy people and blessed men used to take part in different ceremonial and meditational systems. This system is accepted to have been in presence since the fifth century A.D., and it was seen as a technique that would enable an individual saddle to divine cognizance just as their still, small voice. This idea traversed the globe and brought about the cutting edge use of the term Tantra accepting another importance through and through. The term Tantra is prominently connected with the act of Tantric sex. This includes participating in a sexual demonstration with the purpose of collecting divine cognizance together. To lay it out plainly, tantric sex is a training that is used for arriving at sexual nirvana.

History of Tantra

There is some indefinite quality with respect to the birthplace of the idea of tantric sex, however it is a prevalent view that a network, alluded to as the "Lemurian" individuals were viewed as the primary individuals to rehearse this specific type of holy sex. They thought about the human body as an awesome vessel and used different animating procedures for connecting with the senses so as to bring in spiritual liberatedom. A few people will in general accept that Tantra is identified with the old Indian act of "yoga" too, since these two systems use distinctive substantial stances for shaping a bond with the Cosmos.

Tantric sex has increased a great deal of prevalence in the ongoing past and it has gotten well known in the western world with a ton of famous people like Sting, Madonna and even the late Steve Jobs who had confessed to having attempted this system. Presently, it has gradually discovered acknowledgment everywhere throughout the world. A few idealists do have faith in its viability in accomplishing more noteworthy delight.

Tantric sex fulfills individuals genuinely, intellectually and deeply too. Tantric sex gives total fulfillment and causes the whole body to feel incredibly pleasurable, helps in sincerely interfacing with one's partner and on a deep level; it helps in the amalgamation of two spirits and carries them closer to godliness.

Tantra uses two energies; the female and the male energies. The female energy is alluded to as Shakti, and the male energy is known as Shiva. Shakti and Shiva are Hindu divine beings, and their object of worship revere includes the venerating of Ling and Yon. Linga implies the penis and far off methods the vagina. When a couple participates in tantric sex, then the female energy present in the body, Shakti, ascends through the diverse chakras, and it penetrates through the female community that is alluded to as the Kundalini and afterward it converges with the male energy, alluded to as Shiva. This combination of energies helps in framing a bond that outperforms the human domain.

Different parts of Tantric Sex

There are three primary significant parts of Tantric sex, and these are tantric correspondence, tantric positions and tantric working out. Tantric correspondence is a procedure that helps in the converging of a couple genuinely and intellectually. This aides in bringing them near each other and is fit for transforming a standard couple into perfect partners. Tantric positions are sure places that will help in uniting a couple explicitly. There are distinctive tantric activities just as breathing strategies that will help in harvesting the most out of tantric sex. More data about these three parts of Tantric sex has been clarified in the coming sections.

Tantric sex helps in liberating the body, brain and soul. This is conceivable through the act of the systems as referenced previously. Quieting one's psyche is a vital part of any training that includes meditation. So also, for practicing tantric sex, it is basic to facilitate your brain. These procedures have been referenced in the book.

In contrast to normal sex, the lessons of tantric sex focus on making the members mindful of their activities while engaged with a sexual demonstration with their partner. If you are aware of your activities, then you can guarantee that you can initiate a sentiment of veneration and even regard for your partner. It is tied in with respecting your body and that of your partner's also. The essential goal of tantric sex is to assist you with loosening up your body and brain. When you can discover this discharge, you will have the option to communicate without any difficulty that will develop and reinforce the security that exists among you and your partner; the sort of love that would bind together your spirits.

Tantric sex encourages you heal

Maybe one of the best potential employments of tantric sex is that it can help in healing your body and soul. It will likewise assist you with letting go of undesirable thoughts and cause your psyche to feel lighter. You may have been harmed before or might have persevered through some type of dismissal in your past connections. Tantric sex will help you in excusing yourself and will assist you with learning to adore yourself by and by and to appreciate your body as you were intended to. Various strategies have been referenced right now will help you in mending and liberating yourself from any blame or injury that you may have persevered. You will see that you will feel progressively engaged if you follow the guidance that has been given right now. Tantric sex will without a doubt assist you with mending and it is done through the next advances. You should distinguish the occurrence that has harmed you previously. This hurt could have been genuine or nonexistent. In this way, the subsequent stage is decide if it was genuine or fanciful. Sexual incitement will help you in recognizing the distinction. You will have the option to locate the negative feelings connected to this specific damage and can release them. Replace these negative sentiments with positive feelings and encounters that will enable you to heal.

Tantric sex is in fact enchanted. You will find that the different methods that have been referenced right now not just assist you in relinquishing your feelings of trepidation and hurt, yet they will likewise help you in communicating better. Additionally, as an additional advantage these strategies will help you in feeling more youthful and increasingly loose.

Myths And Truths

Tantra is tied in with commending sexuality and sexiness. It is a general misinterpretation that Tantra is about sex. Without being completely mindful of the Tantra, individuals have been known to scrutinize it. This area helps in revealing all the fantasies that are related with Tantric sex and Tantra.

Myth #1: Tantric sex is just about sex.

Truth: Tantric sex involves sex, yet it isn't about genital touch. Tantric sex is about the relationship of the spirits and not simply the bodies. Genital touch or sex will just assistance in expanding this relationship between the spirits. Nonetheless, this is done just when the couple is alright with one another and is prepared for that degree of closeness. Tantric sex includes different perspectives that have literally nothing to do with sex.

Myth #2: If you begin practicing Tantra, then you are just abandoning delight.

Truth: This myth is inexactly founded on the past myth. It is basically a myth. The educating of Tantra do exclude the repudiating of sexual delight, similar to a portion of the yogic practices do. Tantra essentially upgrades the degree of joy that you can understanding. Tantric sex hypothesis doesn't make reference to that you have to deny your wants. Truth be told, Tantric sex energizes the free articulation of your sexual wants. You don't need to imitate a yogi, sit leg over leg or reflect for a long time for shaping an relationship with the Cosmos. Tantra understands the significance of sex in a person's life and it helps in the bridling of the torpid sexual energy present in the body for accomplishing ecstasy. This joy can be accomplished is past anything present in the physical domain.

Myth #3: Tantric sex expands your sexual hunger and the requirement for looking for joy that prompts issues.

Truth: Tantric sex doesn't build your sexual craving or lead you off track as you continued looking for delight. Rather, it will help you in controlling your wants and will likewise help in directing the sexual energy that is available inside your body for a higher reason. You may have not known about your actual potential. Tantric sex doesn't energize participating in sex with various partners. This suspicion has by one way or another advanced into the psyches of numerous and isn't right. As referenced before, Tantric sex will help you in shaping a solid physical and passionate bond with your partner and just develop the deep responsibility that exists between you. Sexuality isn't something that ought to be tossed around carelessly; it should be regarded and valued for accomplishing a more elevated level of cognizance. It isn't tied in with surging towards a climax, however it is tied in with figuring out how to control yourself and your wants. This will help in shaping a more grounded connection towards your partner. You will have the option to shape a relationship that did not depend on physical requirements.

Myth #4: It will transform you into a nymphomaniac.

Truth: Well, this isn't valid, and it is very senseless.

Tantric sex helps in discharging all the sexual energy present in the body and it likewise enables you to communicate as unreservedly as could be allowed, yet this doesn't imply that it will transform you into a nymphomaniac. In any case, there are chances this can be abused. With training, you will have the option to control your wants and quit getting a charge out of unimportant sex.

These normal myths have defaced the picture of Tantric sex in the psyches of the overall population. Is anything but a forbidden and ought to be drilled uninhibitedly if that is your decision.

The Ten promises of Tantra

When you have decided to follow the lessons of Tantric sex, then there are ten promises that you should recollect. Before beginning, it is significant that you recognize what these vows are. You should feel a feeling of harmony while saying these promises. The ten vows are as per the next:

1. I vow to find the godliness that exists inside my body.
2. I vow to regard and seek after the Gods and Goddesses that exist inside my body and that of my partner's also.
3. I promise to investigate my sexuality as well as my exotic nature too, for ensuring that none of my chakras are being blocked as a result of any feelings.
4. I vow to find some kind of harmony between my spirit, connections and my environment.
5. I vow to use this balance for guaranteeing that the remainder of the world finds a sense of contentment too.
6. I vow to comprehend as well as investigate my erotic

nature for guaranteeing that there's congruity in my connections.

7. I vow to ensure that all the psychological pressure and blockages that exist due to my past or even my present have been evacuated. I will free my soul and communicate with no limitations.

8. I promise to progress in the direction of reconnecting with my internal identity.

9. I promise to adore and heal my partner and myself also.

10. I vow to use the revived sexual energy for making myself progressively sure, delicate and associate with my partner and people around me.

You need to take part and watch

As referenced before, you should ensure that your brain is quiet and calm for practicing tantric sex. This is the main manner by which you will have the option to be a member and an eyewitness also. This implies you should be watching your activities as well as those of your partner too while you are occupied with lovemaking.

When you begin focusing on your activities, then you are an observer. This will help you in relinquishing any tension that you may be encountering. When an individual is having intercourse, paying little heed to their sex, there would be a million meditations and questions experiencing their brains. They would stress over whether they can please their partner. Does their partner like what they are doing? Is it accurate to say that they are doing it right? These inquiries add to the nervousness levels and detract from the capability of unwinding. When you begin next the educating of Tantric sex, then you will have the option to observe yourself while occupied with this demonstration. Here are a few systems that will help you in being both a member just as an onlooker.

Mantras

Have you at any point been exhausted to such an extent that you essentially begin murmuring a specific sound ceaselessly? Did this appear to have some sleep inducing impact on you? Mantras are very like this. They are quiet or even spoken sounds and they evoke a specific response from the body in view of their vibrations. These vibrations compare with all the seven chakras that are available in the body. If you have never encountered this, then have a go at saying "Om" and attract full breaths that would compare with this "Om." You will see that you can quiet yourself down and are additionally ready to center your psyche. You will have the option to control the development of energy that is available inside your body. A mantra has a similar impact at the forefront of your thoughts and your perspective as your preferred music does. You will have the option to quiet yourself down. When you use mantras, your brain can meander any place it satisfies and take you along.

The sounds that you make while saying a mantra are short and redundant in nature. This reiteration causes them to have a sleep inducing impact. A mantra can be a solitary word, a sentence or even a stanza. If you don't have the foggiest idea about any mantras, then you can make one up all alone. It could even be a sound that you like.

Yantras

A yantra is a numerical system that is frequently used in Tantric sex. You probably won't be partial to arithmetic, yet you ought to know that geometric figures are basic with regards to Tantric sex. You should concentrate on the picture if you need to invigorate your sexuality and an exact figure should be remembered for inspiring a specific response. If you are feeling apprehensive or even restless while participating in sex, you can concentrate on such figures for relinquishing all the negative feelings. Diverse geometric figures are identified with every one of the seven chakras that are available inside the human body. These chakras are the vortices for energy that is put away in the body. One of the celebrated Yantras is the sex point Star of David.

Things that you should reflect Tantric sex

Everybody will have found out about Tantric sex at some point in time, and from different sources. There's a great deal of data accessible about Tantric sex, and this prompts a ton of perplexity. Thusly, it is very normal that you are confounded about what Tantric sex is about. The explanation behind this is very straightforward; how it has been depicted on TV and motion pictures is very unique in relation to what it's really similar to. In this way, it is nothing unexpected that a great many people are misguided about what Tantric sex contains. This, however a shame is related with Tantric sex. It is viewed as an unusual type of sex entertainment or even voodoo! This isn't valid and is unjustifiable. Tantric sex depends on the lessons of Tantra. Tantra is an old fine art that depends on the standards of accomplishing satisfaction and edification, about making every second count and living it with no pointless cultural limitations. Tantric sex is certainly not an insane practice, and it will, actually, assist you with framing an increasingly significant and more grounded bond with your partner. A couple will have the option to encounter sexual closeness more than ever. Right now, will realize what Tantric sex is about.

It's something other than sex

As referenced before, Tantric sex isn't just about sex. This comes as an amazement to many. The physical part of sex incorporates touching, scouring and petting. You will have occupied with this while having ordinary sex. Then what's the distinction between Tantric sex and customary sex? Tantric sex gives equivalent significance to the physical part of sex, yet additionally the significance of partners being associated on a psychological level as well. It would be very useful if you and your partner could disregard accomplishing a climax, and could rather move your concentration towards the demonstration that you are included. When you let go everything being equal, you will have the option to coordinate all your energy towards getting a charge out existing apart from everything else and valuing each other too. It will help in making a closeness that outperforms all the physical bonds and associates with one another deeply. This improves Tantric sex such a great amount than its ordinary partner does.

It can help in recuperating you

Customary sex has the limit with respect to fulfilling your physical needs and desires, yet Tantric sex can help in fulfilling your enthusiastic needs too. All the awful encounters that you may have suffered previously, your feelings of dread and weaknesses that you have should be possible away with the use of Tantric sex. Tantric sex makes use of various meditational methods, centers around your breathing and furthermore keeping in touch with your partner and doing other easily overlooked details that will improve sex such a great amount than it at any point was. This will likewise help in accomplishing a more advantageous and more joyful condition of being. The delicate touches of Tantric sex will help in shaping a more grounded bond with your partner and wash away the entirety of your unsavory feelings and encounters.

Accomplishing full body climaxes

A full-body climax may appear to be very fascinating and questionable simultaneously. All things reflected, Tantric sex will assist you with accomplishing this. The joy that you can understanding while at the same time taking part in Tantric sex is higher than standard sex. The explanation behind this is, when practiced appropriately, it can to be sure assistance in accomplishing a full body climax, and this is very regular. This happens when you begin concentrating on spreading the torpid sexual energy that is available in your body to all the cells in the body rather than basically confining it to your private parts. This will strengthen the joy you are encountering and make your body wake up.

It tends to be testing

Tantric sex isn't in every case simple to perform. Whether or not or not you have known your partner for your entire life, it can even now be very testing. You will require somewhat more concentration and practice so as to get the hang of tantric sex. Tantric sex is an immaculate type of lovemaking, and so as to appreciate every one of its benefits, it is significant that the individuals who are participating in it can relinquish every one of their hindrances completely. There is certainly not a fast or a simple manner by which you will have the option to get its hang. You should relinquish all the past ideas of lovemaking that you may have had and rethink this whole procedure. You can begin by sitting on the bed or any agreeable surface and look into one another's eyes. It is tied in with framing a bond with your partner and keeping up an relationship with your partner all through the span of sex.

There are Tantric sex courses accessible also. Before you misunderstand any thoughts, these courses aren't bunch blow-outs, nor do they incorporate any realistic shows. These are classes that will show a couple to interface with one another on a more deep level and help in shaping a bond that rises above the physical world. Different themes are canvassed in these courses, and these can be rehearsed with your partner inside the holiness and protection of your own home. There are online courses accessible too. When you have the hang of the nuts and bolts, you can take part in some marvelous sex.

Chapter Two

✑

Benefits Of Tantric Sex

As of now referenced in the past part, Tantric sex will help in uniting two individuals and help in their spiritual, passionate and mental relationship. Right now, will find out about the different benefits that Tantric sex has on offer.

Singular development

Tantric sex helps in expanding the closeness remainder in a relationship. It additionally helps in the development of people also. An individual would have the option to develop intellectually, truly, just as deeply. Tantric sex helps in arousing Kundalini in ladies, and this takes into reflection her ladylike nature to radiate through. She will begin to shine and have an increasingly inspirational standpoint and disposition towards life. The male energy, Shiva causes a man to bridle all his manly energy through harmony and internal quality.

Investigating the breaking points

Quick ones and self-pleasuring methods are turning out to be very normal nowadays, and individuals are as a general rule passing up the benefits that significant and adoring sex can give. This prevents a person from investigating their sexual breaking points. Tantric sex can help turn this around. Tantric sex would help a person in understanding their actual sexuality and their sexual breaking points. When a couple takes part in Tantric sex, they form a deep and important bond that permits each partner to encounter sexual delight. Tantric sex can be thought of like a collaboration where each partner helps the other reach and reel in extraordinary physical, enthusiastic and sexual delight that can be experienced by both.

Increased climaxes

The climaxes accomplished through Tantric sex are more impressive than the customary ones. The different tantric sex positions referenced right now help you in accomplishing pivotal climaxes. The positions are planned with the end goal that they hit all the sweet places and cause your body to sing. It is a general idea that ladies can have a more significant level of climax when contrasted with men, however with Tantric sex, the two people can accomplish a higher condition of climax.

Recognizing what works

When you have figured out how to get its hang, Tantric sex can be agreeable and energizing. With each progressive meeting, you will show signs of improvement comprehension of your sexuality, your triggers and furthermore those of your partner. You will have the option to comprehend what you and your partner appreciate. When you have figured out how to distinguish these delight points, you can begin animating them for accomplishing pure sexual joy. The physical and mental bond that you would have built up with your partner would essentially rely upon him and fortify over a period and you will arrive at a phase where you, as a team, become reliant on one another's sexual energy for their pleasure.

Coordinated happiness

You can time your climaxes with Tantric sex. When an individual has figured out how to oversee their psyche just as body, they can consequently fall into a synchronized example for achieving a common climax. Another type of energy is created, and it courses through every one of them when they have planned climaxes. This amplifies the bond between couples. Lessons of Tantric sex recommend that remaining associated after a sexual demonstration will help in reinforcing the bond that is framed.

Monogamy

It is a prevalent view that Tantric sex can help a couple in remaining together for the remainder of their life expectancy. When two people have figured out how to produce a bond that encourages them to associate on a deeper plane, they become subordinate. This reliance can't be mirrored or repeated with any other individual. When the recurrence of the meeting begins to expand, then the bond between the people additionally begins to extend and fortify.

Medical benefits

Tantric sex helps in advancing great wellbeing. Ladies will profit by this since it will help in making their menstrual cycle progressively ordinary and this, thus, causes them in keeping their bodies fit as a fiddle. Tantric sex helps in creating certain male hormones that produce more beneficial and more grounded sperms, along these lines expanding the couple's richness. A full body climax helps in energizing the body cells and furthermore helps in expanding their solidarity to battle ailment, along these lines expanding the insusceptibility. Ladies and men who have Tantric sex will in general look more youthful because this is an extraordinary pressure buster. It additionally adds another gleam to the face. Aside from all the different benefits that it brings to the table everybody, Tantric sex can additionally help in delivering serotonin that helps with keeping gloom under control. A climax helps in discharging serotonin that helps in keeping cortisol under control and improves a person's temperament.

Restraints

It likewise helps in causing an individual to get familiar with their body and be progressively alright with their body and that of their partner. A great many people right now age will in general get incredibly cognizant about their bodies and these feelings of trepidation that they harbor prevent them from completely appreciating sex and they wind up having fair sex. When you let go of the dread of being judged and have acknowledged your body for how it is, then you will have the option to genuinely give up and relish the experience, as it was intended to be delighted in. If you let go of every one of these feelings of dread, you can appreciate physical joy. Relinquishing your restraints will make sex increasingly pleasant. Tantric sex emforces this deserting.

Force battle

If you follow the mainstream TV arrangement "The Game of Thrones," then you will recall the scene where Daenerys Targaryen breaks all the standards and chooses to assume responsibility for pleasuring her alpha-male spouse,

Khal Drogo. Drogo objects from the outset, yet then he gives in once he understands how pleasurable it truly is. With regards to sex, usually, individuals will in general face an internal force battle. People both will in general like the sentiment of being in charge, through indicating that they are in charge can harm a relationship. There is a distinction between being in charge and getting a charge out of common Tantric sex. Tantric sex will help in disposing of this issue through and through. Tantric sex gives equivalent capacity to both the partners and the various positions will help in permitting both the groups to be in control and they can give every joy the other individual with no limitations.

Satisfaction

Tantric sex helps in diverting all the positive types of energy and this will help in making the individual very happy. Since it is deeply, sincerely and genuinely fulfilling, an individual would be cheerful in every one of these perspectives. The spiritual relationship that it lets you form with godliness makes a difference.

Expanded love

There are a large number of thoughts that experience your brain at some random purpose of time. We will in general reflect various individuals, not really our partners. It's very normal nowadays for couples to sever their connections on the appearance that they aren't feeling "the love" any longer. Tantric sex won't just assistance you in cherishing yourself, yet it will likewise help you in adoring your partner. It helps in building up a supporting relationship that helps in shared development. This sort of solidarity of feeling makes the relationship increasingly strong.

Engages the two people

Most ladies will in general experience the ill effects of low confidence. They have become tormented with thoughts and sentiments that their bodies are flawed. They might not have the ability to disapprove of their partner while occupied with a sexual demonstration. They may not be really ready to have intercourse however are constrained into it as a result of their failure to state no. They probably won't express their actual sentiments and wants openly, and this decreases the joy that they experience. As indicated by the lessons of Tantric sex, ladies are dealt with like goddesses, and they are showered with the reflectation and the regard that they merit. In like manner, even men are tormented with various issues in regards to how they see themselves. Most men stress over how they are performing, regardless of whether they can fulfill their partner if their stamina is sufficient et cetera. Rather than getting a charge out of the demonstration, they are frequently stressed over to what extent they can last. When they follow the lessons of Tantric sex, they will feel engaged since their bodies are regarded as the vessels of God. This will make them increasingly certain and open to new encounters without living with those feelings of trepidation and restraints.

Massive fulfillment

There are times when you may have engaged in sexual relations and felt that something was absent in it. You may feel that there's no fervor or sentiment. This will in general occur since sex doesn't go past intercourse. It stops at the physical demonstration. Sex alone doesn't do anything for a relationship. Tantric sex is progressively pleasurable since it helps in shaping a passionate bond between partners rather than a straightforward physical bond. When an individual is sincerely put resources into a demonstration, it turns out to be progressively pleasurable and charming. When both are, it gets mysterious.

Mitigates despondency

Reflect Tantric sex as your instructor. It will help you in defeating discouragement and even nervousness. Individuals are generally too tired to even reflect eating or rest nowadays. This unleashes devastation on their everyday plan. Tantric sex will help you in handling the issues referenced previously. After a meeting of Tantric sex, you will feel renewed and reenergized, and this freshly discovered harmony and energy will loosen up your body and quiet your psyche, along these lines disposing of all the superfluous pressures that continue focusing on you.

Tantric sex is far beyond simply sex!

Chapter Three

Tantra Sex Basics

When you begin to follow the lessons of Tantric sex, then you will begin to see a positive change in yourself. You will see an adjustment in the manner you see yourself and furthermore observe a positive move in your standpoint towards life when all is said in done. You will wind up taking a gander at long haul connections rather than moment delight.

You will discover that each individual has a specific degree of heavenly nature that is available inside the person in question and this is guaranteed. This adjustment in your viewpoint will make you see sex as a sacrosanct demonstration and not only a physical one. You will likewise figure out how to discover and manufacture a more deep relationship with your partner and accomplish a more noteworthy degree of delight. You will be fruitful just when you have assuaged yourself of any assumptions that you may have. You should quit pondering what you ought to do to satisfy your darling or what your sweetheart must do to joy you. Subsequent to perusing this section, you will have the option to distinguish certain various thoughts that you may have about yourself and furthermore figure out how to give up to have extraordinary sex. This section will help you in understanding the essential ideas of Tantric sex.

The Yin and the Yang

You more likely than not heard the expression that men are from Mars and ladies are from Venus. It is seen that men are progressively self-assured and incredible, while ladies will in general be all the more delicate, delicate and supporting in nature. A few different generalizations exist; men are not fit for communicating their inclination while ladies will in general have a plenty of feelings that are just standing by to be released at any second. Another general misguided judgment is that ladies don't typically prefer to assume praise for the work they do because this is an attribute related with men since they are all the more cordial. In the course of the most recent couple of years, there's been an extreme change in how the two people think.

The standards of Tantric sex immovably accept that people are unique and that they have contradicting qualities. This is a fundamental guideline of Tantra and is epitomized in the Eastern head Yin and Yang. Yin sclimaxs to women's liberation, and Yang sclimaxs to manliness. In any case, this doesn't imply that ladies aren't fit for having and Yang attributes and moreover. As opposed to reflecting people as two elements, concentrating on their energies is a smart thought. Tantra immovably puts stock in the converging of the energies of these two substances.

Shiva and Shakti

One of the most widely recognized pictures of Yin and Yang can be found in Hindu legendary writing. Yin and Yang are spoken to by the heavenly couple of Lord Shiva and Goddess Shakti. Ruler Shiva is viewed as the energy that is available known to mankind and Shakti is viewed as the wellspring of this energy. The relationship of these two ground-breaking divinities is liable for making the yearning in you and every other person for being to be dealt with like a God or Goddess. This has been examined in the coming sections. You will find how to love your partner as a God or a Goddess.

The manly energy that is found in Lord Shiva is euphoria, while the female energy that is available in Goddess Shakti sclimaxs to insight. The reasonable mix of these two outcomes in edification. This couple is constantly spoken to in different positions where they are weaved in some form. They are moving, grasping, or standing together intently. There are additionally a few positions where Shakti is folded over Shiva, and her legs are propped up around his hips. Their moving position is by a long shot viewed as the most sacrosanct one since they are ready to free their energies as well as ready to achieve edification.

Understanding the alternate extremes

There may be a few divisions that exist among you and your partner. The principal thing that you should do is distinguish these divisions and afterward find some kind of harmony between the two restricting forces of energy that exist inside. There may be a couple of cliché attributes that you may have taken note. Take a note of these and furthermore request that your partner do this too. You will then need to make sense of the manner by which you can grasp these attributes about yourself and furthermore figure out how to cherish your partner completely. Just when you can find some kind of harmony between these polarities that exist between both of you, at exactly that point will you have the option to locate an ideal equalization. You should recognize the Yin to your partner's Yang and he needs to distinguish his Yang to your Yin.

You may likely be pondering whether the facts confirm that contrary energies will in general draw in. Why not kick back and investigate all your past connections for addressing this inquiry? Reflect how extraordinary you are from others and recognize the distinctions that kept you both splendidly adjusted. This will likewise help you in breaking down your future connections.

My partner is my darling

Tantra is about holy love, something that goes past physical desire. It is tied in with regarding and valuing your partner while having intercourse. You should give your partner the equivalent unequivocal love that you expect of your partner consequently. While sclimaxing with your partner, use adoring words like 'dear' 'darling' or some other variety of these. These little charms go far with regards to stimulating the sentiments of love in them. Getting out your join forces with these charms out in the open may sound somewhat unusual, however this is the least difficult manner by which you will have the option to impart your love to your partner.

You feel engaged to state what you need!

When you begin feeling enabled, at exactly that point will you have the option to define limits in each part of your life, and this incorporates sex too. You will find a newly discovered feeling of confidence. The lessons of Tantric sex accept that you are the ace of your body and soul. That implies you claim your body and your spirit also. When your partner shows that he needs to enter you, he should look for your consent first. You shouldn't be hesitant to express your genuine thoughts and express yes or no as per your requirements. Open up and state what you appreciate or loath. Enlighten your partner concerning how that you need to and don't have any desire to be touched. You enable your partner by talking reality and will be giving your partner all the data with respect to how you like to be satisfied.

Chapter Four

Communication Essentials

Tantric sex puts a lot of significance on the degree of correspondence that exists between two people. This is an extremely strengthening and personal type of sexual practice and it requires both the people to similarly contribute both verbally just as truly for receiving the rewards that this training must offer. While having Tantric sex, it is extremely imperative to convey. Here are a couple of points that you should remember at the same time.

Investigating the eye

It is basic to keep in touch all through a sexual meeting. You should relinquish every one of your hindrances and look into one another's eyes. It is a typical faith in Tantra that the left is viewed as the looking eye and the correct eye is viewed as the accepting eye. This implies you should focus on your partner's correct eye while you are conversing with him/her. You and your partner ought to adjust your bodies in such a way, that there's a free progression of discourse and you are additionally ready to keep in touch. Try not to close your eyes while your partner is conversing with you and give careful reflection of the various feelings that are acted out while imparting. Eyes are viewed as the reflections of one's spirit. Look into your partner's eyes and let them look into yours. There are no falsifications; eyes never lie.

Grin

Try not to make any interesting appearances or don't look uninvolved while talking. Have a grin all over or only a lovely demeanor all over when you are talking during sex. When you set up a specific bond with your partner, your outward appearance will quickly turn progressively wonderful.

Expressing your real thoughts out

You should state so anyone can hear what you are thinking. You don't need to keep down or onto your meditations and don't hang tight for the correct chance. Tell your partner everything that you are thinking. If you like something, then impart your bliss, and your abhorrence or disappointment if you don't care for something. Talking openly will permit your partner to get a knowledge into how you think and what you feel. Your brain ought to have the option to uninhibitedly communicate what your heart feels.

Act out

Use your hands to make motions while talking. Motions help in including onto your discourse. Make various signs and images to show your partner your gratefulness for what they are doing. Use your outward appearance to pass on what you are stating. Use them notwithstanding your discourse and motions. Try not to be hesitant to chuckle unreservedly, cry, grin or whatever else while you are conversing with your partner. This will help in getting progressively compassionate towards your partner. There are explicit hand mudras that can be used for directing your energy and this will permit you to act out in a superior way. Abstain from doing certain things that can be a significant mood killer, such as breaking your knuckles or crushing your teeth. Rather, focus on looking into your partner's eyes.

Energize and summon

When you are addressing your partner, ensure that you are emforceing him/her to make some noise too. It should be common, and you should ensure that correspondence is a two-way road. Make statements that you realize will evoke a reaction and don't continue talking consistently. Give your partner some an opportunity to react also. Give your partner a chance to communicate his/her sentiments and what he/she is thinking.

Lucidity

While conversing with your partner previously, during or after sex, ensure that you are clear. Balance your voice in like manner and ensure that you are clear and perceptible. Nobody likes it one somebody mutters. It is extremely critical to recognize what you need to state it and the way in which you state this issue too. Put some idea into what you are stating and state it in an appropriate way. Essentially murmuring "I love you" or "you look great" into your partner's ears can be a significant turn on.

Smoothness

Your discourse must be liquid, and you can't continue delaying in the middle of sentences to state what you are thinking and what you need. With regards to Tantric sex, every meeting can keep going as long as you need it to. In this way, you should be readied both genuinely just as intellectually to state all that you need to. Ensure that you don't exhaust yourself by going on and on and channel your meditations and feelings in an appropriate way. Permit this energy to stream unreservedly through your body, and this is the main manner by which you can recite completely with your partner.

Genuineness

Try not to be apprehensive and talk genuinely. Express your real thoughts out, and you don't need to misrepresent or lie about something to make it sound decent. Keep it basic and be honest about it, if you truly need to communicate uninhibitedly.

Relaxing

Start and focus on your breathing and time your breaths so you can match up them with that of your partner. You don't need to talk continually; this will basically hinder your relaxing. Know about how you are breathing and have a decent hold on it. Synchronized breathing can be a serious great encounter. Breathing can likewise support your developments while you are performing tantric sex since it makes you all the more remarkable.

Chapter Five

 ❧

Breathe to Ecstasy

Different practices have been referenced right now will help you in understanding what Tantric sex is about. These practices use various sounds, images and sights that will help you along your approach to accomplishing bliss. A couple of strategies have been referenced right now. You should invest some time and energy for practicing these systems and impeccable them. One of the most significant parts of tantric sex is the one thing that you are doing well currently, relaxing. It is pivotal that you are breathing appropriately to guarantee that you can achieve the most deep conceivable degree of closeness and the most significant level of joy that you can understanding.

Why is your breath significant?

When you are taking in an appropriate way, you are providing your body with the truly necessary oxygen. While you are breathing this likewise takes into reflection the free development of sexiness just as feelings in your body. This will help you in accomplishing various climaxes. Truly, you read it right. Different climaxes! Your breath is the central point that helps in building your stamina and help you to last more while engaging in sexual relations. It will likewise help in ensuring that the love that exists among you and your partner remains close. This sounds excessively simple, isn't that right? There's one issue that you should be tended to right now. Presently, you are holding your breath to an extreme! Each individual will in general do this. Concentrate on your breathing example at this specific minute. You aren't growing your chest, right? Is your breathing shallow? Indeed, this isn't sound. Right now, will find out around three actually essentially breathing procedures that will enable you to inhale as you should.

Concentrate on the wellspring of your relaxing

Have you attempted to distinguish the specific place in your body from where your breathing beginnings? Do you think it begins from your throat, chest or the zone around your stomach? Indeed, it should begin from any of these zones. You should put forth a cognizant attempt to ensure that your breath begins from some place further in the body. To ensure that you are breathing deeply, take a full breath and afterward gradually follow the way of your breath with the assistance of your hand. Unwind, and afterward breathe out. Whenever you are taking a full breath, ensure that it is beginning from some place as low as your private parts. This will help in ensuring that you have adequate energy to prop you up while engaging in sexual relations.

Egg to Eagle Exercise

This is a great system to use, particularly while you are sitting. You should twist up in a ball and keeping in mind that you are bowing, you should breathe out your breath quickly. Presently, carry your hands nearer to your body, and afterward place them on the rear of your head. Do you sense that your back is extending? Breathe in and afterward gradually move into a sitting position. Stretch your hands as far away from your body as you can and ensure that your elbows are twisted despite your good faith. Curve your back gradually and push our chest out. This minute will make all the air return racing into your chest. Proceed with this activity. Your breathing will be all the more significantly after a couple of redundancies of this activity.

The wells work out

The primary point of this specific exercise is to take as a lot of air as you can into your lungs. It is tied in with topping your lungs off with oxygen. This must be done if you begin thinking about your lungs as wells that can be topped off. You should progress in the direction of expanding the virtual limit of your lungs. For doing this, keep your arms close by, and sit in an agreeable place. When you have breathed in, fill your lungs with as much air as you can, then clutch this for a couple of moments and afterward breathe out this air from your lungs with some force. It should seem like a whirlwind hurrying out of your body. Suck in more air, making as a lot of clamor as you can. This will help you in controlling your breathing just as directing the sounds that you make while occupied with sex.

The significance of taking in Tantric sex can't be focused on enough. Each time you feel that you are creeping more like an approaching climax, take a couple of full breaths and pull together your reflectation on getting a charge out existing apart from everything else, rather than pondering the climax. Appreciate and relish each experience.

Chapter Six

Distinguish and Worship the God or Goddess Within You

A great many people follow the way of Tantra to move toward God. God has favored each part of your life; this applies to sex also. You will have the option to interface with God and the heavenly nature, just when you are having intercourse to your partner, since this is the main manner by which you are regarding just as encountering the eternality that dwells inside the human body. The instructing of Tantra immovably expresses that there lies a God in each man and a Goddess in each lady. This infers your body is the vessel for eternality. For accomplishing the critical degrees of shrewdness that are open to you, you will essentially need to relinquish this shell. Your confidence will improve when your partner is regarding you, and you are respecting them consequently. Just when you can see this part of yourself, at exactly that point will you have the option to see the heavenly nature that lives in others also plainly.

Right now, will learn and distinguish the heavenly nature that lives inside you. You will have the option to recognize the God and Goddess inside your body and that of your partner also. This forms the embodiment of Tantric sex. You will likewise have the option to begin to turn out to be progressively edified. This section covers data about various Gods and Goddesses that are famous in Tantric lessons.

The terms 'God' and 'Goddess'

As referenced, the lessons of Tantra express that each man and lady ought to be dealt with like a God or a Goddess. This is to ensure that you not just reflect yourself a vessel for eternality however treat your cooperate with a similar see too. Right now, will have the option to regard and respect your partner in the way that you should. This will likewise guarantee that you can respect the force that exists inside the universe.

The various divinities for the most part revered in Tantric sex are viewed as creatures loaded up with light. They symbolize different energies just as connections. Different terms that are generally used for divine beings and goddesses are Deva and Devi, minister and priestess, and Daka and Dakini separately. These gods are accepted to have force and knowledge. This intensity of theirs can likewise be anticipated inside your body. This projection essentially relies upon the different ethics and characteristics that you have.

Goddess is a term that has over and over been used in Tantra. It is used for depicting a lady who is in touch with the ladylike force that dwells inside her body. The underlying significance of this word as a rule implied a lady who was sustaining and solid. A man isn't alluded to as God since God is viewed as a predominant being in different religions. There are a few religions and even a couple of practices that accept that an individual can turn into a divine being or a goddess by changing a couple of parts of themselves. However, the lessons of Tantric sex express that an individual has a specific degree of heavenly nature that is available inside them since birth and there is no hope to change this.

Tantric sex decides express that paying little mind to race, religion or even station of the individual, there's some heavenliness present in everybody. By alluding to a lady as a goddess, you are essentially respecting her female attributes that make her a sweetheart, a tracker, enchantress and supporting person. Just when a lady deals with her attributes and acknowledges herself for what her identity is, will she have the option to respect herself and be regarded by people around her. By tending to a man as a divine being, you are just regarding his essential attributes of being a defender, healer, supplier and an image of intensity. He should acknowledge these qualities that exist inside him and at exactly that point would his be able to partner respect him. You may know about these qualities, or they may just be available inside you, and you haven't found them yet.

Distinguish your jobs and attributes

When you are beginning with the excursion towards Tantric sex, then the primary thing that you should do is distinguish the divine beings or the goddesses that characterize you. For doing this, you should recognize your essential attributes and the various jobs that you play in your life. Do you believe yourself to be excellent? It is safe to say that you are keen? It is safe to say that you are a business visionary? It is safe to say that you are amazing? Et cetera. You can record every one of your responses to such inquiries. For making things simpler for yourself, you can make a composition, or you can use mind-mapping too. Place an image of yourself in the focal point of a sheet and afterward begin expounding on all the attributes that you think you have.

When you have accumulated data about the different divine beings and goddesses that has been given in the last piece of this section, you can list down the names of gods that you partner yourself. For example, if you have composed that you are ground-breaking, then maybe you can relate yourself to Shiva or even Ares. If you think you are delightful, then you can record the name of Aphrodite.

Look past the shallow layer

You presumably will have heard the expression "never pass judgment flippantly." Everyone has likely heard this expression at some point in time. We will in general appointed authority an individual exclusively dependent on their looks, how they dress, or even the activity that they do. You may have offered expressions like "she is excessively thin," or "he is excessively short." You presumably took a gander at an individual's financial balance before consenting to go out on the town with him. In any case, Tantra manages a person's persona and not their shallow attributes. There are three fundamental advances that you should follow to adore the heavenly nature that exists inside your partner.

The initial step is acknowledge that there is eternality that exists inside you. The subsequent advance is to grasp and distinguish the godlikeness that exists inside your partner too. You should find some kind of harmony between the manly and the female energies of the divinities. The third step is join these gods inside you, through your relationship with your partner. This will help in making the genuinely necessary harmony between the two and assist you with achieving a more noteworthy degree of delight.

Why is it imperative to adore one another?

Each individual is more joyful when they realize that they are being recognized. It feels extraordinary when you are valued by the individuals who are around you. Do you know how you feel when somebody sees you? When somebody attempts to get you? Tantric sex is tied in with venerating yourself and your partner too. This doesn't imply that you should adore each other aimlessly. It essentially implies that you both need to shower each other with unequivocal love. Unqualified love doesn't mean genuine control more than each other. It just implies that serving each other as well as could be expected to achieve common joy.

When you begin next the way of Tantric sex, you will find that it feels great to hear positive things about yourself and you will likewise need to continue praising your partner. This is the importance of being revered and venerating your partner.

Finding out about the Gods and Goddesses

There are diverse male and female divine beings just as goddesses found in various societies around the globe like Egyptian, Greek, Roman and Indian too. These divine beings and goddesses are for the most part from an old time. Let us get familiar with the various goddesses.

The majority of the goddesses frequently sclimax to fruitfulness and life. In any case, they are likewise observed as enchantresses who entice their partners and participate in sex with them. Right now, will find out around a couple of primary goddesses, and you can maybe locate a couple of attributes that you partner yourself with.

Aphrodite:

Aphrodite is viewed as the most acclaimed of Greek goddesses. She sclimaxs to excellence, want, love and sexuality. She additionally sclimaxs to companionship. Aphrodite is regularly spoken to by birds, roses, little dogs and even dolphins too. As indicated by Roman folklore, she is alluded to as Venus. In Roman folklore, she is the image of virtue.

Artemis:

She is viewed as the Goddess of chasing. Artemis is a Greek goddess, and she sclimaxs to the moon and is a virgin goddess. She is a warrior and a tracker, the female partner to supplement Ares, the God of war.

Athena:

The goddess of astuteness and information. She is the supporter goddess of Athens. Technique and arranging are the two attributes that are normally connected with Athena.

Juno:

Juno or Hera, contingent on whether it is the Greek or Roman rendition of folklore is viewed as a mother like figure with a sustaining and a quieting nature.

Hindu Goddesses:

There are different goddesses in India and Nepal, and every one of them has been given a great deal of significance. Different functions are directed to respect each of these goddesses. The fundamental goddesses are referenced here.

Durga is viewed as the mother all things reflected. Tara is reflected to sclimax to astuteness just as graciousness. Lakshmi is the goddess of riches and thriving. Saraswati is the goddess of different works of art and ability. Kali sclimaxs to quality and force. She is likewise the defender of the domain.

Divine beings from Different Cultures

Each religion has various divine beings and goddesses. These divine beings frequently have a partner as a goddess. There are various divinities loved by various societies. They all sclimax to gigantic quality, force, and are frequently thought of as super creatures. This segment covers carious divine beings from various religions. You may have the option to distinguish your qualities or those of your partner right now here.

Hindu Gods:

Hindu divine beings incorporate Lord Shiva who has gigantic force and Lord Vishnu is viewed as the God all things reflected. There are various indications of Lord Shiva, and there are many portrayals of his clouded side also. Shakti is the associate of Lord Shiva. Master Shiva and Shakti form a ground-breaking match and sclimax to pure energy. Ganesh is a famous god also; he is a little youngster with the leader of an elephant. Master Ganesh is known to expel deterrents and spread satisfaction. Master Rama and Sita form a couple that is frequently loved all over India, they are viewed as the ideal couple and sclimax to the concordance that should exist between a husband and spouse.

Greek divine beings:

There are various Greek divine beings, and they have all become well known in view of the quality and force that they hold. Zeus is viewed as the best of all; he is the King everything being equal and the remarkably ground-breaking Alpha-male. Eros is normally alluded to, as Cupid, and he is seraph or a young man who is regularly fiendish and frequently continues shooting bolts of love at individuals around him. He is the God of love. Dionysus is the Greek and the Roman divine force of desire. As indicated by the legends, he generally pursued ladies and enjoyed drinking a great deal of wine. He for sure is the divine force of desire.

Chapter Seven

The Renunciation Path

Buddhism is a remarkable religion. It says that you are the maker of your own world, and only you hold the keys to your own joy. Nobody, not by any means a buddha, can give you illumination – you should be simply the one to spare. Buddhist lessons are not intended to be acknowledged on trust alone, yet tried inside you. Its practices lead to inward harmony and flourishing, and eventually to euphoria. Buddhism is the religion of joy. The way to accomplishing this joy maintains a strategic distance from the boundaries of erotic extravagance and savage self-nullification, and makes a moderate and reasonable "Center Way" (Madhyamā Pratipad). It is a demonstrated way to lasting bliss. The early Buddhist way is known as the Common Vehicle since it is the establishment of all later Buddhist ways. It is basic to have an essential comprehension of its standards for cutting edge Tantric practice.

The Buddha's lessons address the most deep test of all - the issue of human joy. For what reason is it so hard for people to be truly cheerful? You attempt to be happy by having things you figure you will like, creating connections, or achieving activities that you think will satisfy you. Normally, you additionally attempt to maintain a strategic distance from things that will make you troubled.

Lamentably, you are additionally determined by inward motivations that you don't comprehend. You need to unwind and make an incredible most, yet you can't because your meditations and enthusiastic motivations continually pull you along these lines and that. Doing nothing frightens you. You impulsively search out the next action, keeping you from feeling completely the rich experience of being at this very moment. Such an excess of pursuing joy, the Buddha educated, may bring transitory joys, yet it will never present to you the lasting joy you are truly searching for.

History

The Buddha (563-483 BCE) was a man of uncommon knowledge, love, force, beauty, and harmony, whose simple nearness awed and overforceed the individuals who met him. But then he started, as all buddhas do, much the same as a common individual. The genuine importance of his biography isn't just that he turned into a buddha, however that thusly, he showed that everybody can follow in his way and become buddhas as well. The Buddha, otherwise called Śākyamuni (Sage of the Śākya faction), was conceived Prince Siddhārtha Gautama, in Lumbinī (in current Nepal), child of the ruler of the city of Kapilavāstu. His original name Siddhārtha signifies "he who accomplishes his objective." Though living in extravagance, he was crushed by the distress he saw surrounding him and resolved to figure out how to end all affliction. At the age of twenty-nine the sovereign left his castle, spouse and kid to look for edification. He examined with numerous spiritual educators, remembering two for the Hindu Sāṃkhya convention, Āḷāra Kālāma and Uddaka Rāmaputta, from whom he was firmly impacted.

Next six years of training, he found that neither his life of guilty pleasure in erotic delights in the regal castles nor the unforgiving plain disavowal of his educators could achieve his point.

Siddhārtha at last accomplished his objective - he understood what he called the Four Noble Truths. Presently called the Buddha (Awakened One), he spent the next forty-five years instructing and voyaging, building up a network of renunciates set on liberatedom, and showing a way for laypeople to discover bliss right now future lifetimes. He reflected his lessons the Dharma, the Liberating Truth. He increased a deeply committed after, and thousands accomplished edification.

Buddhism is the fourth biggest religion on the planet.

The Buddha's focal lessons remained virtually unaltered for very nearly 500 years. Even though his devotees split into various schools, they shifted for the most part by extremely minor translations of precept and devout principles. Buddhism was a noteworthy religion in India up until the 1200s CE, and almost certainly, significantly after the presentation of the Mahāyāna, the Buddha's unique way (additionally called by later traditions the Śrāvakayāna, the Path of the Disciples) remained the most well-known type of Buddhism all through that time. It is the way despite everything followed today in a lot of Southeast Asia. Twenty-500 years after the Buddha's demise,

It is anything but difficult to reflect the early Buddhist way as simply plain and world denying, yet this isn't at all obvious. The Buddha built up two totally different societies, one devout and one lay. For his priests and nuns, he set up a network committed to revoking life. He instructed monastics to cut off every common tie and live in calm disengagement, concentrating on their selective objective of achieving edification. For the dominant part lay professionals, however, the Buddha needed them to appreciate life serenely and joyfully, live ethically, go to family, collect riches, respect the holiness of the earth, and appreciate common joys without limit. Lay individuals would in general be rich, instructed city-tenants, and the religion succeeded on their help. The lay culture of early Buddhism was happy and disorderly. The sheer energy of realizing that in all the world you had discovered a way to illumination was deserving of serious and blissful festival. The products of training for the Buddha's lay adherents remember bliss for this life and in future lives, a totally different objective than for his priests.

Experts of the Common Vehicle

Vasubandhu

Vasubandhu (c. 330-400 CE), whose name signifies "Riches Holder," was brought into the world a brahmin in Gandhāra (present day Pakistan), and later turned into a priest. In the wake of reading for a long time in Kashmir, he composed The Treasury of Liberating Truth, a synopsis of the Buddha's lessons eagerly concentrated right up 'til today. He additionally composed the splendid critique creating the Five Aggregates, a great book of Buddhist brain science. His sibling Asaṅga attempted to change over him to the Mahāyāna, however from the start Vasubandhu stood up to. Then one night he saw his sibling in reflection by a lake, increased an acknowledgment of the significance of the

Mahāyāna, and grasped it. In the Mahāyāna way Vasubandhu's works are significantly increasingly significant. On the side of the Mind Only way of thinking, he composed two complete writings; The Thirty Verses on Mind Only and The Twenty Verses on Mind Only. He urged reverential practice to the Buddha Amitābha, which stays key to Tibetan and East Asian Buddhism, and established the exploration of Buddhist rationale.

Buddhaghoṣa

Buddhagoṣa (c. 400s CE), whose name signifies "Voice of the Buddha," was the most significant and persuasive pundit of the Common Vehicle on the Buddha's precepts. Initially a brahmin from Bodhgaya, he was vanquished in banter by a Buddhist priest and changed over. Buddhagoṣa made a trip to Sri Lanka, where he composed thirteen analyses on all pieces of the Buddha's lessons. His most exceptional work,

The Path of Purification, plainly sorts out and abridges the Buddha's lessons, and remains the standard guidance manual for devotees of the Common Vehicle today. A mainstream and exceptionally innovative story of his life was written in Burma during the 1400s.

Theory

The Potential for Permanent Happiness

The Buddha resembles a specialist who decides a sickness and offers a fix. He isn't, prefer a logician, attempting to clarify the idea of the real world - he will likely free individuals from misery. In spite of the fact that everybody needs to be cheerful, he says, the vast majority go about it the incorrect way.

The pith of every Buddhist educating is: suffering happens in light of an essential misperception about what your identity is and how to achieve genuine joy. You see things that show up more wonderful and brimming with delight than you are, and you want them. Driven by your hankering wants, you handle at them, figuring they will fulfill you. In some cases they do fulfill you, different occasions not. In any case, they never bring you perpetual satisfaction. Relinquish your bogus ideas "self" and "other," and there is no all the more needing want. Relinquish longing for and there is no misery. Your awareness rests calmly and joyfully in its actual state, and you are free.

The Buddha's way is the way of renunciation. The Fourteenth Dalai Lama expresses, "So as to rehearse the Buddhist way, we have to produce a deep feeling of renunciation of the very idea of our present presence, which is described by mental and physical totals heavily influenced by karma and burdens. We should build up a deep yearning to pick up opportunity from this adapted presence. The core of renunciation is a mission for triumph over the inner foe, the psychological torments." Renunciation is the giving up of want, revultion, and numbness of how life truly is.

The Four Noble Truths

Suffering Exists, Has a Cause, an End, and a Path to its End

The Buddha condensed his message in the Four Noble Truths (Catvāri Ārya Satyāni): 1) suffering is characteristic throughout everyday life (duḥkha), 2) suffering has a reason (samudaya), 3) all suffering can end (nirodha), and 4) there is a way to end all torment (marga).

The Problem: Suffering

Everybody needs to be happy, yet scarcely any discover it. Rather, most suffer (duḥkha). Incredibly, the Buddha characterizes suffering as misery, yet the general unacceptable personal satisfaction since it can never give everlasting harmony and delight. In any event, when you are really glad, the Buddha says, you are still in misery, since that satisfaction will in the end blur. Just when you are for all time cheerful can you genuinely have finished all misery. Perceiving that suffering is natural forever is the primary honorable truth. The Buddha saw three sorts of affliction: 1) normal torment - the suffering innate in fundamental encounters of life, those of birth, mature age, infection and demise, 2) the suffering of progress - where you get yourself glad for some time yet then the conditions change and you lose what brought you satisfaction, and 3) all-inescapable torment - the unpretentious suffering of continually looking for however failing to find lasting bliss.

Saṃsāra

Life right now, in others, is inevitably experienced as torment and can proceed for limitless lifetimes. You are not really free, yet "adapted" (samskṛita dharma) or constrained by different forces, astronomical laws of which you are not by any means mindful. Not realizing these real factors and how to accomplish opportunity, you meander capriciously in ceaseless anguish or saṃsāra.

Fleetingness

Nothing - no item, individual, or experience - right now ever give you perpetual bliss since everything is dependent upon the law of fleetingness (anitya), change and rot. Whatever you think you should be really cheerful – family, work, sweethearts, cash – will be gone sometime in the not so distant future.

Karma

Each move you make, fortunate or unfortunate, prompts an outcome dependent on the nature of the activity and your inspiration. Negative activities bring excruciating outcomes. Positive activities bring bliss, however it is in every case just impermanent. Not understanding the rule of karma (lit. activity) is particularly hazardous, even though solid negative activities can prompt serious and delayed affliction.

Subordinate Origination

Subordinate Origination (pratītya saṃutpāda) is the general law that pushes you forward into unlimited lifetimes of torment. It is a constant causal chain of occasions, driven by your wants, abhorrences, and numbness, that outcomes in a ceaseless pattern of birth, mature age and passing, and keeps you from abiding for all time in harmony and rapture: 1) obliviousness (avidyā), of the genuine idea of the real world, 2) activities (saṃskāra), that outcome in karmic engraves, 3) cognizance (vijñāna), the resources of your brain, 4) name and form (nāma rūpa), your psyche attached to a body, 5) the six sense organs (ṣaḍ āyatana), which produce sensations and discernments, 6) touch (sparśa), the gathering of senses, items, and awareness, 7) sensation (vedanā), the passionate and mental enlisting of articles in your psyche, 8) longing for (tṛiṣṇā), the emerging of wants, 9) getting a handle on (upādāna), your endeavors to have things to achieve bliss, 10) turning out to be (bhava), the aging of the product of your wants and graspings that lead you interminably into common presence, 11) birth (jāti), of yourself into the world, and 12) mature age and demise (jarā maraṇa), and the suffering they definitely bring.

The Cause: Desire

Misperceiving yourself as free and unceasing, you need things that will satisfy you, and maintain a strategic distance from things that will make you troubled. Want (kāma), additionally called desiring (tṛiṣṇā), prompts habitual movement or getting a handle on (upādāna) - attempting to have articles, individuals and encounters that you think will fulfill you. Your voracious longing for exotic delights at times brings you impermanent joy, however it never keeps going. Indeed, even as you scan for bliss, you are constantly diverted by your own senses as they pull you towards objects you hunger for desperately. You resemble a rider who can't control your own pony, yet you are not in any case mindful of your senses' influence over you. Through oblivious constant examples (vāsanā), you respond to things hastily, in light of the propensities for your past meditations and feelings. Your own internal driving forces continually damage you. The Three "Toxins" or obscurations (kleśas) are: 1) want (kāma), 2) abhorrence (dveṣa), including outrage, scorn, dread, or aversion, and 3) numbness (avidyā), the deception in a self, perplexity, mental stirring, and absence of information on the Dharma. You need to be free, yet you can't. You need to be upbeat, however you can't. Nothing you attempt works.

No Self

The deepest reason for your suffering is because you don't exist how you figure you do. All experiencing at last infers sticking to an incredible, autonomous "I" that you attempt to ensure and on which you luxurious reflection. There is no self (anātman). What you reflect as a lasting "I" is only made out of Five Aggregates (Pañca Skandha), elements of your body and brain, which remain together just due to karmic molding. By misinterpreting these different exercises as a solitary, existing unit that doesn't genuinely exist, you make a bogus "I" that prompts languishing:

1. Form (Rūpa): Your physical body, which is made out of the Four Elements: 1) earth, 2) water, 3) fire, and 4) wind. Every single physical item are likewise minor pieces of these components.

2. Sensation (Vedanā): Subtle sense impressions inside your psyche, which enlists all sense encounters as either lovely, excruciating, or unbiased - neither wonderful nor difficult. It likewise incorporates the feelings that emerge from these sensations: 1) distress, 2) bliss, 3) delight, 4) torment, and 5) lack of interest.

3. Discernment (Samjñā): Both the demonstration of seeing items through the senses, and the applied mental action of making essential mental judgments or "signs" (nimitta) of what an article is. For instance, you see an individual out there, and it enlists in your brain with an idea - "a wonderful lady." These discernments can be healthy, unwholesome, or

unbiased dependent on how they influence the nature of your awareness.

4. Mental Formations (Saṃskāra): Mental activities containing such capacities as expectations, interests, wants, repugnances, fancies, decisions, routine inclinations, pride, jealousy, stress, and the forces of care and focus. These can be healthy, unwholesome, or nonpartisan relying on how they influence your brain.

5. Awareness (Vijñāna – lit. Partitioned Consciousness): The workforce of awareness that: 1) knows the world through the Six Senses: eye, ear, nose, tongue, body, and psyche (which sees envisioned items), 2) breaks down encounters, and 3) makes decisions like positive or negative. Awareness has the ability to know of this physical world as well as subtler planes of presence also.

The Solution: The End of Suffering in Permanent Peace and Bliss

Nirodha is the end of anguish. It prompts nirvāṇa (lit. smothered), an unending condition of harmony and euphoria. You are totally liberated from the fever of want, repugnance, the numbness of a deceptive self, the Five Aggregates, and karma. It is outright discharge, immaculateness, soundness, truth, opportunity from cyclic presence, unconditioned and without connection. It is amazing and unfathomable. Achieving it, you never experience the suffering of birth, mature age or passing again.

The Method: The Path

When you perceive suffering as an unaemptyable piece of life, you see that it has a reason, and that it is conceivable to be without affliction, the way (marga) to liberatedom is through developing knowledge, moral lead, and reflective soundness. On a deep level, you understand the genuine idea of yourself as made out of the Five Aggregates, and that these are temporary and constantly subject to karmic molding through the pattern of Dependent Origination. You quench want, discharge your sticking to a self that never truly existed, and you are free.

Path

Lay and Monastic Paths

Generally, most of Buddhist disciples are laypeople, who offer commitment and budgetary help to the network of priests and nuns, and keep on pursueing common delights capably. The monastics, revoking every single common want, surrender their posessions, take robes, take 200-300 promises relying on the methods for their specific appointment genealogy, and carry on with an existence of training and thought. Initially just monastics were told in the Noble Eightfold Path. Today, lay adherents create in the Buddha's calming the psyche practices of Tranquility Meditation, and Insight Meditation is instructed only to priests.

Levels of Attainment

Buddhism is a reviewed way to liberatedom. When you comprehend the Dharma, take the promises, and practice, you are known as an honorable follower (ārya śrāvaka is male, and ārya śrāvakā is female). Four levels in the Common Vehicle are checked, in light of how much you conquer the Ten Fetters (Saṃyojana), internal obstructions that keep you from progress. The five lower chains are:

1) Bogus perspectives, particularly about a self, 2) question, 3) shocking works on, depending for liberatedom on ceremonies that can't bring liberatedom, 4) want, and 5) repugnance. The five higher shackles are: 1) want for the Realm of Form, 2) want for the Realm of Formlessness, 3) unsettling, for example, blame and stress, 4) the vanity "I am," and 5) numbness of the Four Noble Truths. When you achieve the first of these four levels, you are known as an honorable one (ārya pudgala/ārya pudgalā):

1. Stream Enterer

As a stream enterer (srota āpanna/srota āpannā), you have achieved Right View, and discharged the initial three and most significant lower chains of bogus perspectives, question, and shocking practices. You are sure to accomplish liberatedom inside seven lifetimes.

2. Once-Returner

Achieving the degree of a once-returner (sakṛidāgāmin/sakṛidāgāminī), you are fruitful in developing insight, moral conduct, and reflective fixation, and have debilitated the last two lower shackles of want and revultion. You will accomplish liberatedom in your next lifetime.

3. Non-Returner

In turning into a non-returner (anāgāmin/anāgāminī), you have discharged the last two lower chains of want and repugnance. You are for all time liberated from the Realm of Desire. After death you are renewed into an pure domain where you will achieve liberatedom quickly.

4. Liberated One

As a liberated one (arhat/arhatī), or "commendable one," you have achieved lasting harmony and delight. You have discharged every one of the five higher shackles: 1) want for the Realm of Form, 2) want for the Realm of Formlessness, 3) tumult, 4) the arrogance "I am," and 5) numbness of the Four Noble Truths. In spite of the fact that you have accomplished basically a similar acknowledgment as a buddha, you don't have a similar common strategic a buddha and carry on with a mind-blowing rest in detachment.

Benefits

As your comprehension of the Dharma develops, your brain becomes clearer. You realize that you are on the correct way in your life. You are certain, yet unobtrusively so. Through carrying on morally, your psyche isn't disturbed by blame. By creating harmony and ecstasy in meditation, individuals and things that once upset you become untroubling. Physical wellbeing, mental clearness, delight, riches, magnificence, long life and euphoric connections normally come your direction. For lay adherents, the Buddha guaranteed government assistance and bliss right now in future lives. But then, he kept up, none of this will bring about changeless bliss. To accomplish the incomparable objective of the Buddhist way, you should set your expectation on liberatedom through renunciation of every common tie.

Normal Problems

Every spiritual way have dangers. One danger of the Buddhist way is that you might be attracted to the intensity of the lessons and receive a scholarly methodology that penances moral conduct and reflection. So also, practicing excellence without astuteness prompts impermanent resurrection in higher domains that are agreeable yet at the same time saturated by affliction. Another hazard is to concentrate a lot on meditation before you have a decent comprehension of the way. You may turn out to be so captivated of joyful thoughtful states that you don't achieve your last objective. Care can decline into self-ingestion, and nonattachment can get inhumane. And, you can build up a feeling of individual accomplishment with the goal that your personality pride is really fortified as opposed to reduced.

Systems

The Buddha instructed a coordinated arrangement of practices called the Noble Eightfold Path (Ārya Aṣṭāṅga Marga). Taking promises (śīla) and performing practices of dedication (śraddhā), additionally instructed by the Buddha, give the establishment.

Promises

Two arrangements of promises (śīla) mark your passageway into the way, the Refuge Vow (Tri Śaraṇa–lit. Triple Refuge) and Lay Precepts (Pañca Śīla – lit. Five Precepts). The promises of the Common Vehicle are known as the vows of Individual Liberation (Prātimokṣa), in which you take either lay or religious vows.

The Refuge Vow is pith of the way to liberatedom. It is your own promise to look for security from suffering in the Buddha (the educator), Dharma (the lessons), and Saṅgha (the network of professionals). When you take the Refuge Vow, your life takes on new course and significance: you have the best case of human achievement, the best everything being equal, and the best help on your way. The shelter function is a living promise that centers your awareness consistently. It is the day you become increasingly protected in a risky world.

The Lay Precepts are fundamental aides for moral movement that shield you from falling further in torment and bring riches and joy. They bring true serenity and sanitization, and you come to prize them in your heart. You pledge to keep away from:

1. Taking Life: Do not slaughter others, and abstain from murdering creatures, in any event, for food. In any case, it is worthy to buy or get as gifts meat slaughtered by others. Taking life prompts lower resurrection in a damnation domain. The positive part of this statute is developing love and empathy.

2. Taking What isn't Given: Stealing from others because of desiring prompts neediness and resurrection in lower domains. The positive part of this statute is creating liberality.

3. Sexual Misconduct: Sexual offense incorporates having intercourse with: 1) kids who are under the security of their folks, 2) the individuals who have taken ascetic promises, 3) the individuals who are hitched to other people, 4) those ensured by law, for example, the courtesans of a lord, and 5) the

individuals who are another person's darling. Sexual wrongdoing prompts lower resurrection in a hellfire domain. The Buddha's principles for sexual unfortunate behavior take into account incredible opportunity of sexual articulation for laypeople; obviously, all sex must be consensual and peaceful. The positive part of this statute is developing internal happiness that discharges you from longing for erotic delights.

4. Bogus Speech: Lying hurts yourself as well as other people and prompts lower resurrection in a hellfire domain. The positive part of this statute is developing honest discourse.

5. Liquor: Alcohol and different intoxicants diminish the lucidity of your psyche. While taking intoxicants doesn't itself lead to bring down resurrection, it can lead you to do and make statements that bring about awful karma. With respect to real practice, a large number of the soonest statues of Buddhist craftsmanship are of ladies conveying tremendous containers of liquor - so this standard was not generally paid attention to very. Intoxicants are a vital piece of Indian culture, and Buddhism praises erotic joys for laypeople, such huge numbers of followed a "center way" and reflected it on exceptional events, for example, celebrations. The positive part of this statute is developing lucidity of awareness.

Dedication

Buddhism is exceptionally reverential. The Buddha instructed that through extreme dedication (śraddhā) alone, you can arrive at the initial two degrees of accomplishment. Dedication comprises of: 1) worship of the Buddha's, 2) love of divine beings and nature spirits, 3) recognition day practices, 4) praising blessed days, 5) journey, and 6) holy sex ceremonies.

Love of the Buddha's

In the Common Vehicle, the motivation behind commitment to the Buddha isn't, as in many religions, to petition God for help, since Buddha's are for all time past this world. A Buddha, in the case of living or dead, doesn't have the ability to free you, however their lessons and model guide you to free yourself. Dedication centers your awareness, and assists with achieving further degrees of pledge to the way. The Buddha instructed dedication to himself through the starting custom of the Refuge Vow, and the Pali writings notice the names of twenty-eight different Buddha's who are likewise loved. Commitment to Buddha's, for example, the future Buddha Maitreya, the Buddha's mom Queen Māyā, and Gotamī, the main female liberated one, demonstrated well known.

Love of Gods and Nature Spirits

Buddhism is based upon the world perspective on the Vedas. Early Buddhism was firmly impacted by the Vedic religion's confirmation of life and its love of divine beings (devas) and nature spirits (yakṣas). The Buddha stated, "The respectable supporter makes contributions to the devas. This is an instance of riches gone to great use." Since the lay culture of early Buddhism was centered on accomplishing common satisfaction right now the next, revering nature spirits was an ageless method to keep up concordance with the rhythms of life, and increase bounty and joy. The Vedic divine beings keep on being regarded energetically for their job in maintaining the progression of life, the Dharma. While Buddhism is at last classed as a non-Vedic religion in light of its dismissal of the possibility of a spirit and its non-mystical direction, the impact of the Vedic perspective on life is solid and inescapable.

In the Common Vehicle, Mother Earth is the warm, grounded force that ensures the Dharma. The twentieth Century Thai ace Buddhadāsa Bhikkhu persuasively states, "The most suitable lodging for Dharma practice is that nearest to nature, sufficiently close to be called 'in brotherhood with nature.' By building up a way of life that gets physically involved with nature, we are making it helpful for nature to address us. If we are astute audience members, we will hear nature's voice more unmistakably than if we were far away. Closeness with nature can turn into the embodiment of our method of living."

Recognition Days

Upavastha (lit. abiding close): On the four lunar days of the month (Full Moon, New Moon, and the two Half Moons), you take extra vows like an amateur priest, and go through the day in calm Dharma study and meditation. Nowadays create commitment, insight and order.

Blessed Days

The Buddha's birthday, illumination, and demise are completely celebrated on the blessed day (pūjā) called Vaiśākha (a word with no clear interpretation), which for the most part falls on the Full Moon of the fifth or 6th lunar month (April or May).

Journey

Journey (yatra) incorporates visiting the hallowed locales that mark the significant occasions the Buddha's life, for example, Lumbinī (birth), Bodhgaya (edification), Vārānasi (first talk), and Kuśinagara (demise), and to places that house sacred relics of his body.

Consecrated Sex Rituals

The Buddha urged laypeople to appreciate sexual joys morally. In contrast to different strict pioneers of the Axial Age, he never denounced having numerous sweethearts or life partners, bashes, prostitution, homosexuality, sex with creatures, or mistresses. And, sexual customs, generally thought to be just piece of later Tantric Buddhism, were a piece of lay Buddhist practice from the earliest starting point. Numerous students of history have brought up that sexual ceremonies were constantly a component of the Buddhist way even though such a large amount of Indian culture, just as most societies in the antiquated world, was deeply orgiastic. Herbert Guenther, writer of The Tantric View of Life, composes that "Blow-outs have been a piece of life in India since soonest times and are not a specific component of Tantrism." The most punctual Buddhist craftsmanship, for example, at the hallowed locales of Sāñcī and Bhārhut (c. 200 BCE), is blissfully orgiastic, and the craftsmanship student of history Garima Kaushik has composed that the most punctual Buddhist strict locales were really communities for orgiastic customs, brimming with "party" and "lewdness." The most seasoned realized Buddhist statues are not of plain buddhas however sexy female wine bearers (kumbha dāsīs), which The Kāma Sūtra distinguishes as a class of whore. This matches the world getting a charge out of message the Buddha gave his lay adherents, instead of the world denying message he gave his priests.

Two surges of sexual practice impacted early Indian culture. The primary stream is a common stream of lessons on love, for example, The Kāma Sūtra, in which sexual delight is appreciated as a fine art without a deep objective. The second is the Tantric stream, where specialists look to change themselves into divine beings through sexual yoga. Early Buddhist lay culture was emphatically affected by the main stream, and raised it to a hallowed demonstration of commitment to the Buddha that brought merit. Mahāyāna Buddhism was in the end deeply changed by the Tantric stream.

The Noble Eightfold Path

The Buddha built up a wide arrangement of training called the Noble Eightfold Path (Ārya Aṣṭāṅga Marga). It permits you to transcend the distraught drives of common presence. It is likewise a cheerful way, and uses thoughtful delight to achieve the most elevated ecstasy. Determinedly sought after, you can accomplish liberatedom in a solitary lifetime. It includes the three fields of insight (prajñā), lead (śīla), and meditation (samādhi), and every last one of these three depends on the other for progress.

Right View

Through Right View (Samyag Dṛiṣṭi), you build up a comprehension of the Four Noble Truths. You start with a theoretical comprehension by reflecting and thinking about the sūtras, maintaining a strategic distance from wrong perspectives, and end with Insight Meditation (Vipaśyanā) by "making the achievement" - legitimately seeing and understanding the Four Noble Truths. From deep reflection on the unchanging laws of presence (Dharma), you capably use the intensity of your own thoughts to quit taking an interest in all exercises that add to anguish. The last advance right now to ponder the Three Stains (Āsavas), the last main drivers of affliction: 1) want for erotic delight, 2) want for presence, and 3) obliviousness of the Four Noble Truths. Understanding the Three Stains closes languishing.

Right Intention

You hold the Right Intention (Samyak Saṃkalpa) to comprehend the Dharma, act ethically, be liberal to other people, appreciate life, and eventually accomplish liberatedom.

Right Speech

Right Speech (Samyag Vācā) implies using language that is honest, delicate, adoring, and accommodating to yourself as well as other people. You maintain a strategic distance from words that are untruthful, malevolent, damaging, inert, or tattle.

Right Action

You don't act in manners that carry mischief to yourself or others. Abstaining from taking life, taking, sexual unfortunate behavior, bogus discourse, and intoxicants establishes Right Action (Samyak Karmānta).

Right Livelihood

You pick work that helps other people through Right Livelihood (Samyag Ājīva), and live in wellbeing and money related equalization. You evade work that hurts, remembering exchanging for weapons, slaves, meat, intoxicants, and toxins.

Right Effort

You endeavor diligently in Right Effort (Samyag Vyāyāma) to keep away from hurtful thoughts, words or activities, and develop healthy ones. You look for continually to relinquish want and repugnance, create care and thoughtful retention, and straightforwardly see the idea of torment.

Right Awareness

You keep up consistent awareness through Right Awareness (Samyak Smṛiti) of all that you do, say, and think. You remain completely present in every minute as opposed to harping distractedly on past and future occasions, acting with mindful, cautious reflectation. You keep nonstop familiarity with misery, fleetingness, and no self. Care brings you cognizant command over your senses, from which you discharge your erotic longings. You let go of the passionate desires and bogus thoughts that you need anything at all to fulfill you, and live in a condition of nonattachment (aprāpti). With serenity, you stay away from the Eight Worldly Concerns (Aṣṭa Loka Dharma) that keep individuals from ever really accomplishing suffering satisfaction: 1) increase, 2) misfortune, 3) notoriety, 4) offensiveness, 5) delight, 6) torment, 7) acclaim, and 8) fault.

Right Concentration

You develop conditions of thoughtful retention in Right Concentration (Samyak Samādhi) that refine your feelings and psyche through progressively unobtrusive and significant encounters of harmony and delight. Additionally called Tranquility Meditation (Śamathā), you start by resting your brain in single-pointed placelight on an object and accomplish an ecstatic nondual condition of awareness. Peacefulness Meditation incorporates the act of the Four Immeasurables (Brahma Vihāra), in which you accomplish deep reflective assimilations on the characteristics of:

1) Love (maitrī)

2) Sympathy (karuṇa)

3) Happiness (mudita)

4) Composure (upekṣa).

Another training is the Eight Attainments (Samāpattis), comprising of the Four Form Absorptions (Rūpa Dhyānas) and the Four Formless Absorptions (Arūpa Dhyānas). These meditations lead you into dynamic conditions of joyful awareness that briefly lift your awareness into higher measurements. You go through the Three Worlds: the present Realm of Desire (Kāmadhātu), the higher Realm of Form (Rūpadhātu), and the most elevated Realm of Formlessness (Arūpadhātu) – and you find that changeless harmony and rapture can't be found in any of them. Besides, these reflective states just stifle dualistic meditations, they don't dispose of them. By building up yourself in significant harmony and making mental adaptability and transparency, you set up your psyche for Insight Meditation, which at last brings liberatedom. The Buddha additionally showed a joined act of Tranquility Meditation and Insight Meditation called Breathing Meditation (Ānāpāna Smṛiti), through which he himself achieved inward arousing.

Results

An Awakened One

Śākyamuni reflected himself the "Buddha" or Awakened One. A Buddha is an individual who has accomplished perpetual harmony and ecstasy. You have understood the Four Noble Truths, and are liberated from want, abhorrence, and numbness. While alive, your Five Aggregates despite everything capacity together, yet are discharged at death with the goal that it is difficult to be reawakened into any sort of world. You have completely revoked common life. You experience no desire, and are unequipped for getting explicitly excited or engaging in sexual relations. You never again connect to a perpetual self that never genuinely existed. You are somebody who "knows and reflects reality to be it is." All your enthusiastic and mental obscurations are "extinguished," gone. The condition of a liberated one is immeasurable. You are omniscient, brilliant and superb, impeccable in information and lead, adoring and merciful, sorrowless, and absolutely magnificent. A Buddha has every single fantastic quality.

The Buddha additionally reflected himself the Tathāgata, actually meaning the "Along these lines Gone One," one who has disregarded into the lasting tranquility of nirvāṇa. A Buddha is never again human, rising above even the divine beings. He specifies his inexplicable capacities to "travel through the sky like a winged creature," "touch and stroke with my hand the Moon and Sun," and know the meditations and sentiments of others. A Buddha's most noteworthy capacity of everything is to see straightforwardly the Four Noble Truths.

Vows

The Refuge Vow - Tri Śaraṇa

Taking the Refuge Vow (Tri Śaraṇa) implies you look for asylum from suffering in the Three Jewels (Tri Ratna): the Buddha, the Dharma, and the Saṅgha. The promise guides you to harmony and flourishing. You make an inward pledge to adore pictures of the Buddha, treat the expressions of the Buddha with deference, and respect individuals from the Buddhist people group.

Recommended Items

Pratimā - A statue or picture of the Buddha, sclimaxing to the instructor. Sūtra – A book of the Buddha's talks, sclimaxing to the lessons.

Stūpa – A picture of a commemoration internment marker, sclimaxing to the network of professionals.

The Refuge Vow

To take the Refuge Vow (generally done before a priest or religious woman, yet you can do it all alone), bow with your correct advantage and left leg down, hands held in petition, and recite the next in Sanskrit and in English:

My name is (state your name).

buddham śaraṇam gacchāmi dharmam śaraṇam gacchāmi saṅgham śaraṇam gacchāmi

"I go for asylum to the Buddha." "I go for shelter to the Dharma." "I go for asylum to the Saṅgha."

Recite 3x.

Touch your temple with a statue or picture of the Buddha, a sūtra content, and a little stūpa, to worship the Three Jewels of the Buddha, the Dharma, and the Saṅgha.

Congrats! You are presently a Buddhist. Your hair is then shaved off. Generally, the entirety of your hair is shaved as a motion of your change into another and higher period of your life, however in the cutting edge world a great many people simply trim a couple of strands. You likewise get a Refuge name, which your instructor gives you or you can give yourself.

The Lay Precepts - Pañca Śīla

The Lay Precepts (Pañca Śīla) are taken to shield you from lower resurrection, and are the vows of every single lay professional. It is useful to present them every day, or at whatever point you sit for training. Take the Lay Precepts by bowing in supplication and recounting them, in Sanskrit and in English:

māraṇāñ caurikāñ cāpi parapatnīṃ mṛiṣāvacaḥ

tyajāmi sarpavat sarvaṃ pañcamaṃ madyaṃ eva ca

"Murdering, taking, the life partner of another, and bogus discourse,

I will stay away from them like snakes, and the fifth,

intoxicants, too." Recite 3x.

The Fast Day Precepts – Poṣadha Gātha

On the four days of the lunar month, spend however much of the day as could be expected in your sacrosanct space, or in a Buddhist sanctuary or religious community, to peruse the Buddha's sūtras and practice reflection. It is prescribed to take three extra vows for the afternoon, known as the Fast Day Precepts (Poṣadha Gātha – lit. Section of the Observance). Then again, and all the more prevalently, you may go to groups and celebrations and practice reverential holy sex customs. To take the promises, bow and recount the next, in Sanskrit and in English:

vikāle 'pi bhojanaṃ

nṛitya gīta vibhūṣāñ ca vajrayiṣyāmi sotsavān ucchaiḥśayyāṃ mahāsayyaṃ

1. "I won't eat troublesome." Eat once, after dawn and before early afternoon.
2. "I will desert euphoric moving, singing, and sprucing up."
3. "I won't use a high or huge bed." Recite 3x.

Direct - Śīla

Follow the moral rules of the Dharma every day:

1. Right Speech (Samyag Vācā): Sclimax with graciousness and honesty, stay away from unforgiving or inert words.
2. Right Action (Samyak Karmānta): Do not murder, take, or participate in sexual offense.
3. Right Livelihood (Samyag Ājīva): Perform work that

encourages you and others and doesn't hurt.

Heavenly Days - Pūjā

Respect the Buddha's birthday, illumination, and passing on Vaiśākha. You are urged to eat just vegan food, watch each of the eight Fast Day Precepts, be liberal to other people, adore the Buddha, study Dharma and invest energy in meditation. You can likewise be spend them in substantial festivals and inebriated celebration.

Journey – Yatra

Visit the hallowed locales of the Buddha's life in India and Nepal. Respectfully and with collapsed hands, circumambulate these destinations, reflecting the immortal intensity of the Dharma. Then again, visit these places in your brain by perusing the Buddha's biography or looking at pictures of these locales.

Activities

For the individuals who are new to Buddhism, practicing the next activities every day for in any event a month will build up in you a solid establishment for positive living and internal harmony, and set you up for higher Tantric practices. 20 to an hour every day is perfect.

Commitment - Śraddhā

Supporting your way with reverential practices to begin your meditation meeting enormously escalates its capacity.

Making a Sacred Space – Bodhi Maṇḍa

Make a consecrated space for reflection and ceremonies. You can enrich your live with: Buddhist pictures (pratimā)

– Such as photographs of statues and ceremonial destinations.

The Eight Auspicious Symbols (Aṣṭa Maṅgala) of an illuminated ruler: 1) the conch shell (śaṅkha), the call to arousing, 2) the interminable bunch (śrī vatsa), astuteness, 3) the pair of goldfish (matsya), fruitfulness, 4) the lotus (padma), virtue, 5) the parasol (catra), imperial insurance, 6) the fortune container (kumbha), wealth, 7) the wheel (cakra), the law of the Dharma, and 8) the triumph standard (dhvaja), edification.

Set up a sanctuary or raised area (vedi):

Buddha picture (pratimā) - In the inside. A statue or outline of the Buddha. Dharma content (sūtra) – The liberating intensity of the Buddha's words.

Pictures of the four extraordinary snapshots of the Buddha's life (pratimā): 1) an impression (pāda), his introduction to the world,

2) a bodhi leaf (bodhi), his enlivening, 3) a wheel of Dharma (cakra), his educating, and 4) a dedication internment marker (stūpa), his demise.

Oil light (dīpa) - The light is the light of the Dharma.

Incense burner (dāhaka) - Incense is the smell of lovely good lead. Sandalwood, gum guggul, or storax are normal incense.

Blossom container (puṣpa) - Flowers sclimax to fleetingness. White carnations show inward immaculateness. God picture (pratimā) - A common divinity, for example, the earth goddess Pṛthivī (otherwise known as Bhu Devī). She was the Buddha's first observer to his edification, and offers liberally to all.

Each time you enter your holy space for training, offer a respectful bow with your hands in Añjali Mudrā to your Buddha picture. With your hands together respectfully, touch your head, throat, and heart focus, sclimaxing to your dedication through your body, discourse and psyche.

Regarding the Deities of Nature

Respect and recognition the divinities of nature. Give proper respect to their put in the heavenly request, and vow to work agreeably with them.

1. Summon the divine beings and goddesses who manage the characteristic world: "I conjure the celestial couples Indra and Indrāṇī, ruler and sovereign of the divine beings, Dyaus and Pṛithivī, god and goddess of sky and earth, Varuṇa and Varuṇī, god and goddess of water, Agni and Svāhā, god and goddess of fire, and Vāyu and Vāyavyī, god and goddess of wind. I request that you be available with me."
2. Discuss sonnets from The Ṛig Veda, sing your own tunes, or respect them discreetly in your way.
3. Approach the divine beings for their help with making what you want.
4. Thank the divine beings for their assistance, and reject them: "I thank you for your help. You are rejected."

Benefits: Wins the companionship of the divine beings, who help you in achieving common joys and crushing external snags to internal arousing.

Time: 5 minutes.

Reverential Ritual

1. Discuss the opening section of regard to the Buddha, in Sanskrit and in English:

nāmo tasya bhagavāto arhato sama sambuddhāya

"Tribute to the favored one, the arhat, the total and impeccable buddha."

2. Present the Refuge Vow.

buddham śaraṇam gacchāmi dharmam śaraṇam gacchāmi saṅgham śaraṇam gacchāmi

"I go for shelter to the Buddha." "I go for asylum to the Dharma." "I go for shelter to the Saṅgha."

Present 3x.

3. Present the Lay Precepts.

māraṇāñ caurikāñ cāpi parapatnīṃ mṛiṣāvacaḥ

tyajāmi sarpavat sarvaṃ pañcamaṃ madyaṃ eva ca

"Slaughtering, taking, the life partner of another, and bogus discourse,

I will evade them like snakes, and the fifth, intoxicants, too." Recite 3x.

4. Reflect the great characteristics of every one of the Six Remembrances (Saḍ Anusmṛiti): 1) the Buddha, 2) the Dharma, 3) the Saṅgha, 4) moral control, 5) liberality, and 6) the divinities. For the keep going,

reflect the divinities of the magnificent domains, and the excellencies they performed to arrive.

5. Meditate, practicing Tranquility Meditation, Insight Meditation, or both.
6. With happiness and euphoria, close your meeting by presenting a couple of stanzas of the Buddha's lessons, for example, these words:

"Cheerful undoubtedly are the liberated ones! No hankering can be found in them. Cut off is the arrogance 'I am.' Delusion's net is crushed."

Benefits: Develops commitment, which supports practice that prompts inward arousing. Time: 20 to an hour.

Astuteness - Prajñā

Astuteness alludes to Right View (Samyag Dṛiṣṭi) and Right Intention (Samyak Saṃkalpa). It incorporates the aim to turn into a buddha, printed study, and the immediate view of the real world. Put aside some time every week for study and deep reflection on the Buddha's lessons.

Right View – Samyag Dṛiṣṭi

Develop a comprehension of the Buddha's lessons through perusing, and reflect how you can incorporate them into your day by day life. After some time, build up the capacity to straightforwardly see the liberating truth.

Benefits: You gain merit, an amazing nature improves, and you stay away from the snares of anguish. Time: 1 hour seven days; persistently.

Right Intention – Samyak Saṃkalpa

As you develop Right View, set a solid aim to

comprehend the Dharma, carry on ethically, practice reflection, appreciate common joys capably, and eventually achieve liberatedom.

Benefits: Your aim to achieve liberatedom gets solid, and you make the conditions for your illumination.

Time: 1 hour seven days; constantly.

Reflection – Samādhi

Create inward harmony through Tranquility Meditation and Insight Meditation. Right Effort (Samyag Vyāyāma), Right Awareness (Samyak Smṛiti) and Right Concentration (Samyak Samādhi) concern meditation. These practices are regularly best done from the start in brief timeframe periods, and you can expand the time as you become further developed.

Sitting Posture for Meditation

Sit in an agreeable reflective stance on a pad:

1. Your legs are in the Meditation Pose (Dhyāna Āsana, likewise called Lotus Pose or Padma Āsana), with your feet laying on your thighs, or the Half-Lotus Pose (Ardha Padma Āsana), one foot laying on one thigh, or leg over leg. Your hands are in the Gesture of Meditation (Dhyāna Mudrā) either just beneath the navel or in your lap, left hand under the correct hand, the parts of the bargains somewhat touching, and elbows marginally standing out.
2. Your eyes are half open.
3. Your eyes look delicately at the tip of your nose.
4. Your back and neck are straight.
5. Your shoulders are straight, nose in accordance with

your navel.

6. Your lips are tenderly shut.
7. Your tongue leans tenderly against the top of your mouth.

As you hold the stance, let your body be loose. Concentrate your awareness on where the breath enters and leaves your body between the nostrils and upper lip. Breathing is loose, regular, quiet, consistent, and even.

Peacefulness Meditation – Śamathā

Create significant inward harmony through the different acts of Tranquility Meditation:

The Four Immeasurables – Brahma Vihāra

Sit and develop love, empathy, euphoria, and poise towards yourself and all creatures. These characteristics must be pure, without childish inspiration, and without enthusiastic connection to other people. Concentrate first on the nature of love, getting reflectively ingested in it. When you have effectively built up that quality over a time of days or weeks, proceed onward to the next quality and do likewise until you accomplish capability in every last one of them. Then start with love again and develop your acknowledgment.

1. Reflect the threat of loathe and the estimation of love.
2. Create love towards yourself. State to yourself, "May I be glad and liberated from affliction."
3. Reflect a darling instructor, saying, "May this great individual be cheerful and liberated from anguish." With love, become thoughtfully retained in them.
4. Reflect a beyond all doubt adored companion,

saying, "May this great individual be glad and liberated from anguish." With love, become reflectively ingested in them.

5. Reflect an individual you feel unbiased toward, creating love for them just as they were a dear companion, saying, "May this great individual be glad and liberated from torment." With love, become thoughtfully assimilated in them.

6. Reflect an individual you feel disdain toward, and create nonpartisan emotions toward them. Then look to create love for them, thinking, "This individual, as my mom previously, conveyed me in her belly, played with me in her lap, and supported me. And, this individual as my dad fed me by bringing me back riches thinking to take care of his kids."

7. If you despite everything can't create love toward somebody you detest, ponder the benefits of love: 1) you stay in bed comfort, 2) you wake in comfort, 3) you dream no terrible dreams, 4) you are of high repute to people, 5) you dear to nonhuman creatures, 6) divinities monitor you, 7) discharge, toxic substance and weapons can't hurt you, 8) your psyche is effectively focused, 9) your face is peaceful, 10) you pass on without disarray, and 11) you will be renewed into a higher domain.

8. If you despite everything can't produce love towards them, solicit yourself what part from their Four Elements you are furious with: their earth component, water component, fire component, and wind component? Which of their Six Senses would you say you are irate with? Which of their Five Aggregates as you furious with? You find there is

nobody to be furious with.

9. If you despite everything have detest toward that individual, go to them and give them a blessing.

10. When you create love toward the individual you felt detest toward, become reflectively retained in them.

11. Having accomplished a caring thoughtful assimilation, travel through the First to Fourth Absorptions (see the Four Formless Absorptions underneath for guidelines).

12. Generate love overrunning the whole world, similarly to all. Think, "May all creatures be liberated from ill will, pain and uneasiness, and live joyfully."

Benefits: Develops inward harmony and joy right now future lifetimes.

Time: 20 to an hour.

Care Meditation - Smṛiti: The Four Foundations of Awareness

This training is performed with significant awareness and discharging of all feeling of connection to anything right now. Practice care, both as a sitting reflection just as ceaselessly consistently. In every minute bring careful, fair attention to your body, sensations, mind, and the Dharma. Relinquish connection and repugnance as they emerge.

Body - Kāya

1. Breathing: Breathe in and out, and watch your breath. Notice if it is long or short. Know about your whole body as you inhale, and how your breathing turns out to be continuously progressively tranquil.

2. The Four Postures: Be mindful of your body as you:

1) walk, 2) stand, 3) sit, and 4) rests.

3. Clear Comprehension: Maintain constant, away from consciousness of each move you make.

4. Ugliness of the Body: Reflect on the inalienable contamination of the body: 1) head hairs, 2) body hairs, 3) nails, 4) teeth, 5) skin, 6) tissue, 7) ligaments, 8) bones, 9) bone marrow, 10) kidneys, 11) heart, 12) liver, 13) stomach, 14) spleen, 15) lungs, 16) digestion tracts, 17) mesentery, 18) stomach, 19) dung, 20) bile, 21) mucus, 22) discharge, 23) blood, 24) sweat, 25) fat, 26) tears, 27) oil, 28) drool, 29) snot, 30) oils of the joints, and 31) pee.

5. The Four Elements: Be mindful of how your body is made out of the Four Elements: 1) earth, 2) Water, 3) fire, and 4) wind. Your body is anything but a solitary substance, yet a development of components.

6. The Nine Charnel Ground Thoughts: Reflect on your own body as it continuously becomes: 1) a carcass next three days, 2) a body ate up by creatures, 3) a skeleton with substance, blood, and ligaments, 4) a skeleton with blood and ligaments, 5) a skeleton with ligaments, 6) a skeleton with faded bones, 7) stacked up bones, 8) over a year old, and 9) disintegrated to clean. With each subject figure, "My body will resemble that sometime in the not so distant future."

Sensations - Vedanā

Notice whether your physical sensations are wonderful, agonizing, or neither charming nor excruciating. They might be: 1) lewd - charming, excruciating, neither lovely nor difficult, or 2) spiritual - wonderful, agonizing, neither charming nor excruciating. As every sensation emerges, think, "There is a sensation." A licentious sensation is clouded by want, abhorrence, or obliviousness, while a deep sensation is clear.

Brain - Citta

Know about the altering characteristics of your perspective. Notice when it is: 1) with want or without want, 2) with revultion or without abhorrence, 3) with obliviousness or without numbness, 4) contracted or diverted, 5) lifted up or unexalted, 6) top notch or surpassable, 7) concentrated or unconcentrated, 8) liberated or unliberated. As each suspected emerges, think "There is mind."

Liberating Wisdom – Dharma

1. Reflect the Five Hindrances (Nivaraṇa): 1) want, 2) abhorrence, 3) sluggishness, 4) disturbance, and 5) question. Watching them as present or not present, think "There is or isn't this quality in me."

2. Reflect the Five Aggregates: 1) form, 2) sensation, 3) discernment, 4) mental developments, and 5) awareness. Seeing the temporariness of every one, think "Such is form, (and so on.), its emerging and dying."

3. Ponder the Six Senses: 1) eye, 2) ear, 3) nose, 4) tongue, 5) body, and 6) mind. Perceive each sense, what appears to them, regardless of whether the obscuration of want that emerges subordinate upon them is or is absent, and see how it is deserted.

4. Ponder the Seven Factors of Enlightenment (Sapta Bodhyaṅgāni): 1) care, 2) understanding the Dharma,

3) exertion, 4) delight, 5) serenity, 6) reflective ingestion, and 7) composure. Reflect them to be available or not present inside you. Quietness implies calming the brain and feelings, while poise is a more deep condition of awareness that accomplishes the First Absorption.

5. Reflect the Four Noble Truths. Perceive how these are available for you in every minute.

Benefits: Leads to inward harmony and nonattachment.

Time: 20 to an hour; ceaselessly consistently.

The Eight Attainments - Samāpattis

The Eight Attainments comprise of levels of reflective fixation including the Four Form Absorptions and the Four Formless Absorptions. These are levels of rapture, iridescence, and roomy awareness that invade your whole body, and are without upsetting mental thoughts. They are unconstrained acknowledge you gotten mindful of as they emerge. The three characteristics of fruitful fixation are: 1) strength, having steady center, 2) immaculateness, without diverting enthusiastic and mental obscurations emerging, and 3) liveliness, emphatically present.

When you accomplish the Fourth Absorption, you build up a solid establishment to rehearse Insight Meditation and achieve last arousing. You may likewise create supernatural forces. As you accomplish each level, keep away from any ideas of individual accomplishment. Reflect how everyone brings sentiments harmony and joy, yet in addition understand these levels can't prompt perpetual harmony and delight. You find that nothing in all the Three Worlds of

Desire, Form and Formlessness holds your advantage, since they are altogether despite everything planes of saṃsāra. Discharging your longing for them, you set your objective on nirvāṇa.

Access Concentration - Upacāra Samādhi

A condition of awareness close to the First Absorption is called an Access Concentration (Upacāra Samādhi). To accomplish the First Absorption you should incidentally stifle the Five Hindrances: 1) want, 2) abhorrence, 3) sleepiness, 4) disturbance, and 5) question. This is the primary work of a start meditator.

1. With your emphasis on your breath, carry cognizant attention to your psyche, and move delicately into reflective retention. Permit your thoughts and feelings to rise and fall as they may, however don't focus on them. When problematic thoughts and feelings emerge, don't pass judgment on yourself – just pull together your awareness. You are making an effort not to wipe out your thoughts, simply notice them.

2. As you build up your fixation, your awareness gets assimilated into your breath. Harmony and ecstasy emerge, and you develop those sentiments by concentrating on them. The Five Hindrances are smothered, and the First Absorption unexpectedly rises.

3. When negative thoughts emerge, you can: 1) center around something healthy, 2) look at the risk of those thoughts, 3) overlook them, 4) still your thoughts, and as a last resort, 5) grip your teeth, place your

tongue on the top of your mouth and coercively oblige your brain.

The Four Form Absorptions – Rūpa Dhyāna

1. First Absorption - Five variables are available in your awareness: 1) the object of meditation (grāhya), your breath, 2) in number, absorptive fixation on the item (samādhi), 3) energized joy or delight (prīti), 4) quiet joy or joy (sukha), and 5) one-sharpness (eka gratā). You are without sense wants, as your awareness briefly disengages from the Desire World into the Form World, which comprises of forms without want. Loaded up with happiness, your physical body encounters no agony. Your thoughts are as yet present, and your awareness effectively keeps up one-pointed placelight on your breath. Your care and focus might be shaky, and poise might be feeble.

2. Second Absorption – Releasing your reflection on the object of meditation (your breath), three residual components are available: 1) joy, 2) rapture, and 3) one-pointed awareness on the absorptive experience. You are liberated from thoughts, and your discernment is "signless," liberated from reasonable marks. Care and focus are steady. Your awareness is discharged into a higher and progressively refined degree of form. Composure is available.

3. Third Absorption - The two components present are rapture and one-sharpness. Energized satisfaction falls away. Ecstasy is more grounded. Care and fixation are solid. Composure is solid.

4. Fourth Absorption - The two elements present are composure and one-sharpness, and both are solid.

Euphoria is discharged. Care and fixation are exceptionally solid and pure. Liberated from agony and joy, your psyche and body are iridescent and rest in deep stillness.

The Four Formless Absorptions – Arūpa Dhyāna

1. Base of Infinite Space (Ākāśānantya) – Meditating on unbounded space, you see space yet never again see any forms or tactile encounters (sight, smell, and so forth.) inside it. Incidentally discharged from both the Desire and Form universes, you experience the Formless world. You increase significantly more deep serenity and one-sharpness.

2. Base of Infinite Consciousness (Vijñānānantya) – No longer seeing either form or space, you see just endless awareness. You gain ever more deep poise and one-sharpness.

3. Base of Nothing Whatever (Akiñcanya) – Passing past awareness, you see just total nothingness. You increase reflectably more deep serenity and one-sharpness.

4. Base of Neither Perception nor Nonperception (Naiva Saṇjñānasanja) – From supreme nothingness, you discharge any feeling of the demonstration of recognition, but then an unpretentious lingering discernment remains. You increase deep conditions of composure and one-sharpness.

5. The Ninth Special Supramundane Attainment - Nirodha Samāpatti

6. The Cessation of Perception and Feeling (Nirodha Samāpatti) – This ingestion is the complete discontinuance of awareness. It is the most elevated

and most refined achievement, and sanitizes you deeply. It is just achievable by nonreturners and arhats, not normal experts. However, it is still just an impermanent reflective achievement - it can't all alone bring liberatedom.

Benefits: Develops significant inward harmony that turns into the base for Insight Meditation. Time: 20 to an hour.

Understanding Meditation - Vipaśyanā

Understanding Meditation - Vipaśyanā

Reflect with deep inward placelight on the laws of common presence. As you show up at genuine comprehension, desert the basic inclinations toward suffering inside you.

1. Ponder what is unwholesome and healthy: the Three Poisons and the Lay Precepts.
2. Reflect the continuing variables of life: 1) food, 2) touch, 3) mental developments, and 4) awareness. Understanding the continuing variables of life closes languishing.
3. Ponder the Four Noble Truths. Understanding the Four Noble Truths closes languishing.
4. Reflect mature age and demise. Understanding mature age and passing closures languishing.
5. Reflect birth. Understanding birth closes languishing.
6. Ponder common presence. Seeing common presence closes languishing.
7. Reflect connection. Understanding connection closes

languishing.

8. Ponder want. Understanding want closes languishing.

9. Reflect sensation. Understanding sensation closes languishing.

10. Reflect touch. Understanding touch closes languishing.

11. Reflect the Six Senses. Understanding the Six Senses closes languishing.

12. Reflect name and form. Getting name and form closes languishing.

13. Ponder cognizance. Understanding cognizance closes languishing.

14. Reflect mental arrangements. Understanding mental developments closes languishing.

15. Reflect obliviousness. Understanding obliviousness closes languishing.

16. Reflect the Three Stains (Āsavas). These are the last main drivers of misery: 1) want for erotic delight, 2) want for presence, and 3) numbness of the Four Noble Truths. Understanding the Three Stains closes languishing.

17. Deeply understanding these certainties, you are liberated.

Benefits: Develops the shrewdness that prompts liberatedom.

Time: 20 to an hour.

The Union of Tranquility and Insight Meditation – Yuganaddha

Breathing Meditation - Ānāpāna Smṛiti

Breathing Meditation joins the thoughtful ingestion of Tranquility Meditation with the entering intensity of Insight Meditation. The following advances are dynamic: start with the initial four stages, taking as much time as is needed with every one, and gradually move into more deep and subtler degrees of retention. Include different advances gradually after some time, continually starting every meeting with the initial steps and in the long run advancing toward the end. Play out each progression while concentrating deeply on your own breath as you normally take in and out.

Body – Kāya

1. Mull over the long breath. Take long, slow breaths, and notice how they influence your brain. Is it lovely or unsavory? Is it quieting or energizing? Does it make you cheerful or troubled?
2. Ponder the short breath. Take short, speedy breaths, and notice how they influence your psyche. Is it wonderful or unsavory? Is it quieting or energizing? Does it make you glad or miserable?
3. Experience the entire body. Watch your breath as it conditions your body. Perceive that your physical body is consistently influenced by your breath.
4. Quiet the entire body. Concentrate one-distinctly on your breath to quiet your breath, which quiets your physical body and brain. Inhale long breaths to discharge any negative feelings and reflections, and arrive at inward harmony. Perceive how your breath

impacts the characteristics of your body and brain. Long breaths bring harmony and bliss, short breaths excitation and inconvenience.

Sensations - Vedanā

1. Experience euphoria. Notice as vibes of energized satisfaction or delight (prīti) emerge and how they influence your psyche.
2. Experience rapture. Notice as impressions of quieting joy or euphoria (sukha) emerge and how they influence your psyche.
3. Experience the psychological developments. Know about delight as a coarse, animating and upsetting quality that disturbs your body, breath, and brain. Know about happiness as an unobtrusive, quieting and mending quality that placates your body, breath, and psyche.
4. Quiet the psychological developments. Drive away your impressions of energized delight through developing reflective focus, and develop your consciousness of quieting happiness. Right now, deal with your sensations.

Psyche - Citta

1. Experience the psyche. Know about your brain in every minute in the entirety of its characteristics. Observe if there is: 1) want, 2) revultion, or 3) numbness, which may emerge as expectation or dread, obsession or constant mental stirring regarding a matter that inconveniences you. Is your psyche clear or vague? Concentrated or not concentrated? Preeminent or not incomparable?

Liberated or unliberated?

2. Carry satisfaction to the psyche. Develop preeminent euphoria, pleasure, and happiness by thinking about how glad you are that you found the Dharma and how it will carry you as far as possible of all anguish.

3. Concentrate the psyche. Through reflective retention, drive away undesirable meditations and set up yourself in the three characteristics of fruitful fixation: steadiness, immaculateness, liveliness.

4. Free the psyche. Discharge all connection to any material articles, wrong perspectives, unliberating ceremonies, and all meditations and sensations you use to characterize yourself through the figments of "I" and "mine." Release the Five Hindrances and the Three Poisons.

Freeing Wisdom - Dharma

1. Reflect temporariness. Reflect the fleetingness of every single adapted wonder. Reflect suffering, and no self.

2. Mull over disintegration. Having perceived the genuine characteristics of common presence, permit every one of your connections to break up. Permit your psyche to stay composed, quiet, and equipoised.

3. Reflect discontinuance. Discharge totally your connections, fears of birth, mature age, and passing. End all your passionate conditions of misery. End your craving, repugnance and obliviousness to everything. End your thought that any of the Five Aggregates establish a "self." As suspension emerges, nirvāṇa emerges.

4. Examine opportunity from connection. With

incredible composure, discharge every last remainder of "I" and "mine." You are totally liberated.

Benefits: Leads to liberatedom. Time: 20 to an hour.

Couples Sacred Sex Ritual - Maithuna Vidhi

You can rehearse your own Buddhist consecrated sex custom next in the methods for the Common Vehicle. While the buddhas are past giving favors and help, you can seek them for motivation and build up your commitment. Concentrate on producing pure love without connection among you and your sweetheart.

Proposed Items

Sacrosanct Space: A special raised area, two or three cushions on the floor, a few covers, towels and tissues. Gifts: Small blessings to provide for one another, for example, a gem, a shell, or a bloom.

Garments: Wrap-around skirts for people, both topless, and some straightforward and exquisite gems. For the lady, a thin midriff belt can be extremely exquisite and sexual. Assemble a few blossoms and make them into two wreaths for offering crowns.

Bloom laurels: One fragrant wreath for every one of you.

Food: Fruit cuts or other reduced down food, heavenly and effectively absorbable, served in a little bowl. Drink: Wine served in copper cups or coconut shells. Conjure the goddess of wine (Madhu Devī) to sanctify your beverage before the custom: "Goddess of wine, favor this beverage with the goal that it might bring us love and delight and motivate us on our way to liberatedom."

Plates and Utensils: Large green leaves for plates, and use your fingers to eat. Music: Indian music, for example, sitar and tabla, vīṇā (lute), or hip twirl.

Individual Preparation

Clean your bodies, give each other back rubs, scrub down, wear custom dress, and practice a couple haṭha yoga presents.

The Ritual

nāmo tasya bhagavāto arhato sama sambuddhāya

"Reverence to the favored one, the arhat, the total and immaculate buddha."

3. Recite the Refuge Vow.

buddham śaraṇam gacchāmi dharmam śaraṇam gacchāmi saṅgham śaraṇam gacchāmi

"I go for asylum to the Buddha." "I go for shelter to the Dharma." "I go for asylum to the Saṅgha."

Recount 3x.

4. Reflect on the temperances of the Three Jewels.
5. Practice Tranquility Meditation on one of the Four Immeasurables.
6. Practice Insight Meditation, pondering the Four Noble Truths.

7. Invoke the divine forces of love, Kāma and Ratī, and request that they support you in your lovemaking. "We conjure the divine forces of love, Kāma and Ratī, and request that you support us in our lovemaking."

8. Give gifts to one another, and crown each other with a wreath of blossoms.

9. To animate the feeling of hearing, share expressions of fondness for one another.

10. To animate the feeling of sight, every lady finds a good pace seat and moves for her sweetheart. She sits down. Each man finds a good pace seat and moves for his darling. He sits down.

11. To invigorate the feeling of smell, offer each other a laurel of fragrant blossoms.

12. To animate the feeling of taste, she moves to sit on his lap; offer each other food and drink.

13. To invigorate the feeling of touch, offer each other sexy satisfying touches.

14. Arouse each other through suggestive touches and satisfying your cooperate with your mouth.

15. Make love to one another, using different situations as you appreciate them.

16. Cuddle together thereafter.

17. Give gratitude to the divine forces of love for helping you in your custom and reject them. "We offer gratitude to the divine forces of love for helping us in our custom. You are expelled."

18. Venerate the Buddha's with deep regard. "We love the Buddha's, whose ideal acknowledgment has carried them to flawlessness. We look for

consistently to develop your valuable characteristics."

19. Sit on cushions facing one another, and bow respectfully with Añjali Mudrā.

Benefits: You make great karma among you and your darling for the love and joy you share. You get the gifts of the divine beings and nature spirits who will enable you to make what you want. Creates dedication, internal harmony, and happiness, and legitimacy that prompts higher resurrection.

Time: 2 hours, including 1 hour getting ready for the custom, and 1 hour performing it.

Chapter Eight

⟨℘⟩

Prepare Your Body

The lessons of Tantric sex accept that your body is a sanctuary of love and that it is extremely significant that you keep in solid. If you need to accomplish more elevated levels of rapture, then you should stay in shape. Right now, will find out about the various tips that you can use for keeping your body fit and sound. There are explicit yoga places that you can use if you need to encourage the development of energy in your body. The practices that have been referenced right now supportive in helping you in directing just as controlling sexual energy in your body.

As a general rule, we will in general underestimate our bodies. We don't stress over it, and we don't understand that the body is the scaffold that will help you in accomplishing rapture. You should venerate your body and treat it with the consideration and love it merits if you need to achieve a more elevated level of joy.

Building love for your body through the mirror

One of the most significant things that you should do while you are setting up your body for Tantric sex is to relinquish all the distinctive negative musings that you may harbor about your body. You should see all aspects of your body, including your privates and see whether they are sound. If you feel that you are fat, just disclose to yourself that you are awe-inspiring. You should do this routinely to ensure that you let go of any negative emotions that you may have towards your body and rather have a ball and have a ton of fun while engaging in sexual relations.

When was simply the last time you have seen bare? Have a go at standing stripped before a full-length reflect. You can do this subsequent to washing up if you want to do this. Investigate every last bit of your body. Start from your feet straight up to the highest point of your head. If you notice that you are scrutinizing yourself, then stop without further ado and rather offer yourself a commendation. Replace each negative idea with a positive one. If you feel that your rear end is fat or that your thighs are thick, just imagine that you have a tasty figure! You needn't stress over what you resemble. Change each negative inclination into a positive one. Then watch your private parts. You should concentrate on each and every part of your privates, the hues, shape and furthermore the sogginess specifically territories. It is extremely significant that you do this to be sure about your body.

You can watch your first chakra, the base chakra that is situated toward the finish of your spine and the butt-centric area. This chakra gives you the possibility of security, and you have to take some time and watch this territory in a similar way where you watched your private parts. Use two mirrors if you have to.

The relationship between yoga and tantric sex

Yoga is maybe probably the most ideal manners by which you will have the option to set up your body for Tantric sex. Yoga and Tantric sex are firmly related.

Accordingly, it wouldn't come as an unexpected that the vast majority of the Tantric experts have additionally aced the craft of yoga. Learning yoga will help in dealing with their bodies. Rehearsing yoga will likewise help you in dealing with your brain and body. It will likewise help in controlling your body developments. Overseeing your body will let you experience different climaxes and furthermore have force over your discharge. This will positively affect your wellbeing and your sexual coexistence also.

Basic yoga developments

This area will assist you with learning a couple of essential yoga represents that you can perform to improve your general wellbeing and stamina. In the next area, you will find out about the distinctive tantric activities that you can, and your partner can perform together. This will help in expanding your closeness and solace level with one another.

The Head lift

Ensure that you are standing up straight for this. Then tilt your head upward and tilt it in such a way, that string from the sky was pulling it upwards. Keep your mouth shut, and you should breathe in through your nose. When you are breathing in, ensure that you are moving your shoulder bones in reverse so it would appear that they are attempting to touch one another. It should feel like your feet are fixed to the ground. Loosen up your position and afterward repeat this procedure.

The Cobra posture

You can rests on the floor or a yoga tangle. Presently

stretch out your body to ensure that your stomach is touching the floor. Then place your hands under your shoulders with the goal that your elbows are set at the back. Lift your chest off the floor and tilt your head so it would appear that a bend. Ensure that you are looking upwards. This posture should like a cobra that is going to strike. Loosen up your position and afterward repeat this procedure.

The Cat posture

When you are finished with the Cobra posture, you should delicately bring down your head and gradually ascend on your knees. This should appear as though you are hunching, so stretch your spine the other way than what you did in the Cobra posture.

The Resting posture

When you have completed the Cat posture, you should expect the Cobra posture. Stretch your arms outwards. Take in deeply and uninhibitedly. Ensure that your brow is laying on the ground and that your chest is touching your knees.

Tantric activities

If you need to add some use to your act of Tantric sex, then you can begin rehearsing a couple of activities and breathing procedures that will help you in making your sexual experience far and away superior. These activities, just as breathing systems, are most appropriate when finished with your partner, however they should be possible all alone also. These activities and breathing systems have been referenced right now.

Shoulder stand

Shoulder stands are useful for ladies for expecting the different Tantric postures easily, however on the other hand men can rehearse them too. For playing out a straightforward shoulder represent, the individual should rests level on a tangle or even the floor with his/her legs extended straight and their hands resting close by. The individual will then need to lift the legs at a 90-degree edge so their upper middle stays stuck to the floor. Their legs ought to be lifted somewhat higher than their lower back, and their hands ought to be put on their back for supporting this stance. Rehearsing this system will help in building up the genuinely necessary adaptability for accepting different Tantric sex positions.

Pontoon posture

This posture is by and by accommodating for ladies. The individual playing out this posture ought to sit with a straight back, and their legs ought to be loosened up. Then the individual should lift their legs at a 45-degree edge and afterward stretch their hands outwards so their fingers are pointing towards their feet. Attempt to keep up this posture for three minutes and afterward unwind. Repeat this posture multiple times.

Three legged canine posture

This posture is useful for extending the hamstring muscles, and these are frequently used in Tantric sex. For playing out this represent, the individual must rests on their stomach on a tangle while their hands are set on their sides. Your palms ought to be put alongside the chest and support your feet with your toes. Lift your body in such a way, that your toes support your body pressure. This position ought to appear as though your body is making a triangle, with the floor shaping the base of the triangle. The correct leg should then be gradually lifted upwards. Lift your leg to the extent your body would allow. Then come back to impartial position and repeat the equivalent with the other leg.

Extension posture

This is a represent that is appropriate for both the genders. For playing out this procedure, you should rests on your back and afterward twist your legs in such a way in this way that your knees are pointing upwards. Your feet ought to be put near your bum. The lower middle ought to be lifted, and your hands should lie on either side of your body for offering help. Repeat this multiple times.

Kegels

This posture will help ladies in fortifying their pelvic muscles. This aides in fixing the grasp of the pelvic muscles and for causing the vaginal section to appear to be more tightly, along these lines making it an unmistakably additionally invigorating experience for the two groups. For playing out this activity, the lady should focus on the vaginal muscles and pull them in and discharge. The suction can be clutched for whatever length of time that conceivable and afterward discharged. This activity should be possible anyplace and anytime of time. It additionally assists muscle with controlling impressively.

Kapalbhatti

This is a simple breathing method, and the man can play

out this privilege before his climax. This can likewise be played out each morning for better outcomes. For playing out this procedure, you will basically need to take a few short and sharp breaths. It is ideal to do this while sitting upstanding with your legs bungled. The focal point of this activity is more on the exhalation of air than inward breath. The mouth ought to be shut while breathing out and this ought to make a noisy sound while allowing the aerial. Play out this in sets of 3.

Pranayama

This is another activity that can be performed by both the genders and it helps in helping and controlling your breathing during Tantric sex. For playing out this strategy, the individual can sit upstanding in the lotus posture and place the correct thumb on their correct nostril and point a finger at the focal point of your temple. Breath in through your left nostril, hold the breath for a couple of moments and afterward discharge it through your correct nostril. While doing this, the correct nostril ought to be liberated, and the left nostril ought to be squeezed up. Repeat this multiple times. This can help the energy levels to increase and furthermore helps awareness.

Chapter Nine

Purification Path

The Mahāyāna (Great Path or Vehicle) is a sensational reevaluation of the Dharma. It is, undeniably, the Buddha's unique arrangement of lessons flipped completely around. The uncommon topics of the Mahāyāna are: 1) the objective isn't to achieve liberatedom for yourself alone - yet for all creatures, 2) the way of thinking isn't just that people are without self-presence - however all appearances are without self-presence, 3) the way isn't to repudiate the world - yet to take part in it completely out of empathy, and 4) the outcome is that a Buddha is no longer inconveniently settled - yet strongly and forever associated with carrying everybody to edification. While holding to the Buddha's most fundamental standards of the Four Noble Truths, the Mahāyāna rises above his unique lessons, while likewise professing to be disclosures of his own actual words given sometime in the not too distant future to bodhisattvas in higher measurements. The Mahāyāna doesn't see its lessons as repudiating the Buddha's, however as an increasingly significant elaboration on them.

The Mahāyāna starts with the Buddha's acknowledgment that all creatures who are not edified are in affliction. Considering deeply this somber condition, adherents of the Mahāyāna promise out of extraordinary sympathy to bring themselves as well as all creatures in all the universes to finish and immaculate illumination. Seeking illumination just for yourself is seen as childishness, the very malady the Buddha was attempting to fix.

Moreover, the Buddha's guideline of benevolence is deeply rethought. An "individual," in the early Buddhist view, has no suffering self, however is a blend of the Five Aggregates that give off an impression of being a self, held together by karma and ongoing propensities. However "you" are not genuine, these totals are genuine and the world is genuine. In a conclusive understanding, the Mahāyāna writings uncover, not exclusively are people not genuine, yet in addition all that you involvement with your reality has no self-existent reality. The intensity of this thought turns out to be promptly apparent: by survey all appearances as deceptions, you can discharge your wants and repugnancies for anything a lot quicker. Moreover, the Mahāyāna writings guarantee that since arhats have accomplished just "the benevolence of people" and not "the magnanimity of appearances," their acknowledgment is deficient. The spiritual fulfillment of an arhat is just the devastation of passionate obscurations, not mental ones, and an arhat, while abiding in internal harmony, is as yet not a Buddha. The astuteness and empathy of the arhaats must be energized so they may enter the Mahāyāna way and accomplish total and impeccable Buddhahood.

The Buddha's lessons center around yourself - and every one of your musings, emotions and activities to pick up freeing awareness. The Mahāyāna's direction, nonetheless, is towards others. By benevolently serving others while holding the observation that they are as fanciful as dreams, you help assuage them of misery, and you draw nearer to illumination. As opposed to the Buddha's training that Buddha's are perpetually "gone to the next shore" of nirvāṇa, the Mahāyāna encourages this is the very thing it is outlandish for a Buddha to do. This is because a Buddha, understanding the genuine idea of the real world, likewise suddenly acknowledges incredible empathy. Out of maritime sympathy for other people, a Buddha radiates incalculable forms in endless universes and vigorously helps with freeing all creatures no matter what. It is these sacrificial demonstrations joined with the intelligence of incomparable benevolence that are the most significantly cleaning. The Mahāyāna is the way, not of renunciation, since you stay on the planets, yet sanitization.

The Three Refuges - the Buddha, Dharma, and Saṅgha - the core of the Buddhist way, are significantly rethought. The Buddha isn't simply tranquilly quiet, yet everlastingly carrying on of sympathy. The Dharma isn't only a lot of lessons however an incomprehensible nearness. The Saṅgha isn't only the network of priests and lay supporters, yet the unending span of deeply acknowledged bodhisattvas who are an imperceptible yet ever-present and caring reality.

Significantly more so than in the Common Vehicle, the natural perils of the world are firmly underlined. Right now philosophy (rather than the later "Tantric" Mahāyāna), the world is by its very nature suffering, and a bodhisattva never stays right now make the most of its delights. While the Indian Buddhist siddhas grasped the fundamental lessons of the Mahāyāna, the Tantric attestation of the world would turn into their most significant purpose of distinction.

History

A few hundred years after the Buddha's passing, Buddhism was altered as the Mahāyāna, or the Universal Way, showed up with a moving new arrangement of lessons. The Mahāyāna development started with the sacrosanct disclosure of the Perfection of Wisdom sūtras. The soonest content of this class was The Perfection of Wisdom Sūtra in Eight Thousand Verses, which emerged around 100 BCE. This content instructs that, similarly as in a fantasy, there is no self and no other, no saṃsāra and no nirvāṇa, appearances are meager in nature, and buddhahood is on a very basic level the view of this fact. The Perfection of Wisdom Sūtras turned into the establishment for the philosophical custom that shows Emptiness (Śūnyatā), called the Middle Way (Madhyamaka).

From the First Century CE, a few writings developed with extra deeply new lessons. The principal content to instruct that all that you see is the Mind Only (Citta Matrā) is The Unraveling the Mystery of Thought Sūtra, which declares that its lessons supercede even the perspective on the Middle Way. Around a similar time, The Buddha Essence Sūtra presents the principal lessons on the way of thinking of Buddha Essence (Tathāgata Garbha), the possibility that there is a genuinely existent extreme reality comprising of an endless field of early stage light, and that the way to illumination is the acknowledgment that you are that light. Following the lessons in the Mahāyāna sūtras themselves, most Indian Mahāyānists may have followed these higher ways of thinking instead of the way of thinking of the Middle Way, albeit after c. 600 CE the Middle Way seems to rule in the colleges. Additionally in these earaly hundreds of years, The Flower Garland Sūtra sets up the sensational perfect of the bodhisattva, who acts with knowledge (prajñā) and empathy (karuṇa) to free all creatures from affliction.

The Mahāyāna's ascent in fame appears to have been moderate, and was likely constantly a minority development. By the 400s, in any case, it turned into the dominating educating at Nālandā and other lofty colleges. Mahāyāna philosophy and practices kept on creating until the 1200s when Buddhism was lost in India.

The Buddha himself didn't present these lessons right now, was stated, on account of their profundity and force - individuals were essentially not prepared for them, so they stayed covered up in different measurements until insightful experts could uncover them sometime in the future. However they stay consistent with the substance of the Buddha's lessons, and are strongly and, to their aficionados, much more significantly Buddhist. In the Mahāyāna, the Buddha's sūtras are known as the principal "turning of the wheel" or introduction of the Dharma, the transitional lessons on the Middle Way the subsequent turning, and the most noteworthy lessons of Mind Only and Buddha Essence are the third.

As the Mahāyāna created, the lay network remained solidly grounded in praising the delights of life, respecting the holiness of nature and getting a charge out of orgiastic celebrations. The sluggish erotic nature and splendid happiness found in the Buddhist craft of the time, for example, Ajantā, remain demonstration of the suffering grasp of life by lay Mahāyāna adherents. The two Buddhist societies, religious and lay, kept on running corresponding to one another, until at long last the lay networks, drove by the Tantric siddhas, ruled the Buddhist creative mind for a long time.

Bosses of the Mahāyāna

Nāgārjuna

Nāgārjuna (Bright Serpent Spirit; c. 100s) established the Middle Way (Madhyamaka) lessons of Mahāyāna Buddhism. Brought into the world a brahmin close to the town of Nāgārjunakoṇḍa (in current Andhra Pradesh), he later changed over to the Dharma. Perceived for his profundity of knowledge, he got the Perfection of Wisdom Sūtras as a blessing from submerged snake spirits (nāgas). He left broad compositions, of which The Fundamental Verses of the Middle Way is generally significant, and clarifies with splendid and stunning rationale the way of thinking of Emptiness. While the Perfection of Wisdom Sūtras present the idea of Emptiness and welcome it to be acknowledged on trust, Nāgārjuna contends compellingly that Buddhism, and reality itself, can just bode well coherently inside a right comprehension of emptiness. His writings stay key to about all Mahāyāna customs.

Philosophy

When You Perceive Both Your Self and Appearances as Not Being Independently Real, You Attain Buddhahood

Mutual Views of the Mahāyāna

The Inconceivability of the Dharma

In the Common Vehicle, the nature of a Buddha is

unfathomable. In the Mahāyāna, the Dharma itself is unfathomable. The Mahāyāna separates itself by its lessons on knowledge, and contends that on account of the impediments inalienable in the lessons of the Common Vehicle, that way is constrained in its capacity to achieve total liberatedom. The Common Vehicle, it says, depends on a dualism of self and other, when the truth isn't dualistic. All convictions, for example, positive or negative, reality or nonexistence, saṃsāra or nirvāṇa, are close to mental developments, theoretical overlays that your brain places onto a reality that is never kept by any of them. The Mahāyāna trains that if you could just observe reality unmistakably, you would see the huge scope of harmony and delight that pervades and genuinely is everything. Dharma broadens limitlessly past the sacred texts as an ever-present force, so any snapshot of your life can be an open door for higher acknowledgment. The Mahāyāna sūtras rouse marvel and awe through their dreams of universes immense and significant, imparting dedication to its astounding lessons.

Saṃsāra and Nirvāṇa are Perceptual

The Mahāyāna instructs that the extremely significant qualification in the Common Vehicle among saṃsāra and nirvāṇa is only perceptual - they are not genuine places. When your mindfulness is clouded by obliviousness, you are in saṃsāra. When your mindfulness is liberated from numbness, you are in nirvāṇa. Saṃsāra is essentially the misperception of nirvāṇa. The Mahāyāna reclassifies the nirvāṇa of a buddha as nonabiding nirvāṇa (apratiṣṭha nirvāṇa) - a buddha evades latently withdrawing into nirvāṇa, and simultaneously maintains a strategic distance from individual suffering in saṃsāra while remaining completely occupied with the world out of empathy for other people.

In any case, liberatedom doesn't bring about a happy festival of appearances. Karmic obscurations are what make the universe of appearances (saṃjñā) in any case – and appearances are involved the very texture of karmic molding. There will never be the point at which you are illuminated and just unwind and appreciate the excellence of the world. The White Lotus Sūtra clarifies, "This world is delivered by karma, and this world shows by methods for karma. All creatures are delivered by karma. They show up through the reason, karma." Appearances are conditionally started from karmic molding and experienced as affliction. In liberatedom you would hypothetically encounter nothing by any means, because your karmic obscurations that produce appearances would be totally discharged. However, due to sympathy, Buddha's stay in the realm of appearances simply to free others from anguish.

The Mahāyāna View of Life

The universal Mahāyāna perspective on the sūtras, instructed primarily by researcher priests, holds the key life-invalidating places of the Buddha on the idea of life - that it is characteristically languishing. In spite of the fact that the Mahāyāna instructs that saṃsāra and nirvāṇa are at last perceptual instead of physical places, the handy reality remains that for conventional creatures and bodhisattvas they are as various as night and day, adequately just as they despite everything are places. Saṃsāra is abiding in the six domains (ṣaḍaloka) of creatures (people, divine beings, enemies of divine beings, evil spirits, hungry phantoms, and creatures), and nirvāṇa is the pure harmony and euphoria that lies outside them. The body is inevitably suffering; birth, mature age, and demise are unaemptyably encounters of torment, and liberatedom from them is intrinsically quiet. It is difficult to accomplish lasting bliss right now. The Mahāyāna sūtras decry sexy articles as "like nectar spread on a razor's edge," apparently pleasurable yet seriously risky. Ladies stay second rate compared to men - they can't achieve edification in female form and should resurrect as men. And, a bodhisattva who stays on earth does so exclusively out of empathy, not out of any natural joy in it. Just nirvāṇa brings lasting harmony and rapture – it remains the most significant standard of the Mahāyāna way for all creatures to stay in it.

The Liberating Purpose of Philosophy

The Mahāyāna sūtras present three methods of philosophy: the Middle Way, Mind Only, and Buddha Essence. They may appear to be so not quite the same as one another that they don't share anything for all intents and purpose, yet every one supplements the others well. They all assistance to free you from your enthusiastic and mental obscurations so you can see reality straightforwardly and carry a perpetual end to your affliction. The Middle Way philosophy frees you from connection to appearances, the Mind Only way of thinking frees you from connection to the subject/object split of your psyche, and the Buddha Essence theory frees you into early stage insight. Key qualifications among the three methods of philosophy incorporate how they address the Two Truths (Dvi Satya), alluding to the world as it shows up and the world as it genuinely may be, and give a dream of buddhahood (buddhatva).

These ways of thinking are for the most part significant instruments for deep individual reflection, however just when they are joined with meditation can they genuinely free you into the immediate view of reality whose nature is unfathomable, past all ideas and methods of philosophy. The last objective of Buddhist way of thinking is never just to see intellectually how reality "truly" works, however to furnish you with calculated instruments that lead you to internal arousing. In the Mahāyāna, Buddhism can never be a fixed tenet or convention. The Dharma is absolutely not a thought of "no self" or "self" - it is whatever frees you. The pith of Buddhism can never be contained in words, even though the embodiment of Buddhism is ecstasy.

The Middle Way

The truth is the Absence of Inherent Existence

You and your general surroundings seem to comprise of strong, separate things that exist forever. It is the ordinary method for seeing. However to consider appearances to be having their own self-presence isn't just mixed up, it is a risky fancy that outcomes in misery. The Heart Sūtra proclaims this educating: "Form is emptiness and empty is form." To know the significance of this one sentence is Buddhahood:

1. Form is empty – Direct discernment into a definitive nature of things uncovers that no forms can be found by any stretch of the imagination. All forms break down into a total absence of natural presence.
2. Emptiness is form – Though missing of any self-

existent nature, appearances emerge due to karmic molding.

This is the insight of emptiness.

To see unmistakably and achieve immaculate knowledge is to see empty (śūnyatā). Emptiness is the rule that everything is meager, related, emerging out of Dependent Origination, fleeting, persistently changing, and at last incomprehensible. What you see as things is just the appearances of things. These appearances (dharmas) emerge and fall away consistently. And, there is no basic plane of extreme reality from which any appearances emerge.

The term Emptiness implies that everything is vacant of innate self-presence (svabhāva). With no characteristic, interminable nature that is autonomously your own, you and the world seem to exist just because of karmic molding. From the lessons of the Perfection of Wisdom Sūtras, appearances are clarified as transient and meager as: 1) the impression of the Moon in water, 2) a performer's stunt, 3) a face in a mirror, 4) a delusion from water, 5) the sound of a reverberation, 6) mists in the sky, 7) a bundle of froth, 8) a water bubble, 9) the unfilled center of a plantain tree, and 10) a glimmer of lightning.

This way of thinking is known as the Middle Way (Madhyamaka) even though it dismisses as outrageous perspectives both of the two thoughts that: 1) appearances have any sort of everlasting presence, or 2) appearances don't exist by any stretch of the imagination. Empty doesn't amount to nothing exists by any stretch of the imagination, rather the mindfulness appearances need inalienable presence and emerge just due to karmic molding.

Simultaneously, emptiness is certainly not a nature of an alleged plane of extreme reality from which appearances emerge and return. When you straightforwardly see the absence of intrinsic presence everything being equal, you enter the ecstasy of nirvāṇa.

The significant and freeing estimation of this instructing is that there are no things for you to append to, no people to stick to, no plans to consider, and no objective to accomplish even though there are no creatures in affliction and no Buddha's who free them. It is the stunning disclosure that every one of your ideas about the truth aren't right even though the very idea of reality can't be enveloped by ideas. You will never get reality. There is nothing to pick up, and nothing that can be lost. Furthermore, without anything to achieve, and no hindrances to restrict you, there is definitely no motivation behind why you can't be totally and consummately serene and ecstatic right now minute. Upon straightforwardly seeing empty, all appearances break down into their characteristic inadequacy, and your psyche is normally purged. You then see the boundless potential outcomes for freeing yourself as well as other people from misery.

The Two Truths

The Middle Way reasoning shows Two Truths (Dvi Satya), or methods for seeing reality. The differentiation is basic - from one emerges saṃsāra, from the other, nirvāṇa. However these facts are not two separate real factors, even though saṃsāra and nirvāṇa are indistinguishable. They are only two distinct methods for seeing a similar reality. Through your recognitions, you make your own jail and you free yourself from it.

The primary truth is relative truth (saṃvṛiti satya) - the customary world you know in which appearances emerge and appear to be freely genuine. It is the universe of how things give off an impression of being to a great many people. Relative truth is the thing that you experience as genuinely existent, yet isn't. It is a "bogus truth." Appearances don't have the self-presence (niḥsvabhāva) that they appear to, however emerge absolutely due to the karmic molding of Dependent Origination. It just because of your own enthusiastic and mental obscurations that you experience appearances. All things considered, appearances don't not exist – they have a nearness for those whose psyches are clouded. Even though itself empty of self-existent reality, the standard of Dependent Origination wins in universes made from relative truth. Kamalaśīla (c. 800s) watches, "Albeit at last every one of these wonders need personality, expectedly they unquestionably exist. If this were not the situation, how might the connection among circumstances and logical results, etc, win?" Appearances, however deceptive, ought not to be coolly rejected as "negligible hallucination" since they convey the sting of karmic molding.

The subsequent truth is extreme truth (paramārtha satya), which is the genuine idea of things. As a liberated being, you see straightforwardly the absence of inborn presence of appearances. It is the world as things really may be. Extreme truth is simply the immediate recognition that appearances emerge because of karmic molding and that they are without self-nature, which means they come up short on any sort of extreme, characteristic, perpetual presence of their own. No changeless spiritual guideline or force called "Empty" is declared. Extreme truth isn't an unceasingly present substratum to presence that is nothing, since appearances would never emerge as a causal outcome from complete nonexistence. Rather, extreme truth is essentially the nonappearance of self-nature of appearances. Empty is an assignment for the direct nonconceptual experience of the nonattendance of self-nature of appearances, an encounter that is in itself unsclimaxable yet feasible. Nāgārjuna portrays extreme truth (tattva - reality or suchness) right now: "reliant on another, tranquil and not manufactured by mental creation, not thought, without differentiations - this is the character of the real world."

Buddhahood as Wisdom and Compassion

A Buddha is a being who comprehends and sees empty. This observation discharges all torment and brings total flawlessness. Nāgārjuna clarifies through significant rationale that a Buddha is past every single applied class: "Since he is commonly vacant, the idea that the Buddha exists or doesn't exist after nirvāṇa isn't proper." Buddhahood, as nirvāṇa, can't be spoken about regarding what it is, however just as far as what it isn't. When you are completely present to the empty of what is, that is Buddhahood.

Hypothetically, a Buddha would see nothing by any means. The Song of the Dharma Sūtra says: "When empty is seen, there is no observing. Not seeing all wonders is seeing impeccably. Seeing nothing at all is seeing suchness." However, after acknowledging empty, extraordinary empathy emerges, and this brings a Buddha's mindfulness once more into the universe of appearances, where you look to free all creatures from misery. A Buddha constantly sees appearances and their empty all the while - the last acknowledgment of the character of saṃsāra and nirvāṇa.

Since everything emerges just from karmic molding, even Buddha's, however they are great, emerge just because of the karma of creatures in affliction and the Buddha's' assurance to free them. Not the slightest bit do Buddha's exist as autonomous creatures. Their sanitized totals and sympathetic goal to free others keep them in the realm of appearances. It is exclusively from the releasing of the maritime intensity of sympathy that Buddha's emerge.

The truth is Mind

The Mind Only (Citta Mātra – lit. Brain Mother) reasoning instructs that, as opposed to your ordinary perspective, outer items don't exist freely - all that you experience is a projection of your psyche. It is much the same as a fantasy. But since you don't understand this, you respond to things just as they were genuine when you made them from the start. When you don't see how mind functions, you make languishing. Getting it, you know the way to liberatedom.

Psyche is an all-inescapable field of cognizance, not something secured your head how Westerners will in general consider it. The Mind Only way of thinking isn't a solipsistic thought that says everything is "your" mind, since it totally dismisses the possibility of "you" and "others" in any case. There is just one brain. Psyche is a common dream-like involvement in others, yet we as a whole make various adaptations of what that the truth is, producing struggle. Your psyche makes a deceptive and dualistic mental overlay among "yourself" and the "objects" around you. This polarizing conviction torques separated the solidarity of experience and makes want. Subsequently, your psyche needs you to have things it accepts are outside of you that it thinks will fulfill you. And, want makes karma, which prompts languishing.

By understanding your psyche effectively and rehearsing meditation, the standard clashed mind (vijñāna) is cleaned and turns into the knowledge mind (prajñā). Dualistic reasoning stops, want stops, karma is finished, and liberatedom is accomplished. Sympathy spontaneoiusly emerges, and you try to free all creatures from misery. At long last conscious to the truth that everything is a fantasy, your forces are incredible. This way of thinking, whose center lessons are found in the Mahāyāna sūtras, is prominently called Yogācāra (lit. Yogic Practice), in spite of the fact that Yogācāra really envelops both the Mind only and Buddha Essence lessons.

The Three Natures

The guideline educating of the Mind Only way of thinking is known as the Three Natures (Tri Svabhāva). These sclimax to the three different ways your brain can see the appearances it makes of the world: 1) the Imaginary Nature (Parikalpita), harrowed cognizance, in which appearances are created in a completely anecdotal manner by your passionate and mental obscurations, 2) the Dependent Nature (Paratantra), dualistic awareness, in which appearances are delivered once you clear your enthusiastic obscurations, yet you are still darkened by the root mental obscuration of separating your encounters into subject and article, and 3) the Absolute Nature (Pariniṣpanna), pure cognizance - as you are liberated from any passionate or mental obscurations, no appearances are created. By understanding the Three Natures of your psyche and rehearsing meditation, you achieve edification.

The Imaginary Nature is the condition of the vast majority who mistakenly see reality through want, revultion, and obliviousness, and make their own affliction - in Western terms masochist projection. You see and react to things that don't exist in any capacity by any means. In any case, the Mind Only way of thinking goes a lot further than Western brain science to express that to have any understanding of anything whatsoever as "genuine" totally nonexistent, pure projection is. The standard force that supports the Imaginary Nature is language. By ceaselessly appointing mental names and sincerely charged implications to appearances, you make your own snare of anguish.

The Dependent Nature of brain is the condition of the individuals who have cleared their enthusiastic obscurations, discharged connection to their own marks through language, and effectively see mentally the genuine idea of reality as without division of subject and item, however have not yet acknowledged it straightforwardly. You consider appearances to be they emerge, without enthusiastic projection, in any case your discernment is still darkened by the root dualism. This is the thing that Western brain science calls the perfect of an intellectually sound individual, yet in Buddhist brain research is still intellectually darkened and open to affliction. The Dependent Nature is continued by the root stains of "I" and "mine," the unobtrusive however deep faith in self and other. This state is known as the Dependent Nature since, similar to an appearance in a mirror, its method for being doesn't exist freely yet exists subject to karmic molding, and is reliant upon the Absolute Nature, which has genuine presence.

The Absolute Nature is accomplished by those whose psyches are liberated from all passionate and mental obscurations, wherein your brain sees just itself. Vasubandhu expresses, "The Absolute Nature opens the entryway of astuteness to the domain of suchness," even though you are at long last observing reality obviously. It is pure cognizance without appearances, immaculate harmony and joy.

The Eight Consciousness

You ordinarily consider yourself having only one psyche, yet the Mind Only way of thinking encourages that you have Eight Consciousness (Aṣṭa Vijñāna), each with completely separate capacities, that together unconsciously bunch together and call your brain. To accomplish illumination, you should cleanse them all totally. The initial five consciousness are the Five Senses - sight, hearing, smell, taste, and touch - which get and subtlety decipher the sense impressions of your reality.

They can get darkened through injury or disease, and the sensations emerging from them that you decipher as wonderful, horrendous, or aloof can likewise turn out to be karmically clouded.

The 6th awareness, the Conceptualizing Mind (Mano Vijñāna – lit. the brain that isolates knowledge), gets the sense encounters of the initial five consciousness. It is inside this cognizance that meditations happen that mark and separation encounters, that you recollect the past, think about the present, and plan for the future, make visual pictures of things, and make decisions of fortunate or unfortunate. This cognizance doesn't see the world legitimately, yet makes a psychological picture of it inside it, which might possibly be near what the world truly resembles. It works under befuddled conditions, driven by propensities for dualistic idea and activity. Reflection happens at the degree of the 6th awareness, which precipitously sanitizes the various consciousness.

The seventh is the Afflicted Consciousness (Kleśa Vijñāna), an exceptionally inconspicuous level that holds firmly to the deception in self and other, and makes your essential disarray and unclarity of discernment about existence. Its central trait is that it has the Three Stains (Āsavas), the most deep main drivers of affliction: 1) want for exotic joy, 2) want for presence, and 3) numbness of the Four Noble Truths. It is the place your urgent wants and revulsions effectively drive you in your musings, words and activities. The forces of the seventh stream into the 6th, veiling your cognizant psyche with passionate and mental obscurations, and clouding your substantial sense consciousness's too. By legitimately seeing the fantasy of self and other at this level in reflection, you discharge the seventh cognizance, and it is changed on arousing into the Wisdom of Equality (Samatā Jñāna), in which all appearances are seen as equivalent.

The eighth is the Store Consciousness (Ālaya Vijñāna). This is the oblivious plane of mindfulness, and is in every case completely mindful of every minute. Vasubandhu watches, "Store awareness contains all appearances known to mankind." It is the place karmic engravings of past activities are put away, age, and later emerge, causing you with surprising and undesirable affliction. The seventh cognizance emerges from and is supported by the karmic seeds (bīja) put away in the eighth awareness that constantly dark your encounters and make the suffering you involvement with your life. When the eighth awareness is totally decontaminated, it changes into the Wisdom of True Reality (Dharmadhātu Jñāna), and Buddhahood is accomplished.

The Two Truths

In the Mind only way of thinking, relative truth is simply the mixed up thought that and appearances exist freely and independently from the brain. The Imaginary Nature makes all the bogus sincerely charged projections you force onto appearances. The Dependent Nature, however increasingly unadulterated, also emerges as the bogus yet deeply established conviction that you and others exist separate from the one brain.

Extreme truth is the arrival of the off base recognition that subject and item are an option that is other than mind. When you achieve this reality, which is the Absolute Nature, the lighting up nondual Buddha mind precipitously emerges. You see straightforwardly that appearances emerge as in a fantasy, yet lead to suffering even though they are karmically molded. Extreme truth is the truth of the all-inclusive psyche - it is neither a solipsistic mind nor the early stage mindfulness educated in the way of thinking of Buddha Essence - it is basically cognizance liberated from subject and article, particular, not partitioned into knower and known, lasting, normally clear, unadulterated mindfulness.

Buddhahood as Wisdom and Compassion

Buddha's are creatures who have refined their brains totally; all karmic seeds in the Store Consciousness are depleted, and their psyches are of the Absolute Nature. Right now of the last arrival of karma is an unconstrained internal arousing called the Reversal of the Basis (Āśraya Parāvṛitti), because the experience of the Eighth Consciousness, the oblivious premise of your psyche, shifts from suffering to delight. A Buddha would normally encounter no appearances by any stretch of the imagination - just the unadulterated awareness of nirvāṇa. In any case, out of sympathy for all creatures, you stay in the realm of dreams to free others. Since all encounters are dream-like, all the marvelous forces of the Buddha's emerge for you easily.

Buddha Essence

The truth is Primordial Wisdom

Buddha embodiment is early stage Buddha intelligence (Buddha jñāna), a limitless field of unadulterated illuminated mindfulness, and just that extreme reality exists, and everything else is deceptive. Its fundamental nature (tathāta) is similarly present in all creatures, just incidentally clouded inside them. Buddha embodiment is the internal potential and intensity of all creatures to achieve edification.

Its ever-present force travels through all creatures looking to free them. Without Buddha substance as of now inside you, accomplishing Buddhahood would be outlandish and every one of your endeavors would create nothing. Since just the ecstasy of nirvāṇa exists, you are as of now a Buddha. But since you don't remember it, you suffer. Buddha Essence (Tathāgata Garbha) theory is the most noteworthy articulation of the Mahāyāna sūtras on the idea of the real world.

The way of thinking of Buddha Essence instructs that past every fanciful appearance extreme reality genuinely exists – it has its own actual, inherent self-nature (svabhāva) that can be straightforwardly seen by a Buddha. It is a vast field of unfathomable mindfulness with its own: 1) endless shrewdness (jñāna), 2) otherworldly characteristics (guṇa pāramitā), and 3) self-existent nearness (anābhoga). It is unadulterated mindfulness (pratyātmavedya) without the familiarity with any appearances. The Supreme Continuum depicts its limitless and indistinguishable every great quality, taking note of particularly that it has four extraordinary characteristics:

1. Virtue (Śubha) - It is clean by karmic obscurations.
2. Self (Ātman) - It is early stage, all-unavoidable, mindful intelligence.
3. Delight (Sukha) - It is the wellspring of extreme euphoria.
4. Lastingness (Nitya) - It is interminable and perpetual.

These four characteristics are significant even though they totally upset the Buddha's own regulations on presence as having the characteristics of 1) karmic polluting influence, 2) no self, 3) suffering, and 4) fleetingness. Buddhists who follow the initial two turnings of the wheel of the Dharma don't put stock in a self – Buddhists who follow the third turning of the wheel do. Buddha quintessence is early stage, still, and all-unavoidable. It doesn't emerge out of karmic molding. Nothing other than it genuinely exists. All appearances (dharmas) are absolutely deceptive and have no presence in any capacity by any stretch of the imagination.

Buddha pith is hard to discover and acknowledge, however it is the best of all fortunes since it is your own actual nature. It resembles: 1) a Buddha in a rotting lotus, 2) nectar in the midst of honey bees, 3) grains in their husks, 4) gold shrouded in rottenness, 5) an underground fortune, 6) shoots penetrating through organic products, 7) a statue of a Buddha inside a heap of torn clothes, 8) a ruler in the belly of a poor and pitiful lady, and 9) a valuable picture inside earth. The Buddha Essence reasoning distinctions your own capability to achieve inward arousing and is expected to give you extraordinary certainty. The objective of its lessons is for you to see the gleaming Clear Light of extreme reality and sympathetically free yourself and all creatures from anguish.

The Two Truths

In the lessons on Buddha Essence, relative truth is the bogus impression of any appearances whatsoever. It is seeing appearances escaped the immediate experience of Buddha substance by your passionate and mental obscurations. These obscurations are totally incidental (āgantaka) and deceptive (bhrānti). The Supreme

Continuum says, "The issues are accidental," and "The obscurations resemble covering mists, naturally non-existent." not the slightest bit do obscurations influence extreme reality. Appearances don't exist by any means. No emerging of appearances ever happens, Dependent Origination is itself deceptive, so any appearances you see are just fanciful. The foundation of the intensity of relative the truth is your own mixed up faith in self and other.

Extreme truth is the capacity to see straightforwardly the indissoluble field of primordially existent extreme reality (svabhāva). Extreme the truth is early stage awareness and radiance, limitless knowledge, love, harmony and rapture. The Supreme Continuum is broad in its portrayals: it is the Clear Light, endless, uncaused, the open territory, "constant like space," "nondual," "indestructible," "perpetual," and "everlasting." It is unconditioned, free, changeless, and euphoric. It is vacant of dreams, fleetingness, appearances, and languishing. It is self-started basic virtue, impeccable, always having immaculate characteristics. In spite of the fact that it seems to act to those with betrayed minds, it is actionless. It is boundless, all-inescapable, omniscient astuteness, sympathy, liberated from theory, uncompounded by Dependent Origination. "It is simply the invariable reality... It is valid (Ātman) because the entirety of the difficulties of self or no self-have been completely controlled." Seeing extreme truth, you are liberated.

Dolpopa, the principal Tibetan reporter on Buddha Essence, contends that to state that nirvāṇa and saṃsāra are "indistinguishable," as the Middle Way philosopohy claims, is unreasonable. In truth, he says, saṃsāra doesn't exist, and nirvāṇa does. While concurring with the Middle Way reasoning that extreme the truth is unsclimaxable, Buddha Essence theory sees that by embracing that all encounters of any sort are only self-unfilled (niḥsvabhāva), the Middle Way reasoning can really misdirect you into missing a definitive reality that isn't self-void by any stretch of the imagination. Buddha Essence reasoning says it isn't sufficient just to consider appearances to be not genuinely existent. The Ornament of the Light of Wisdom Sūtra alerts against the Middle Way reasoning, saying "The obliteration of appearances through acknowledgment of void isn't the suspension of torment," because an a lot more noteworthy experience anticipates you through acknowledgment of Buddha Essence. While the Mind Only lessons express that extreme the truth is your brain, Buddha Essence lessons watch early stage the truth wouldn't fret (citta) in the customary sense, and even psyche doesn't exist as a free element, so reflecting on "Psyche Only" could lead you to miss the genuine extreme reality too. What just exists is the boundless, early stage astuteness mind (jñāna), likewise called the Clear Light nature of your brain (Prabhāsvara citta).

Buddhahood as Wisdom and Compassion

The Supreme Continuum uncovers, "Buddhahood is the brilliance of early stage insight." In this exact second, you are a Buddha – there is nothing else you would ever conceivably be. Your total flawlessness as a Buddha is as of now completely present however quickly clouded by figment. Buddhahood, primordially existent, is the main thing that exists. It doesn't emerge because of causes and conditions, yet is "uncreated," "the self-existent," "the preeminent nirvāṇa," and "the self-nature." Its self-nature is its indestructible extensive size, shrewdness, and brilliant clearness.

Since all appearances are deceptive, even the appearances of Buddha's are fanciful. "These are simply appearances," The Supreme Continuum notes impartially. Pictures of Buddha's emerge from the beguiled personalities of creatures, and are false arisings - "Customary creatures don't comprehend the way that these are the appearances of their own brain." There is no activity that buddhas really perform; they are consistently in impeccable harmony. Simultaneously, their exercises towards creatures caught in fantasy are boundless, easy, unending, and immediately emerging.

Path

The Bodhisattva

At the core of the Mahāyāna is the assurance to end languishing over all creatures. As troublesome for what it's worth for even one individual to accomplish illumination, a bodhisattva (lit. stirred being), roused by incredible empathy (karuṇa), looks to bring all creatures all through boundless existence no matter what to definite freedom. Kamalaśīla rouses with a model, saying "Similarly as a mother reacts to her little, adored, and suffering youngster, when you build up an unconstrained and equivalent feeling of sympathy toward all creatures, you have idealized the act of empathy. Also, this is known as extraordinary empathy."

As a bodhisattva, you produce bodhicitta (lit. stirred psyche) - the empathetic desire for edification. Bodhicitta is simply the significant aim to free and all creatures from torment. It is the special driving intensity of a bodhisattva that gives the person in question their incomprehensible forces of shrewdness and empathy, without which it is difficult to accomplish illumination. It isn't just a longing for all creatures to be upbeat, yet a significant duty that you will free them. The Ornament of Clear Realization proclaims, "The desire for totally ideal illumination for the government assistance of others is bodhicitta." It is your affirmation of the most noteworthy conceivable aim a being can hold. It is just through developing the desire for general edification that illumination can ever be accomplished, even though just bodhicitta has the ability to get through the figment of self and other.

As a bodhisattva, bodhicitta isn't just a desire yet in addition a persistent action. You don't withdraw from the world, yet remain sympathetically occupied with it, while perceiving the genuine idea of the real world. Empathy isn't a condition of being hopeless from continually observing other's anguish, yet a warm delicacy of heart and sympathetic association. Astuteness frees empathy from distress in its acknowledgment that nobody ever truly suffers - they just figure they do. What's more, empathy frees intelligence from indifferently watching the nonexistence of creatures. Together, knowledge and sympathy manage you and all creatures to edification.

Levels of Attainment

The Mahāyāna is a continuous way to edification. Your way is guided by your expectation for widespread freedom, maritime empathy, significant reflective ingestion, and infiltrating astuteness into a definitive nature of things. It is a way of cleansing, and as The Supreme Continuum characterizes it, "Immaculateness is the nonappearance of want."

In the wake of taking the Bodhisattva Vow, you are known as a respectable child or little girl (ārya putra/ārya duhitā). When you achieve an immediate impression of extreme reality in meditation, you are a bodhisattva/bodhisattvā, additionally called a respectable one (ārya/āryā). You then go through the Ten Stages (Daśa Bhūmi) of a bodhisattva to edification, all so troublesome they take three boundless ages to finish. The bodhisattva way is a constant exercise in creating merit (puṇya), great deeds in helping other people that present to you the great karma to accomplish illumination, and astuteness (prajñā), the immediate view of extreme reality. Legitimacy clears passionate obscurations and intelligence clears mental obscurations. These two, legitimacy and insight, called the Two Accumulations (Dvi Saṃbhāra), when developed together, lead to the Two Accomplishments (Dvi Siddhi) - mystical forces and omniscience that you use to free others.

1. Incredible Joy

Accomplishment over lifetimes of training brings about an upwelling of happiness as you at long last achieve direct view of extreme reality in meditation - you arrive at the level called Great Joy (Pramuditā). When you sit in reflection, you quickly accomplish nondual familiarity with genuine reality. In post meditation, in any case, you can't keep up direct impression of extreme reality. You have gained some ground in clearing your enthusiastic and mental obscurations, and can move others in their way. Liberated from common feelings of dread, the focal point of your training is on liberality. When you achieve the primary level, you may intentionally pick resurrection right now another.

2. Placeless

At the stage called Stainless (Vimalā), you free yourself of the stains of dishonest conduct. Your attention is on moral order.

3. Brilliant

For the bodhisattva at the degree of Radiant (Prabhākarī), the light of your knowledge normally emanates to other people. Your training stresses acknowledgment.

4. Light Giving

For those at the phase of Light Giving (Arciṣmatī), your familiarity with the fanciful idea of self and different develops. Your own inward light tries to please. You develop primarily exertion.

5. Hard to Master

When you arrive at the level called Difficult to Master (Sudurjayā), your training shifts all the more completely into preparing others. You ace your own feelings as you manage the individuals who are regularly so far untamed inwardly. Having filtered your passionate responses, you refine your own internal authority. You grow mainly thoughtful ingestion.

6. Confronting the Transcendent

When you accomplish the degree of facing the

Transcendent (Abhimukhī), you face the fairness of saṃsāra and nirvāṇa, and reside in neither of them. In your development, you are especially handy in placating self-importance in creatures. You center primarily on developing intelligence, and come to comprehend the fanciful idea of enthusiastic and mental obscurations.

7. Gone Afar

For the bodhisattva at the level called Gone Afar (Dūraṃgamā), you ace going into and emerging from the immense spread of extreme reality, the Dharmadhātu, and understand the fundamental similarity all things considered. Through extending acknowledgment, you disavow self-getting a handle on. You create capable action in freeing others, constantly guided by otherworldly insight.

8. Ardent

In the initial seven levels, as a bodhisattva you despite everything have enthusiastic obscurations that emerge in reflection. At the eighth, Immovable (Acalā), you achieve impeccable reflective solidness, undisturbed by any inward or external observations, unadulterated nonconceptual mindfulness. It is the degree of the genuine resistance of the incomprehensibility of the real world. It is additionally the degree of irreversibility. You gain the capacity to see straightforwardly the unobtrusive types of the Buddha's (saṃbhogakāyas) on higher planes. Your accentuation is on heightening quality. You discharge your deep situated faith in a different self. Your goal for complete and ideal Buddhahood for yourself and all creatures elevates.

9. Commendable Wisdom

When you accomplish the ninth level, Meritorious Wisdom (Sādhumatī), you gain the Wisdom of Discriminating Awareness (Pratisaṃvedanā). This incorporates: 1) the capacity to encourage the Dharma as indicated by the limit of understudies, 2) the capacity to comprehend the genuine significance of the lessons, 3) the gift of using language ably to show the significant nuances of the Dharma, and 4) the total self-assurance that slices through questions. Your primary focal point of advancement is on unconstrained edified action.

10. Dharma Cloud

At the tenth level, Dharma Cloud (Dharma Meghā), just the faintest stays of passionate and mental obscurations keep you away from complete illumination. There is basically no distinction at all between your mindfulness in thoughtful states and post reflection. You increase boundless, omniscient astuteness equivalent to the sky, pouring down a downpour of Dharma. Your primary accentuation is on developing omniscient astuteness, discharging the last leftovers of your most unobtrusive karmic obscurations. Entering the Adamantine Samādhi (Vajra Samādhi) that gathers up the last unpretentious remainders of your obscurations, you legitimately see the overall truth of appearances and a definitive truth of the nonappearance of appearances at the same time, and accomplish total freedom.

Benefits

By following the Mahāyāna, you concede to the genuine way of illumination. You increase incredible legitimacy, become a help to different creatures, and sanitize negative karma. Suffering and disarray fall away. The benefits are really endless as every great quality create inside you. Riches, long life, wellbeing, delight, harmony, clearness of psyche, satisfaction, lovely dreams, and numerous amazing characteristics start to show for you. You increase common enchanted forces through reflective focus, and easily make what you want. Harmony and concordance encompass you, the divine beings ensure you, and you normally pull in numerous companions. You are high-minded, your passionate obscurations decrease, sympathy emerges, you can put forth solid attempt practically sclimaxing, you surrender all interruptions to your way, and you neither append to nor dismiss this life. Also, you guarantee the most awesome future lives, and accomplish flawless Buddhahood.

Regular Problems

The Mahāyāna lessons are broad, significant, and spectacular – and it is anything but difficult to get diverted by the way of thinking and disregard practice. If you misconstrue the lessons on the Middle Way and mistake vacancy for nothingness, you probably won't care about anything anymore. Thinking karma is only an "unfilled" idea, you may submit negative acts that lead to bring down resurrection. The danger of the Mind Only lessons is that, while you perceive appearances as mental projections and can discharge your connection to them, you may append to internal encounters of harmony and rapture and make a repugnance for different feelings, easing back your actual way. From the lessons on Buddha Essence, pompous in realizing that you are as of now a Buddha, you may choose not to practice, and cut yourself off from consistently acknowledging Buddhahood.

Since the Mahāyāna way takes unfathomable lifetimes to accomplish freedom, you may not be spurred with the direness to rehearse and get lethargic. Attempting to be a bodhisattva, you could turn out to be only a decent deed practitioner – helping other people without infiltrating into a more deep attention to extreme the truth is classified "debased goodness" (kliṣṭa puṇya), and ought to be maintained a strategic distance from. Your developing sympathy could expand your connection to other people and lead you into more prominent affliction. At last, without a genuine and true pledge to freeing yourself and all creatures from torment, you are not a devotee of the Mahāyāna, yet the Common Vehicle, and will always be unable to pick up the legitimacy important for buddhahood.

Procedures

Vows

In the Mahāyāna custom, the Bodhisattva Vow (Praṇidhāna Samvara – lit. Yearning Vow) is the most significant act you will ever take to accomplish illumination. It is a definitive pledge of astronomical obligation. You concede to huge lifetimes of self-improvement, as you look to help all creatures all through unending existence to accomplish illumination too. The promise guides you on your way, keeping you from the threats of saṃsāra and the dormant delight of nirvāṇa. The Bodhisattva Vow is discussed regularly so as to produce the knowledge and incredible empathy that energizes your way to edification. Progress is outlandish without keeping it.

Dedication

Dedication (bhakti) is significantly more significant in the Mahāyāna than the Common Vehicle. Not at all like in the Buddha's unique way, you can't achieve acknowledgment totally all alone - you need the assistance of the Buddha's and their nonstop lessons. Through dedication, you make a solid heart association with them. Buddha intelligence overruns the universe, and Buddha's can show at any minute, in any capacity, for any individual who calls upon them with genuine commitment. You give your dedication to the Buddha and bodhisattvas, to the Mahāyāna sūtras as holy disclosures of astuteness, to your instructors, and to ubiquitous insight itself. However Buddha can just instruct and motivate, they can't really expel your karmic obscurations - no one but you can do that. Your chief demonstration of commitment in the Mahāyāna is the Bodhisattva Vow (Praṇidhāna Samvara).

Holy Sex and Sexual Yoga

The Mahāyāna proceeds in the use of holy sex ceremonies as demonstrations of commitment to the Buddha's, and without precedent for the Buddhist way additionally consolidates sexual yoga - the use of sexual energies to achieve illumination. In The Ornament of the Mahāyāna Sūtras, Asaṅga states, "Preeminent poise is gotten in the inversion of sex, in the happy Buddha equipoise and the unhindered vision of one's life partner." The "inversion of sex" alludes to the yogic acts of driving sexual energies up into the inconspicuous body instead of out into your partner to enable your edification. Sexual yoga is a vital piece of the bodhisattva's way.

Astuteness

Astuteness is the capacity to straightforwardly see the genuine idea of things. To develop shrewdness, you examine and think about the Mahāyāna sūtras, bringing their exercises deep into your heart. You start by building up an applied comprehension of the Mahāyāna, and create confidence and feeling about its worth. And afterward through training you accomplish the most noteworthy insight of placeless, direct knowing.

Sympathy

Sympathy (karuṇa) is developed through the Bodhisattva Vow, setting a solid aim for the freedom everything being equal. Your empathy turns out to be warm, delicate, unsentimental and easy in light of the fact that it is educated by the astuteness that there are no creatures to free. To create empathy without shrewdness, or intelligence without sympathy, is servitude, becauseneither alone can free you from connection to self and other.

Moral Conduct

Moral direct in the Mahāyāna is called capable methods (upāya), becauseyour activities are proposed to diminish and free creatures from anguish. After some time, you create extraordinary aptitude in liberative procedure.

The Six Perfections

As a bodhisattva, you develop the inward characteristics of a Buddha while serving others in carrying them to higher acknowledgment. The Six Perfections (Ṣaṭ Pāramitās) are the fundamental activities of a bodhisattva: 1) liberality (dana), 2) moral lead (śīla), 3) acknowledgment (kṣanti), 4) perseverence (virya), 5) thoughtful focus (dhyāna), and 6) intelligence (prājña). Liberality lifts you out of your self-sticking, and furthermore brings you enough riches because of your great karma with the goal that you have the opportunity to rehearse meditation. Moral direct makes you innocuous to other people, forestalls awful resurrections, and gives you a psychological clearness liberated from blame and stress, an internal establishment for higher reflective states. Acknowledgment implies opportunity from expectation and dread, essentially permitting whatever is available, a resilience for the incomprehensibility of the real world. Exertion implies proceeding with force in care and practice. Thoughtful fixation alludes to creating reflective retention in Tranquility Meditation, developing inward harmony, solidness and mental concentration through placating your feelings. Knowledge is the most significant of all, building up the view that in all activities there is no on-screen character, no activity, and nobody being followed up on.

Brain Training

The Mahāyāna arrangement of Mind Training (Citta Patha) extends the acts of the Six Perfections to sanitize you of all antagonism. These incorporate practices, for example, 1) Seven-Point Cause and Effect (Sapta Krama Hetu Phala), respecting others as having been your caring mother from beginningless previous existences, 2) Equalizing and Exchanging (Parātma Parivartana), taking into account that you are on a very basic level equivalent to others in wishing bliss, 3) Giving Up Self-Cherishing (Anupādāna Ātman), setting out to discharge self-getting a handle on and, out of sympathy for other people, consistently put the premiums of others over your own, 4) Giving and Taking (Dana Graha), imagining yourself taking in the suffering of others and sending them unadulterated love, and 5) Poison and Antidote (Viṣa Pratipakṣa), finding a toxin in your brain, for example, a hurtful feeling, and figure out how to develop its inverse. In the Mahāyāna, you don't take out your obscurations as in the regular Vehicle through the commanding exertion of disavowing them and avoiding them away. Rather, by decontaminating them, in the long run they are discharged.

Meditation

In the Mahāyāna, the inspiration for meditation is no longer exclusively for yourself. Reflection must be spurred out of all inclusive sympathy or you won't accomplish internal arousing.

In Mahāyāna Tranquility Meditation (Śamathā), the initial four thoughtful states instructed by the Buddha, the Four Form Absorptions, stay of significant worth to the way. The Four Formless Absorptions, however, are kept away from in light of the fact that their extreme harmony and delight can too effectively persuade that you are illuminated when you are not, and may prompt higher resurrection into unclean domains to which you may get connected. Exceptional directions called the Nine Levels of Mental Stability (Nava Bhūmi) help you to accomplish the First Absorption, called Even Placement (Samāhita), all the more no problem at all. Through Tranquility Meditation, you accomplish a steady, sans thought, resolute concentration with lucidity of mindfulness, and the establishment for Insight Meditation.

For Insight Meditation (Vipaśyanā), you ruminate over the three shroud entering ways of thinking of the Middle Way, Mind Only, and Buddha Essence, and look to see extreme reality legitimately. You consider comparative with be as regular, deceptive, and prompting suffering, and extreme truth as placeless and freeing. Understanding Meditation is never just a psyche calmed of its considerations, which alone can't evacuate the center misguided judgment of self and other. When you play out the deep examination of Insight Meditation, you would then be able to move into nonconceptual reflection. The most elevated Insight Meditation builds up a nonconceptual, brilliant, clear mindfulness. Considering your to be and considerations as with no self-presence, they are normally appeased without compelling exertion.

Through the association of Tranquility Meditation and Insight Meditation, you quiet your mind and enter a significant thoughtful absoption, play out an examination of the Two Truths, and afterward rest your brain in a deep, nonconceptual reflective ingestion on the genuine idea of the real world. It is this association that wipes out the entirety of your obscurations and prompts Buddhahood.

Results

Buddhahood

Buddhahood in the Mahāyāna is definitely more huge and magnificent than in the Common Vehicle, and is progressively celebrated. The exercises of the Buddha's are unfathomable. In early Buddhism, a solitary buddha emerges in a time, instructs, and afterward dies into nirvāṇa. In the Mahāyāna, buddhas rise above reality and are multitudinous. The Mahāyāna rejects the first Buddhist objective of individual illumination finishing off with tranquil confinement. As a Buddha, your Five Aggregates are not discharged however filtered, and you remain everlastingly occupied with the world to soothe the suffering of others. You react to everybody from unadulterated shrewdness and sympathy so every being can achieve Buddhahood. You have boundless phenomenal forces that you use to free others.

The Three Dimensions of a Buddha

The immeasurability of a buddha involves the Three Dimensions (Tri Kāya, lit. Three Bodies). These measurements emerge precipitously once you achieve edification, and are the methods buddhas use for all their vast freeing exercises: 1) the dharmakāya, 2) the saṃbhogakāya, and 3) the nirmāṇakāya.

The Dharmakāya

The dharmakāya (measurement of freeing truth) is the unending, all-inescapable, region of extreme reality, space-like, which you know to be indistinguishable from yourself. It is the ceaseless field of unadulterated early stage cognizance that knows itself. It is inconspicuous, unitary, undifferentiated, indissoluble, and without birth and demise. It is all the immense great characteristics of Buddha substance: Purity, Self, Bliss, and Permanence. It is iridescent Clear Light, liberated from the stains of want, repugnance and obliviousness. It is unfathomably significant, interminable astuteness and sympathy. Its basic quality is brilliance. Upon illumination, your psyche perceives itself as the dharmakāya. The dharmakāya is the equivalent for all Buddha's, and is the interminable and constant wellspring for the other two Buddha measurements. It is the ceaseless wellspring of a Buddha's insight and adoring movement, and can allow all wants.

The Saṃbhogakāya

The saṃbhogakāya (measurement of delight) is the transmission of a Buddha on the unpretentious plane, wherein you serve more significant level bodhisattvas and guide them to edification. As an unpretentious radiation of a Buddha, you exude an unadulterated buddhafield, alongside an unobtrusive body that is flawless in form, has no characteristic reality, and however shows everlastingly out of empathy for those in torment. You manage with your following of bodhisattvas. It is in every case at the same time inside the dharmakāya. Its basic quality is suddenness. Upon illumination, you show a saṃbhogakāya on the unpretentious plane. A Buddha on this measurement trains the Dharma as per the Mahāyāna, and its activities are unconstrained and free. From the saṃbhogakāya type of a Buddha, deeply acknowledged bodhisattvas get the most noteworthy lessons they have to achieve acknowledgment.

A Buddha field (Buddha kṣetra) is a field of unadulterated illuminated mindfulness produced out of empathy by a Buddha, either on a higher measurement or on earth, which filters creatures who abide in it. Right now, cleaning exercises of a Buddha are ceaseless. Inside a Buddha field, creatures are suddenly evolved in their positive idea, prudence, high purpose, and insight. Staying in your widely inclusive Buddha field, creatures can accomplish illumination all the more rapidly.

The Nirmāṇakāya

The nirmāṇakāya (measurement of physical radiation) is the physical transmission of a Buddha, existing out of empathy for common creatures. A nirmāṇakāya has as its premise the dharmakāya, from which it emerges out of affection and empathy for other people, and shows to help creatures on the earth to free them. Its fundamental quality is constant sympathy. Upon illumination, your physical body changes into a nirmāṇakāya. A buddha can genuinely show in different forms at the same time to serve others. A nirmāṇakāya is never again a physical body contained karmic molding, yet a transmission of the dharmakāya. You have no applied musings and no tainted developments, and your activities are unconstrained and easy. Your discourse announces the Dharma easily and enthusiastically. A nirmāṇakāya is changeless, and constantly joined with the dharmakāya. The motivation behind a nirmāṇakāya is to get creatures this world to revoke saṃsāra and educate them in how to filter their own obscurations. You likewise have extraordinary forces which you use to impart motivation and trust in the Dharma.

Promises

Bodhisattva Vow - Praṇidhāna Samvara

Take the Bodhisattva Vow by remaining before a picture of the Buddha, or envisioning endless buddhas and bodhisattvas every which way in space, stoop and discuss these refrains, first in Sanskrit and afterward in English: viśuddham dhārayiṣyāmi yathā buddhena deśitam tena jitvā śaṭhamāram prāpya buddhatvam uttamam bhaveyam bhavakhinnānām śaraṇam sarvadehinām

"I will look after immaculateness, as educated by the Buddha.

Vanquishing the evil spirit Mara, and accomplishing preeminent buddhahood, I pledge to be an asylum for all creatures, exhausted of saṃsāra."

Recount 3x.

Congrats! You are presently a supporter of the Mahāyāna. You get another bodhisattva name. See the Appendix for a rundown of Buddhist names.

Bodhisattva Conduct – Bodhisattva Caryā

Your progressing promises in day by day practice are to be aware of the Bodhisattva Vow, practice the Six Perfections and Mind Training, and look for approaches to free others from anguish.

Bodhisattva Vow – Praṇidhāna Samvara

Be aware of the Bodhisattva Vow consistently, and fortify your responsibility to accomplishing illumination to serve all creatures.

1. Think about the significance of freeing all creatures from torment, despite the fact that they have no characteristic presence.
2. Develop your responsibility.
3. After some time, genuine desire emerges suddenly, completely present with you consistently.

The Six Perfections – Ṣat Pāramitās

Practice the Six Perfections every day. Play out these without connection to any outcomes, to any idea of a self, an activity, or a beneficiary.

1. Liberality – Cultivate benevolence by providing for other people. This frees you from self-getting a handle on.
2. Ethical quality – Practice moral lead. This makes your brain understood and stable by and by, makes you innocuous to other people, and keeps you concentrated on helping other people instead of yourself.
3. Acknowledgment – Accept what occurs in your existence without expectation or dread, since everything is the deceptive play of early stage cognizance.
4. Perseverance – Vigorously put forth a concentrated effort by and by to accomplish achievement.
5. Fixation – Cultivate reflective serenity and significant conditions of retention, from which you can understand intelligence.
6. Astuteness – Reflect on and acknowledge: 1) all appearances are vacant of innate self-nature, 2) appearances originate from your brain, and 3) your psyche is indistinguishable from early stage insight.

Brain Training - Citta Patha

Seven-Point Cause and Effect – Sapta Krama Hetu Phala

1. Create serenity toward all creatures.
2. Create a feeling of passionate closeness and closeness with all creatures.
3. Perceive that you can't hold up under the suffering of others.
4. Submit yourself actually to end the suffering all

things considered.

5. Create cherishing graciousness.

6. Submit yourself actually to carrying bliss to all creatures.

7. Create bodhicitta - seek to profit all creatures and free them into nirvāṇa.

Evening out and Exchanging - Parātma Parivartana

1. Think about deeply your fundamental equality with others - you wish to be upbeat, thus do every others.

2. See that you are just a single individual, while every single other being are vast in number – their need is more prominent than your own.

3. See that everybody is interrelated. What befalls one individual influences all others.

4. Perceive that every one of your endeavors to satisfy yourself by seeking after your very own joy above others have been fruitless.

5. Get that if you put forth an attempt to put the bliss of others first, you will in the long run achieve edification.

Surrendering Self-Cherishing - Anupādāna Ātman

1. Perceive that every incredible being, for example, the Buddha achieved edification by relinquishing self-appreciating and esteeming the requirements of others.

2. Make plans to discharge self-getting a handle on and, out of sympathy for other people, put the government assistance of others over your own.

Giving and Taking – Dana Graha

When you see somebody who is in suffering somehow or another:

1. Picture yourself as Avalokiteśvara, the bodhisattva of sympathy.
2. Picture a white, flaring hot hriḥ seed syllable in your heart place.
3. Picture pulling a dark haze of contrary energies of the other individual through your nose and down to your heart, where it is totally singed.
4. Picture conveying a white fog from your heart to the next individual, and envision that they become unadulterated and upbeat.

Toxic substance and Antidote - Viṣa Pratipakṣa

1. Consider the passionate and mental obscurations that keep you away from Buddhahood.
2. Pick an obscuration, and purge it by building up its cure. For want, consider grotesqueness. For revultion, ponder love. For obliviousness, consider Dependent Origination. For desire, think about yourself as equivalent to other people. For pride, work on Exchanging Yourself and Others.

Day by day Conduct - Caryā

In the wake of ascending from your thoughtful retention, in post contemplation approach your day with a care that brings you lucidity of mindfulness in the entirety of your exercises. In your Illusion-Like

Samādhi (Bhrānti Samādhi), see all appearances assimilated in a mindfulness that they are not substantively genuine but rather dreams. You consider everything to be unfilled of self-nature, similar to a fantasy created by your psyche, or as unadulterated and impeccable Buddha knowledge.

Activities

Play out the following activities for at any rate a month will set you up well for Tantric practices.

Recommended Items

Add to your special raised area in your hallowed space:

1. A copy of a Mahāyāna sūtra.
2. A picture or pictures of Mahāyāna buddhas and bodhisattvas to whom you feel dedication.

Insight – Prajñā

Create intelligence every day by considering the significant bits of knowledge of the Mahāyāna sūtras. Advantages: You understand the inescapability of torment and develop approaches to support all creatures. Time: 1-2 hours out of each week; constantly.

Opening Practices - Sevā

Start each training meeting with the following:

1. Recount the Refuge Vow.

buddham śaraṇam gacchāmi dharmam śaraṇam gacchāmi saṅgham śaraṇam gacchāmi

"I go for asylum to the Buddha." "I go for shelter to the Dharma." "I go for shelter to the Saṅgha."

Recount 3x.

2. Recount the Bodhisattva Vow.

viśuddham dhārayiṣyāmi yathā buddhena deśitam

tena jitvā śaṭhamāram prāpya buddhatvam uttamam bhaveyam bhavakhinnānām śaraṇam sarvadehinām

"I will look after virtue, as instructed by the Buddha.

Overcoming the evil presence Mara, and accomplishing preeminent buddhahood, I promise to be an asylum for all creatures, fatigued of samsāra."

Discuss 3x.

3. Practice Meditation on the Buddhas.

Advantages: Develops solid yearning for edification, cleans obscurations. Time: 9 minutes.

Contemplation on the Buddhas - Buddhānu Smṛiti

Reflect on Buddha Amitābha and his unadulterated domain of Sukhāvatī. You can likewise play out this reverential practice with different buddhas.

1. Envision Amitābha before you: He is red, with one face, two arms, wears the streaming pieces of clothing of a buddha, and sits on a red lotus. His hands are in the Gesture of Meditation (Dhyāna Mudrā). The bodhisattvas Avalokiteśvara and Mañjuśrī remain to one side and right.
2. With dedication, present his mantra om amideva hriḥ ordinarily.
3. Go to Amitābha for what you want.
4. Disintegrate the representation into vacancy.

Advantages: You get the assurance and gifts of perhaps

the best buddha. Time: 5 minutes.

Reflection - Samādhi

Peacefulness Meditation - Śamathā

Peacefulness Meditation follows similar acts of the Common Vehicle, yet includes a refinement of steps driving continuously to the accomplishment of the First Absorption. It is up to you how you need to form the measure of time you spend on each progression. This technique is known as The Nine Levels of Mental Stability (Nava Bhūmi):

1. Sitting in a reflective stance, start by removing stale air multiple times from your lungs, breathing out totally and with somewhat more force than expected. Keep your psyche effortfully engaged to slice through interruptions and build up nonconceptual retention. To address sluggishness, look upward. To address fomentation, look descending.
2. Ruminate over a statue of the Buddha. Proceed with this training until you accomplish some level of reflective strength, not permitting your psyche to meander.
3. Equipoise (Samādhāna) – Your psyche is unexpectedly still, undistracted with resolute center, and dynamically conscious. You are focused in yourself, settled, in a basic, without thought, nondual reflective assimilation.
4. Ruminate over the Four Form Absorptions as instructed in Chapter 1: The Common Vehicle.

Advantages: Develops inward harmony and delight. The conclusive outcome subsequent to achieving these levels is the First Absorption, called Even Placement.

Time: 20 to an hour.

Knowledge Meditation - Vipayśanā

Knowledge Meditation is created through continuously developing comprehension and at last legitimately seeing the perspectives on void, mind just, and buddha embodiment. Start by perusing a couple of pages of a Mahāyāna content that portrays the genuine reality, for example, The Heart Sūtra, Vasubandhu's stanzas on Mind Only, or Asaṅga's The Supreme Continuum, ponder it, and addition a solid feeling about its fact.

1. Contemplate vacancy:

   a. Sitting in contemplation, see the universe of relative truth where appearances appear to have self-nature. See that all appearances emerge due to karmic molding, and they are of the idea of misery. This is saṃsāra.

   b. Discharging connection to relative truth, don't see a self, sensations or any appearances as having a self-nature of any sort. Try not to acknowledge, handle, or reject anything. Try not to lay your mindfulness on any single appearance. Try not to conceptualize anything.

   c. Accomplishing thoughtful ingestion, rest in nonconceptual samādhi.

   d. Permit a definitive truth of vacancy to emerge suddenly in your mindfulness. Appearances and vacancy are indivisible. As feelings emerge, unwind into them, and see their unfilled nature. As musings emerge, unwind into them, and see their unfilled nature. As nonconceptual mindfulness sunrises, your obscurations disintegrate. The total, direct impression of vacancy is to see no appearances by any stretch of the imagination. This is nirvāṇa.

e. Perceiving that creatures are in suffering their connection to a deception in a self and to purge appearances, permit sympathy to emerge normally. Nondual mindfulness liberated from self and other suddenly sunrises. Your discernment comes back to the universe of appearances. Considering all to be as dreams, you maintain a strategic distance from saṃsāra's snares, however you stay out of empathy for other people.

f. When you know there are no Buddha's, you are a Buddha.

2. Ruminate over psyche as it were:

a. See that external articles are mind as it were.
b. Verify that no external articles are ever seen.
c. Discover that a brain that cognizes objects isn't seen.
d. Incapable to see either protests or an awareness that sees them, rest in nondual ingestion.
e. Recognizing that creatures are in suffering their connection to deception in a self and to appearances as mental projections, permit sympathy to emerge normally. Nondual mindfulness liberated from self and other unexpectedly first lights. Your observation comes back to the universe of appearances. Considering all to be as hallucinations, you dodge saṃsāra's snares, however you stay out of sympathy for other people.

f. When you know it all is the pure idea of psyche, you are a Buddha.

3. Think about Buddha quintessence:

a. Think with dedication on Buddha pith. Sure that the genuine idea of extreme reality has the otherworldly characteristics of Permanence, Bliss, Self, and Purity, you rest normally and equitably in tranquil nonconceptuality, without fixing on any object of core interest.

b. Direct view of the Clear Light of early stage astuteness day breaks.

c. You perceive your karmic obscurations as fanciful, and your obscurations break up.

d. As your acknowledgment develops, you consider all to be as totally deceptive. Nothing to expel, nothing to include - no appearances ever emerge. Deceptions fall away. You never again think "on" extreme reality however are extreme reality itself.

e. Perceiving that creatures are in suffering their connection to a deception in a self and to appearances that have no presence by any means, permit empathy to emerge normally. Nondual mindfulness liberated from self and other unexpectedly first lights. Your observation comes back to the universe of appearances. Considering all to be as hallucinations, you maintain a strategic distance from saṃsāra's snares, however you stay out of empathy for other people.

f. When you realize you are a buddha, you are a buddha.

Advantages: Cultivates buddha knowledge prompting omniscience. Time: 20 to an hour.

The Union of Tranquility Meditation and Insight Meditation – Yuga Naddha

1. As you create yourself in ever-more deep degrees of thoughtful assimilation, ponder the genuine idea of things through the methods of reasoning of the Middle Way, Mind Only, and Buddha Essence.
2. Achieve nonconceptual retention in Tranquility Meditation. Your psyche is steady and centered.
3. While keeping up your reflective assimilation from Tranquility Meditation, accomplish clearness of mindfulness through Insight Meditation. Your psyche is splendid, still, and clear.
4. You accomplish the undefined association of serenity and understanding, and rest easily in that mindfulness. After three inestimable ages of training, you accomplish immaculate Buddhahood.

Advantages: Cultivates inward harmony and intelligence that prompts internal arousing. Time: 20 to an hour.

Closing Practices - Visarjana

Commitment of Merit - Pariṇamana

Toward the finish of all training meetings, end with a petition devoting the legitimacy you created be given to profit all creatures. Recount the accompanying petition, in Sanskrit and in English:

puṇyaṃ prabhūtaṃ yad ihāpi sarvaṃ saṃbodhaye tat

pariṇāmayāmi

"I commit all legitimacy emerged here for the objective of complete and flawless illumination."

Advantages: The legitimacy you picked up from training helps boundless creatures. Time: 1 moment.

Gathering Sacred Sex Ritual – Maithuna Maṇḍala Vidhi

Coming up next is a gathering holy sex custom in the convention of the Mahāyāna.

Recommended Items

Set up your hallowed space as portrayed in Chapter 1: The Common Vehicle, with extra things for every individual in your gathering. You can likewise add the extra Mahāyāna things to the raised area.

Pads: Place cushions around the space for every one of the members, in sets of two. Ladies sit on the left cushion, men on the right. The main couple sits in the middle.

Individual Preparation

Get ready yourselves as in the couples hallowed sex custom in Chapter 1: The Common Vehicle.

Direct of the Ritual

1. Sit on your pads and face your darling.

2. Discuss the Refuge Vow.

buddham śaraṇam gacchāmi dharmam śaraṇam gacchāmi saṅgham śaraṇam gacchāmi

"I go for asylum to the Buddha." "I go for shelter to the

Dharma." "I go for shelter to the Saṅgha."

Discuss 3x.

3. Discuss the Bodhisattva Vow.

viśuddhaṃ dhārayiṣyāmi yathā buddhena deśitaṃ

tena jitvā śaṭhamāraṃ prāpya buddhatvam uttamaṃ bhaveyaṃ bhavakhinnānāṃ śaraṇaṃ sarvadehinām

"I will look after virtue, as instructed by the Buddha.

Overcoming the evil presence Mara, and accomplishing preeminent Buddhahood, I promise to be an asylum for all creatures, fatigued of saṃsāra."

Discuss 3x.

4. Practice Tranquility Meditation as rehearsed in the Mahāyāna convention.
5. Practice Insight Meditation as rehearsed in the Mahāyāna convention.
6. Conjure the gifts of the Buddha's and approach them for what you want in your life. "We summon the buddhas, and request their direction and motivation during the custom."
7. Summon the divine forces of adoration, Kāma and Ratī, and request their help during the custom. "We conjure the divine forces of adoration, Kāma and Ratī, and request your help during the custom.
8. Bow to your darling with Añjali Mudrā.
9. Offer gifts to one another, and crown each other with a wreath of blossoms.
10. To animate the feeling of hearing, share expressions of love for one another.

11. To animate the feeling of sight, every lady finds a good pace seat and moves for her darling. She sit down. Each man finds a workable pace seat and moves for his sweetheart. He sit down.
12. To invigorate the feeling of smell, offer each other a laurel of fragrant blossoms.
13. To invigorate the feeling of taste, she moves to sit on his lap; offer each other nourishment and drink.
14. To invigorate the feeling of touch, offer each other exotic satisfying touchs.
15. Stir each other through sexual touchs and satisfying your join forces with your mouth.
16. With your sweetheart, have intercourse to one another. Use the different situations as you appreciate them.
17. Following 10 minutes, bow to your sweetheart with Añjali Mudrā.
18. The ladies move to one side and start again with another partner, rehashing stages 15-17. Leave your psyche alone liberated from any decisions of your partners.
19. When all the ladies have had intercourse with all the men, the circle is finished.
20. The lady comes back to her unique partner, and you nestle together.
21. Offer gratitude to the Buddha's and expel them.
22. "We offer gratitude to the Buddha's for their direction and motivation. You are rejected."
23. Offer gratitude to the divine forces of affection, Kāma and Ratī, and expel them. "We express gratefulness to the divine forces of affection, Kāma and Ratī. You are expelled."

24. The gathering bows to the lead couple in the inside with Añjali Mudrā.
25. Recount the Dedication of Merit, devoting the value of your lovemaking to all creatures.

puṇyaṃ prabhūtaṃ yad ihāpi sarvaṃ saṃbodhaye tat pariṇāmayāmi

"I commit all legitimacy emerged here for the objective of complete and flawless edification."

Advantages: You create internal harmony and joy, and win the help of the Buddha's. Time: About 4 hours; 2 hours to get ready and 2 hours for training.

Chapter Ten

Positions And Techniques

Right now, will find out about various Tantric sex positions and procedures that you can use for spicing up your sexual coexistence.

The Sidewinder

This position is enlivened from the yoga position of a similar name, and this procedure takes into account deep entrance. It likewise accommodates the couple to keep in touch. For playing out this method, the lady should rests on her side and supports the heaviness of her chest area with the assistance of her hands. She should lift one of her legs and place it on her darling's shoulder while the other leg is lying on the bed. A variety of this equivalent position is that then again the man can rests behind the lady and enter his partner from behind.

The Yab Yum

The Yab Yum position is viewed as probably the best situation for having tantric sex. It is a genuinely simple situation to perform, and it takes into consideration synchronous climaxes. This position helps in animating quite a few places. Likewise, the man's hands happen to be free right now, he can touch his darling's body however he sees fit, since the couple would confront one another, it takes into consideration enthusiastic kisses also. The man should sit leg over leg on the bed or some other agreeable surface and hold his back straight. The lady should straddle him and fold her legs over his lower back. It takes into account delayed here and there developments that can help the couple in accomplishing an all-around planned climax.

The latch

This posture permits the man to get a decent see his sweetheart's face and the other way around. This is an extremely attractive posture and aides in pleasuring both the partners. For playing out this procedure, the lady should be situated on a high stage like a table or even the kitchen counter. She will then need to recline and adjust her upper middle and her head with the assistance of her hands by inclining onto her elbows. The man should remain between her separated legs and enter her. This is one represent that doesn't need to be limited to the room and is ideal for an off the cuff cavort.

The butterfly

This method is accepted to allow both the partners to achieve a significant level of rapture and takes into consideration deep entrance. For playing out this system, the young lady should rests on the table so that her butt lies at the edge of the table and the man should help lift her lower back marginally off the table and afterward place both her legs over his shoulders. Her vagina would be free for him to infiltrate while remaining in the middle of her legs. Since her legs are shut together, this fixes the vaginal waterway and gives a tight fit. The man should enter her while her butt is in midair.

The double decker

This is an amazingly suggestive posture and will help in accomplishing a climax no problem at all. The man will likewise be given a decent perspective on all the activity that is going on down there, and his hands will likewise have unlimited access to lay with his sweetheart's butt. This position is very enabling for ladies since they have all the control here. For playing out this system, the man should sit on the bed while his legs are collapsed under his body. The lady will then need to confront away from him and place her feet one either side of her darling while her feet are set level superficially to give her some help. When she has brought down herself onto his erect penis, then she will just need to begin moving advances and in reverse or can even decide on a here and there movement. The man should basically kick back and have fun.

The last place anyone would want to be

This is an extraordinary posture since it permits both the gatherings to have a similar measure of control and ooze a similar measure of pressure for having a great sexual encounter. People will have equivalent balance right now. For playing out this represent, the man should sit on the bed and support his chest area with his knees. He will then need to move the lower some portion of his legs in reverse and place them marginally separated. The lady will then need to expect a similar position yet she will do as such while confronting ceaselessly from him and her run would be squeezing into his scrotum and her back against his chest. Her legs would be joined and afterward set in the space that is accessible between his legs and the man should enter her from behind. For this situation to be compelling, both the partners should remain as near to one another as could reasonably be expected.

Skiff

This position is a slight adjustment of the lady on top position. Right now, bodies should be situated so that both the partners will find a good pace great take a gander at one another's face while occupied with the demonstration. For playing out this, the man should sit down on a seat that can marginally twist in reverse. The lady will then need to put herself on his lap and afterward place her legs on either side of the seat. The young lady should fire an allover development without anyone else, or her partner can help her by setting his hand under her bum and helping her move in an upwards and downwards way.

The mermaid

This is a somewhat fluctuated adaptation of the butterfly, and it takes into consideration a more solace and better hold. Right now, man can play with his darling's feet. Remember that feet are viewed as one of the most touchy and erogenous pieces of a lady's body. For playing out this method, the lady should expect a similar situation as she did in the butterfly, however her butt ought to be propped with the assistance of a pad. Her legs should loosen up and ought to be at a 90-degree edge. The man should stand near the table and infiltrate her.

Tsunami

This posture is very agreeable, and it is a sensual treat. This will knock your socks off. This posture is a slight alteration of the exemplary minister style. Right now, lady should expect the job that a man as a rule does in the teacher style. For playing out this, the man should rests level on his back, and his arms should be put close by. The lady should lie over him, and the man should embed his penis into her vagina. The lady should totally loosen up her legs with the goal that they are resting on his. Her palms ought to be put on his lower arm for giving her some help. The lady will then need to begin moving her pelvis in an upward and descending development.

Lap dance

This is a great posture for a man to encounter his darling's body in the entirety of its magnificence. His hands will be allowed to meander around her body, and he can do what he needs. The lady will face away from him as she would have, had she been giving him a lap move. For playing out this represent, the man should sit down on a seat, and his back should be kept straight. The lady will then sit on his lap and parity herself by setting her hands on his upper thighs or even his stomach. She will then need to lift herself gradually and place the backs of her calves and brings down herself onto his penis. Another variety of this would be that the lady should bring down herself onto his penis while confronting her darling and this will give him a serious decent perspective on her bosoms. He can choose to prod and play with them for whatever length of time that he satisfies.

Pretzel

This is another represent that is satisfying to take a gander at and even simple to expect. This will cause the couple to feel incredibly attractive. For playing out this procedure, the couple should stoop before one another. The man should move advances, and the lady will fold her arms over him. The lady will then lift herself up and place her left leg by her darling's correct foot; her foot will confront downwards. The man will then need to put his left leg close to her correct foot. When taken a gander at a couple occupied with this posture, they look like a pretzel, an extremely provocative and mouth-watering pretzel.

The spread

This is an essential and an amazingly hot position. This permits the lady to get incredible delight since it lets her stroke her sweetheart and permits him the entrance to joy her. For playing out this system, the lady should sit at the very edge of the couch or even the bed and spread her legs separated. The man will then need to remain in the middle of her legs and infiltrate her. She can draw nearer to him and kiss him while his hands have the entrance to her full body.

The entwine

This posture looks intense and about difficult to copy, however then it very well may be pleasurable if it's done appropriately. This posture is tastefully engaging. For playing out this strategy, the couple should sit near one another and face each other. The man should put his legs on either side of his partner. The lady will then need to lift both of her legs and place them on either side of her sweetheart's sides, under his arms. The man's upper arms will secure the lady's legs, and the lady will then need to lift her upper arms and place them over his elbows. The man will then lift his legs and place them over her hands. This does sound very muddled, isn't that right? All the exertion that goes into it will merit your time and energy.

The G-force

This is maybe one of the most blazing tantric sex presents there is. This is the piece de opposition of all sex presents. The man has full oversight over his darling right now, both the people included will get extraordinary delight from this posture. For playing out this position, the lady should rests on her back on the bed, and the man must bow by her legs. He will then gradually lift her middle off the bed so she's offsetting herself with her head and her shoulders put on the bed. The man can either extend her legs at a 90-degree edge or infiltrate her, or he can likewise pull them separated and place her feet just beneath his chest and enter her.

The waterfall

Right now, lady should put her hand on her sweetheart's penis and afterward let her fingertips brush his scrotum gradually and tenderly. It is a smart thought to use some ointment for making it progressively pleasurable. Her hands should be set on either side of his gonads, and afterward she should gradually slide her hands up till they arrive at the touchy tip of his penis. When this is done, the lady should give the man some time to chill off, and he will then need to respond the administration he got. The man needs to cup his sweetheart's vagina and touch all her delicate spots. He should slide his hands over her clitoris and her vaginal external lips.

The snake

For this, the lady should gradually extend the pole of her sweetheart's penis with one of her hands and let the other hand follow little circles directly under the leader of the pole. This is like giving a slow and delicate hand work. Proceed with these movements a clockwise way and afterward once you arrive at the leader of the penis move to anticlockwise heading. Keep this up for whatever length of time that your sweetheart can suffer it.

Tantric triangle of touch

The lady should rests on her back and spread her legs somewhat and twist them at the knee. The man will then need to embed his list and center finger into her vagina and marginally twist them upwards till they make a come here development. This will give the ideal incitement to her G-Spot. This will make her groan in delight. While doing this, he should put the palm of his other hand on her lower midriff and apply a little delight. This consolidated incitement will rapidly push her off the edge.

The teeter-totter

There is nothing remotely guiltless about this specific teeter-totter. This is exceptionally suggestive. The lady should rests on her back on the bed, and her pelvis should be somewhat tilted upwards. A pad can be propped under her pelvis for doing as such. The man will then need to lift her feet and tenderly overlap them with the goal that her knees are laying on her bosoms and the bottoms of her feet are touching his chest. This position permits unhindered access to a lady's vagina, and the upward tilt will guarantee that he hits her G-Spot each time he pushes into her.

Tub Tangle

Get your man to lean back in a tub that is loaded up with water and the lady should straddle him while her back is confronting him. When his penis has entered her, he should sit up so you both are confronting one another. Then she should fold her legs over him, and he will do likewise with the goal that their elbows are under their partner's knees. Clutch each other as firmly as you can and start an influencing to and fro movement. This allows for some enthusiastic kissing.

Love Triangle

The lady should rests on her back on the floor or the bed and afterward she should lift her left advantage into the air. Her correct legs ought to be loosened up to her correct side, with the end goal that both her legs are lying opposite to one another. She will then need to move her correct hand and catch her correct knee and form a triangle on the bed with the use of her correct leg and her correct hand. The man should hunch a little and enter her while holding her knee. This position would give the man better pelvic control and furthermore the chance of touching from multiple points of view as you would need to. A slight variety can be added to this posture by requesting that the man pivot his hips in a roundabout movement while pushing into the lady; this will push the couple to their verge.

Presently and Zen

This posture can be used for giving a snapshot of relief from the approaching climax. Tantric sex isn't tied in with discovering speedy discharge; it is tied in with enjoying the experience. What better approach to do as such, than to control yourself directly before arriving at the final turning point. When you feel that it is possible that you or your partner is near climaxing, enjoy a couple of moments and reprieve liberated from the position that you both are in. The man can just roll onto his side and remain inside his partner at the same time. This position just requests a snapshot of break. Slow pushing is passable, however if you feel that, you are going to climax, then pause for a minute, delay, maybe appreciate a tad of kissing and touching before proceeding with where you had given up. This position gives the genuinely necessary closeness during the sex to make the entire experience additionally adoring and healthy.

Torrid Tug-of-War

The lady should sit leg over leg on the floor or some other agreeable surface and afterward gradually sink onto his erect penis and fold her legs over his back. This position will permit the couple to confront one another and this implies you can grasp each other's elbows for offering some help and incline toward the bearing endlessly from your partner. This resembles playing a round of shy back-and-forth. If you both happen to be adaptable, then one partner can tilt their heads back and lean in reverse, away from the other partner. This position will take into account the arrangement of your bodies, and it will cause you to associate with your partner. It frames a close association and aides in gathering speed. Both the partners find a good pace player's right now the entrance can be controlled on the other hand by the partners.

The Python

The man should rests right now, his legs ought to be kept near one another while his arms are resting by his sides. The lady should bring down herself onto his penis and mount him gradually. When the man has entered her, then she can extend herself above with the goal that she's laying completely on his body. Both of your bodies would be superbly adjusted, and you can get a handle on one another's hands for gathering some speed and furthermore for offering some help. The lady will then need to gradually lift her middle off his with the goal that it nearly appears to be a snake that is ready to strike. She can push against his feet for including some greater development. You will both be touching each other completely, and her bosoms would rub against his chest, your hands would be gotten a handle on firmly, and his thighs would rub against hers. It takes into consideration deep entrance, however it additionally takes into account clitoral incitement. Since the couple would confront one another, this takes into account some enthusiastic kissing too. All the erogenous zones in the body would be animated.

Indeed! Indeed! Truly!

Right now, lady will lie face down on the sleeping pad, and she should hurry forward till her head and her middle are hanging off the side of the bed and she should support her chest area with the assistance of her palms put on the floor. The man will then need to slither between her legs and afterward infiltrate her from behind. The man can generally clutch his darling's hips for showing signs of improvement influence. The couple occupied with this position appears to be a sideways Y and in this way the name of this position. All things considered, yes it is very shameless. This position is great for fast in and out developments that will send you both pulling in delight. This is a topsy turvy represent that additionally takes into account the blood to go hurrying directly to the head. This position can be somewhat dubious and debilitating too and subsequently you probably won't have the option to keep at it throughout the night. In any case, it adds a particular colorful flavor to your ordinary cavorts and zest things up. A slight variety that can be added to this posture is that the lady can add some crushing movement to this situation to take into consideration double incitement.

X Marks the Spot

Right now, lady must rests on the bed or some other delicate surface of decision with her head propped on a pad. She should bring her knees up to her chest and fold her legs at her lower legs. The man will then need to stoop before her and gradually lean in some time pulling her hips towards his crotch. She should keep her thighs squeezed together while he begins pushing into her. This will take into account a to and fro movement and the intersection and clipping of legs will basically include some more touch. If the lady can begin getting her PC muscles, it will turn out to be much increasingly pleasurable.

Time Bomb

The man should sit down on a low seat with his legs in a casual position. While confronting ceaselessly from him, the lady should straddle him and spot her feet on the floor while gradually bringing down onto his penis. Her knees should be twisted at a 90-degree point. She should put herself at the tip of his penis, and afterward he should push into her. It is a serious loving posture and takes into account most extreme touch between the partners. Ladies will expect all the control right now men have the opportunity to fold their arms over their darling's body and investigate it however much they might want. He can likewise animate her clitoris for her additional joy.

Arc de Triomphe

This is a serious hot posture. The man should sit down on the bed with his legs extended before him. His sweetheart should slither up to him and afterward straddle his erect part. When you both are agreeable right now, should curve her back as much as she can. Being adaptable will prove to be useful right now. Ladies should be cautious while doing this because the pointless strain on their lower back can have genuine repercussions. She can tenderly move back and reach back to hold her lower legs. Presently, the genuine enjoyment starts. The man should lean forward and begin pushing into her. Ladies should prepare themselves for the invasion of development by clutching their lower legs. The man will find a workable pace all-encompassing perspective on his sweetheart's body and devour it. If the man wishes along these lines, he can lean down and kiss her chest too.

Head Game

Right now, lady should rests on the ground or some other level surface while her face is confronting upwards. Her hands should support her lower body; she will then need to lift her advantages, and her back too with the goal that they are lying opposite to the ground. She can support her pressure by propping up her arms against her lower back. While she is clutching her lower legs, the man should stoop before her and bring his knees towards her shoulders. He can generally clutch her hips so it will keep them both consistent and she can clutch his thighs for some additional help. This is topsy-turvy activity, ensure that you are delicate with your darling and it very well may be very dubious to get it directly in the first go itself. Ladies, every one of those Kegels that you have been rehearsing can be put to some great use right now. For making it progressively pleasurable, begin getting your PC muscles and begin draining your darling's penis.

Supernova

This is a represent that essentially begins by appearing as though a standard cowgirl position. Rather than the lady mounting him the long way, she should mount him while lying opposite to him on the bed. When she detects her man moving toward a climax, she can tenderly crush on his middle and incline toward her knees and continue crawling forward towards the edge of the bed with the goal that his head and shoulders are hanging off the side of the bed. Presently, she can continue her ride by and by. This position puts all the control with the lady, and she can ride her man, in any case, she satisfies. It additionally takes into consideration more deep infiltration, and since all the blood would race to the man's head right now, will encounter a marvelous climax. It is very engaging to the Goddess to see that she has the reigns right now. Tastefully, it is a serious sight for the man to view.

Love Seat

The man should rests on his back and prop his head with the assistance of a couple of cushions and spread his legs marginally. The lady should bring down herself onto his erect penis while confronting endlessly from him. It resembles the turnaround cowgirl position. She should put her feet between his legs on either side of the floor or the bed that he's lying on. Her right-hand should be put on the correct side of his hip and the left one on the left side. By using this for help, she can gradually bring down herself onto his penis. The lady's hands and feet will let her control the movement, and she can establish the tone. The man simply needs to rests and appreciate the work that his partner is doing. His hands are allowed to wander her body. Indeed, the inward goddess will be glad and will savor the control that has been put in her grasp.

Bed spread

The lady should twist around her side with the goal that her bosoms are laying delicately on the sleeping pad and her feet are holding tight the floor. The man will then need to move behind her and enter her from behind. While doing this, he can hold or lift her legs somewhat with the goal that it considers better infiltration and furthermore gives him the vital influence for pushing as he might want to. Since the lady's legs have been lifted off the floor that she should simply let the person accomplish all the work and make the most of his endeavors. This position gives all the control to the man, and he is responsible for the profundity and the speed of developments.

Chapter Eleven

Multiple Orgasm And Tantric Sex

One of the most significant parts of Tantric sex is that it separates between climaxing during sex and discharging. If you feel that you aren't completely fulfilled significantly in the wake of having discharging, which is because you probably won't have encountered a climax. Accordingly, it isn't fundamental for a man to discharge to have a climax. By using the various techniques for controlling a climax that has been referenced in the way of thinking of Tantra, you will have the option to encounter different climaxes and climaxes that will keep going for longer than the ones that you are typically used to. Doesn't this sound awesome? Who said ladies alone are fit for encountering various climaxes?

There's a specific Tantric method that you can use, and it will permit you to have different climaxes. However, before getting yourself familiar with this specific degree of sexual ability, you should accomplish power over your climaxes. There are three distinct procedures that you can use for dealing with your climaxes.

Keep your cool

This may sound bizarre, yet the most ideal manner by which you can delay your intercourse is by keeping your cool. If you feel that your climax is quick drawing nearer, and afterward you will essentially need to quiet down, hinder your breathing and your pushing movements also. Remember this may likewise prompt some ponderousness with your partner if you don't convey about it. Try not to feel ungainly and tell your partner your explanation behind easing back down.

Go slowly

When you begin engaging in sexual relations with your partner, ensure that you are taking things gradually during the underlying stage. The slower the sex is, the more exceptional your climax would be a direct result of all the development. Ensure that your breathing is standard and when you feel that, your climax is drawing nearer; follow the means referenced in the past points. Quiet yourself, hinder your breathing, and grasp your pelvic muscles.

When you feel that your climax is dying down, and afterward you can continue your pushing movement by and by. Continue rehashing this procedure for whatever length of time that you can hold off. Construct your energy and continue going. This development will make your climax last more, and it will be all the more impressive. When you feel that you are near climax, attempt and grip your pubic muscles while it is going on. This won't just keep you from discharging, yet it will let you experience the delight of a climax and not lose your erection. This implies you can prop up considerably in the wake of encountering a climax, doesn't that sound great? After a little practice, you will have the option to hold off for some time longer and engage in sexual relations for quite a long time together.

Chapter Twelve

Female Orgasm

Tantra not just furnishes an approach to manage issues that men face during sex, it even addresses the issues that ladies will in general face while engaging in sexual relations. This is the motivation behind why there are various practices material to ladies right now of living. It is a typical confidence in Tantric way of thinking that the most impressive sex organ for a lady is her brain. This implies her sexual excitement is equipped for being hosed by her negative reasoning and feelings that limit her desire. These considerations and feelings can be caused because of uneasiness, outrage, or even blame. Despite the explanation of their root, these feelings can negatively affect the sex drive of a lady. This would make a lady occupied while engaging in sexual relations.

It is pivotal to put less significance on the showy behavior that are associated with the procedure of sex and more on what the lady is feeling while at the same time making an insincere effort of sex. Here are a couple of methods that will help a lady in accomplishing a climax.

Clitoral Stimulation

Most men are generally unconscious of the way that not do just ladies get turned on or energized by vaginal entrance. There's nothing incorrectly in not having the option to accomplish a climax through infiltration. Truth be told, it is just a little division of ladies who will in general climax through infiltration. Sex, in itself, is a significant invigorating act, however the clitoris is the pearl that gives most of the sexual delight that a lady encounters. Thusly, it is extremely essential to focus on the clitoris also. Men, recollect that you should be delicate while you are animating a lady's clitoris. It is very touchy and being harsh would simply cause your partner to feel outrageous distress. Furthermore, the pressure of having to climax likewise will in general take out the enjoyment from the demonstration of sex. Along these lines, don't pressure your partner to climax.

G-Spot

The lessons of Tantra show that there lies a sacrosanct spot inside a lady's vagina that is alluded to as the G-Spot and it is very touchy. When animated in the ideal way it can deliver staggering climaxes. The G-Spot is accepted to be situated at the highest point of the vaginal waterway, a couple of creeps inside the vagina. You can animate your partner's G-Spot by tenderly rubbing the highest point of the vaginal trench. This spot would feel like a slight knock against the smooth vaginal wall. Delicately brush it to inspire a response from your partner. You will have the option to acknowledge when you have discovered the enchantment button from your partner's response. Dominant part of ladies can climax if this consecrated spot is animated appropriately. On uncommon events, when animated appropriately, ladies can discharge too. The G-Spot is additionally accepted to be the resting spot of Kundalini, the torpid sexual energy that is available in ladies. When animated appropriately, the Kundalini stirs and courses through the body.

Chapter Thirteen

Tantric Sex Teachings

Right now, us investigate the lessons of Tantric sex that will help in improving the degree of closeness as well as the sexual delight that you and your partner experience. This will positively affect your relationship. When these lessons are used in the best possible way, then it will put you a bit nearer to accomplishing edification. Every single one of these lessons can be used in a sexual and a non-sexual way.

Relax

Make sure to continue relaxing. You likely would have comprehended at this point the significance of breathing with regards to Tantric sex. It isn't just about tantric sex; any of the lessons that have begun in the East, in regards to the achievement of edification, will in general spot a lot of significance on relaxing. It is urgent that you comprehend the motivation behind why this is done and the way in which it is identified with Tantra just as the profound improvement of a person.

The response to this is very straightforward, each living thing relaxes. We inhale constantly, and if we do quit relaxing for delayed timeframes, it will at last outcome in death or even obviousness. Right now, could be essentially comprehended that breathing can be identified with our condition of awareness. Consider breath energy. Each breath that we take fills our body with oxygen and removes carbon dioxide right now. This oxygen that we breathe in is then provided to various cells in the body. Oxygen and breathing are crucial for the working of our bodies. Breathing is definitely not an intentional or cognizant capacity. It is something that our body has been intended to do. You may never give any consideration to how you are breathing, however you never truly quit breathing when you are alive. Isn't it scaring how our life relies upon a capacity that we don't do intentionally?

Things being what they are, what might occur if you begin to make breathing a cognizant capacity rather than an automatic activity? All the lessons that have started in the East, including the lessons of Tantra, accept that breathing ought to likewise be an intentional activity. Like referenced before, breath is energy, and by having the option to control your breathing, you will likewise have the option to manage the development of energy inside your body.

It is very intriguing to take note of the advantages of cognizant and directed breathing can have on various parts of your life, including your sexual coexistence. It is regular that while individuals are occupied with any sexual action, they will in general hold their breath, this is definitely not a known capacity. Each time you get energized, you may see that you will in general hold your breath. You most likely clutch your breath without understanding that you are doing as such. When you quit breathing, this will disturb the progression of energy in your body also. Making breathing a cognizant demonstration while occupied with sex will help you in figuring out how to control your energy and the development of energy in your body. This educating of Tantra is tied in with taking breaths in a loose and quiet way. Let your breath stream gradually through your body. If you need to accomplish a full body climax, then you should ensure that your breathing is profound and even. When you begin concentrating on this, you will understand that you can peak all the more no problem at all.

Unwind

The pressure in your muscles and body will go about as an obstacle in a way that is like shallow relaxing. The strong strain that you will in general experience when you are occupied with any sexual action is certifiably not a cognizant one. One of the standards of Tantric sex is that you should know about this strong strain that exists in your body thus that you know about all the various muscles that are being held up because of pressure. You do require a tad of pressure for encouraging development in the body and furthermore for holding up the body, however that is it. Strong strain isn't required in all aspects of the body.

If you fire settling on the choice of worrying your muscles a cognizant one, then you will see that you are presumably worrying a couple of muscles in your body pointlessly while engaging in sexual relations. For example, a man may wind up straining every one of his muscles while accepting oral sex. Though he's essentially expected to give up and appreciate the consideration being showered by his partner, rather he is worrying the muscles in his middle and legs. In such a case, all the additional pressure is superfluous, and this essentially deters the free progression of energy in the body. Concentrate on loosening up all these strained muscles. Concentrate on your breathing and appreciate the sexual warmth that is coursing through your body.

In any case, it is critical that unwinding doesn't just incorporate the relinquishing the physical pressure, however the psychological strain also. Relinquish all the pointless contemplations and desires. Relish the experience, appreciate the glow, the sensations, and don't keep yourself down.

Sounds that can help

Sounds are essential with regards to the development of energy in the body. A few people may not be agreeable, or they may even be cognizant about the sounds that they make when stirred. These contemplations shouldn't be paid attention to while participating in Tantric sex. Relinquish all the restraints that are keeping you down. Communicate as unreservedly as you need to. There is no limitation separated from the ones that you have forced on yourself. Cause all the sounds that you to feel like making. These sounds are automatic responses to the joy that you are encountering, and they are associated with the feelings and impressions that you are encountering. If you are quiet or calm, then the development of sexual energy in your body gets moderate. When you are vocal in communicating what you are feeling, the energy begins to move in the body. Tantric sex is tied in with arousing the torpid sexual energy that is available inside the body and afterward using it for accomplishing illumination. Indeed, in what capacity will the energy move when you are restless about something as inconsequential as how you sound?

You don't need to unravel the various sounds that are related with the various feelings that you are encountering. You groan, moan, or take a sharp breath relying on the joy that you are encountering. All the different sounds that you make add to the joy that you and your partner would get from sex. The sounds delivered needn't be rational; it is only the statement of the feelings that you may be encountering at a specific minute. While you are having intercourse, there would be a couple of cases that may cause you to feel overjoyed, and this will be spoken to in the sounds that you would make. There may be a couple of horrendous encounters also. You should verbally communicate your disappointment just as pleasurable sentiments, and you needn't keep yourself down. You have to convey your pleasure or disappointment to your partner. It isn't just about being vocal. You can be verbal in your appearance also. Sounds, yet words can likewise be used for conveying the equivalent. If you feel that, you are getting a charge out of something that your partner is doing, and afterward you ought to impart the equivalent to them with no hindrances. This gives some support as well as tells your partner that they are accomplishing something right. In a similar way, if you don't care for something, then you should communicate your distress to your partner. Relinquishing your hindrances is the main manner by which you will have the option to genuinely encounter unbridled joy.

Eye to eye connection is basic

This may seem like an undeniable thing. All things considered, it enhances the general sexual experience. Taking a gander at your partner while occupied with any sexual demonstration will make the experience increasingly exceptional eye to eye connection doesn't imply that you gaze thoughtfully into your partner's eyes. Move over to the aching look an adoration struck doggy has in its eyes. We are discussing some genuine X-appraised looking, so prepare for it. This will assist you with accomplishing some additional closeness. For beginning, you and your partner can locate an agreeable spot to sit with the goal that you both will have the option to investigate each other's eyes. Pause for a minute to assemble your considerations; typically, a full breath will do the stunt for you. When you feel that you are prepared, you can open your eyes and look into your partner's eyes. Permit your partner the entrance to see you, your actual self, sans any misrepresentations and likewise, you can look at them. This may feel somewhat inept at first, however it will end up being very viable.

Permit yourself to convey through your eyes and not simply your privates. You can let your eyes meander over one another's body. Let your partner recognize the desire clearly and the wanton relinquishment. Nothing would be a superior turn on than realizing that your partner wants you and necessities you. In the way, that sounds and contact can impart, similarly, you can convey significantly more by using only your eyes alone. This will help you both speak with one another in a sincere way.

Exploration of your senses

Tantra is an antiquated craftsmanship, and it's been around for a considerable length of time. It is essential to observe the way that Tantra isn't just about improving the physical nature of engaging in sexual relations, however it is additionally about upgrading the passionate experience.

All your tangible organs will in general participate as far as you can tell. Sex isn't a disengaged procedure. Thusly, Tantra is tied in with improving your tangible experience also. If one of your senses has been undermined, then, different senses will in general become touchy.

Take motivation from this, and you can presumably fuse this into any of the sexual experiences that you may have with your partner. It isn't just about taking an interest in the demonstration; it is likewise essential to investigate all the senses of your partner and yourself. You both ought to have the option to make a situation that will help you in lighting your sexual flames. You needn't make a decent attempt to do this. The earth ought to be sexual and exotic. It should allow you to unwind. You can attempt to blindfold your partner. This will help in invigorating their other tangible organs. You can tempt their olfactory senses by consolidating different sweet-smelling basic oils and aromas into your daily schedule. You can animate their feeling of sound by playing some moderate and alleviating music, something that will develop some expectation. Going to the feeling of taste, you can take care of one another some delicious berries or even lick off some cream off their fingers. Different things should be possible for invigorating one's detects. Bother their body and bother their senses too. Let your creative mind go out of control, and there are no limitations. You can stroke their body with quills, silk, or some other material. When you have figured out how to prod every one of their senses, evacuate the blindfold and let your partner see what you have been doing. That seething look of unquestionable want in their eyes would be astounding.

Focus on a full body climax

Who wouldn't have any desire to have a climax? A full body climax does sound enticing, isn't that right? Thus, without burning through whenever, let us begin with this entrancing idea.

One way in which you can condition your body to have a full body climax is by rehearsing the development to a looming climax and afterward letting it die down without yielding to the delight. You should drive your partner to the verge of a climax and afterward let it blur away, without allowing them to peak. When you let it die down, you should fire developing it again and let it blur away once more. Use all your resolution and continue playing at it for whatever length of time that you can.

You can take your partner to the verge of a climax orally or through some other strategy, yet you ought not to give them the help that they are wanting for, in any event not for some time. Continue expanding upon this joy. Subsequent to keeping at it for some time, you can at last let go. When your darling gets to encounter the much-anticipated climax at last, it will be really staggering.

The excursion tallies

Climaxes are awesome, yet Tantric sex isn't about essentially accomplishing a climax. It is tied in with deferring your climax for some time longer to get better outcomes. A climax can be thought of as a brilliant result of participating in Tantric sex. Tantric sex is more otherworldly and holy than customary sex. It is the association of the contradicting sexual energies present in the partners. The pressure of accomplishing a climax will in general remove the joy of taking part in a sexual demonstration. This pressure is very hurtful, and it negatively affects the individual's presentation. The excursion in Tantric sex is nearly as significant therefore. Climax isn't the principle point. It is tied in with making the most of your body and your partner also. It is tied in with adoring each other's bodies and loving your time together. Sex implies far beyond a negligible physical act that a couple would take part in. Have a go at moving your concentration to various things that you appreciate and furthermore the things that your partner finds pleasurable. There will unquestionably be sure things that you both appear to appreciate. Locate those basic things. It might be kissing, foreplay, holding one another or any oral action and consolidate these into your lovemaking procedure.

Stunts for joy

The thigh high

Select your preferred fundamental oil and pour a couple of drops of this scented oil onto your hands. Ensure that your plasma are very much oiled and afterward place these on your partner's thighs, a little over their knee. Start by delicately massaging and move upwards. Take as much time as necessary and let the expectation manufacture. This development of sexual strain will simply add to the experience and make it progressively pleasurable. Try not to contact your partner's private parts; rather, center on the zones around the privates.

Take the nail street

Use your nails and delicately follow examples of figure eight on your darling's thigh or run your nails softly along the length of their back or their calf. Bother every one of those regions that are delicate to contact and fluctuate the strain to evoke various responses from your partner.

Attempt the aural sex rub

Take some time and attempt and back rub your partner's ear. Ensure that you are being delicate and use light contacts. Use your fingers and begin working from the external overlap of the ear towards the internal ear. Run your little finger along the external edge of the finger. You can say romantic things and charms into your partner's ear while doing this. You can tenderly lick and look around with your tongue if you are feeling marginally brave.

Presently, turn up the warmth

After all the prodding and the tempting foreplay, the time has come to turn up the warmth. You and your partner can enjoy some oral sex or investigate one of the numerous tantric sex places that you have found out about in the past section. It is up to you, the way where you need to turn up the warmth in the room. Take as much time as is needed as you did with all the foreplay. Is anything but a fast in and out; it is tied in with relishing the experience and respecting each other's bodies.

These standards will help you in improving your sexual encounters. Tantric sex is tied in with connecting with your senses and your cognizance at the time and determining the most extreme joy you can.

Chapter Fourteen

Improve Tantric Sex With These Tips

The principle motivation behind Tantra is to assist you with accomplishing splendid climaxes that you have been precluded in light of the fact that from securing your standard sexual practices. Notwithstanding, this doesn't imply that Tantra ought to be dealt with daintily. Consider Tantra an erotic exercise. Tantric sex is viewed as more charming than going through hours together at the rec center, yet the measure of physical effort that your body encounters can be contrasted with that you may understanding while at the same time playing out any overwhelming activities.

Additionally, there are various degrees of Tantric sex. Essentially bouncing into Tantra with no experience or primer practice may improve your sexual coexistence, yet it is so much better when you participate in some type of pre-sex warm up practice that will help in setting the mind-set and working up some expectation concerning what is yet to come. There are a few manners by which you can heat up, however perhaps the most ideal way that could be available is give your partner a back rub and have your partner give you one also. This will extricate up your muscles, which is significant in light of the fact that solid muscles can hinder a full body climax.

The back rub that you are providing for set up your

darling for tantric sex has some particular standards that are joined to it, alongside a system that is intended to uplift the sexual affectability and make the body progressively open to assist sexual incitement. Additionally, this back rub can be combined with a procedure that can be used on a lady to cause her to accomplish a climax. This will contribute extraordinarily to the nature of tantric sex in light of the fact that accepting one climax makes an individual patient for the following one, and this furnishes you with the fundamental open door o coax your partner and draw out the sex.

The Use of Oil

The main thing that you need before you can give your sweetheart a pre-sex knead is oil. Oil is an incredible instrument that can be used if you need your back rub to be increasingly compelling. It helps in extricating the skin up and giving grease to your hands. If your hands can slide and coast easily over your darling's body all the more adequately, then it will likewise help in making the back rub increasingly sexy and causes in paving the way to the real sex!

The best oil that you can use in a pre-sex rub is grape seed oil. This is because grape seed oil has minimal number of individuals that are oversensitive to it, and can be incredible for your skin. In this manner, by giving your sweetheart a grape seed oil rub you will be helping him, or her get milder skin too, and isn't this a fantastic special reward? You can generally include a couple of drops of your preferred scented or basic oil to make the experience far and away superior. Distinctive fundamental oils can be used relying on the specific explanation behind which it is being used. For example, lavender can be used for unwinding and alleviating muscles; rose can be used for giving an increasingly erotic feel to the back rub.

If grape seed oil isn't accessible, go for whatever other oil that has been made with the end goal of back rubs.

The Technique

The primary thing that you should do is clearly begin spreading the oil over your sweetheart's body. Ensure that the oil is conveyed uniformly everywhere throughout the body, and remember that too little oil won't give sufficient oil and result in teasing. In any case, using an excess of would simply wind up getting chaotic, and this can be irritating. Attempt to locate the fair compromise! While you are spreading the oil over your partner's body, you will find that the skin ingests the oil rapidly. Thus, you should keep habitually spreading more oil over their body, if the grease quits being adequate.

When the oil has been spread over your partner's body, the back rub can appropriately start. At first, it would be a smart thought to begin with essential pressure of the entirety of the significant muscles. The muscle you ought to go for while applying wide and vague pressure are the thigh muscles since this zone is normally under the most strain for the duration of the day.

When the muscles have been relaxed up in your partner's legs, you can move their back, the second-most tense region of the normal body. Simply apply pressure with your straightened palm, and make sure to speak with your partner as much as you can about what feels better and what is excruciating.

Attempt gently slapping territories that you feel are as of now free to invigorate blood course in these zones. Recollect not to slap so hard that it harms except if your partner needs you to obviously!

When you have finished this back rub and released up the significant muscle gatherings, the time has come to start centered pressure with the tips of your fingers and your clench hands. There are explicit territories that you ought to focus during centered pressure, and these zones are determined in the following segment.

Territories to Target

Bosoms: The bosoms are one specific territory of the human life systems that will in general draw in a great deal of consideration, and it so occurs, that they are additionally an astounding wellspring of sexual incitement for some individuals. They likewise will in general have exceptionally thought purposes of strain that, when discharged, wind up causing the individual to feel fantastically loose and quiet.

Along these lines, bosoms are clearly going to be one of the most significant zones of the body that you should target. Purposes of pressure here are most likely going to be on the lower half of the bosoms. It is significant that you search, attempting to discover the zone where the pressure exists.

This little wad of strain can be discovered right beneath the areola, and your partner may likely shout out when you hit this specific spot. In any case, don't confound this torment and stop the back rub. This torment is entirely charming, with numerous individuals contrasting it with the inclination once gets while scratching a tingle.

Something imperative to note while performing such a back rub is the source of these little wads of strain that are available in the body. They are not just strong pressure. Their root is more mystical than physical in nature.

You are as of now acquainted with the different chakras present in the body. In any case, you most likely don't know that these chakras are the significant stops in an immense system of energy that is streaming inside your body, vortices through which energy continually streams. However, there are sure circumstances where the progression of energy can get disturbed.

This typically occurs because of a less than stellar eating routine or a physical issue in a previous existence that may residually affect your body right now. Therefore, when you apply profound strain to these points the energy begins to get discharged, consequently expelling the impediment that was formerly hindering the progression of energy in your body.

Discharging energy is agonizing and yet very charming in light of the fact that the progression of energy gives essentialness and expanded sexual affectability to your body. This implies when you knead these points, your partner is going to feel an extraordinary tingling vibe that will regress into a stimulating sensation as the blockage is expelled from the energy pathways in the body.

The most ideal manner by which you can apply strain to

this specific point is by pushing down using the tips of your fingers. Start by applying pressure and moving your hands in a round movement. This will discharge the energy blockage in a mellow and proficient manner. The round movement extricates up stuck energy and afterward permits your hand to move away to an alternate piece of the blockage, permitting the relaxed up energy to stream into the energy pathway without being impeded by the pressure of your fingers.

You can likewise apply serious strain to this point. This is exceptionally valuable since it will discharge energy from the blockage in a very serious way, and this will wind up opening your partner up for extraordinary sexual incitement.

Butt: This is another zone of the body that a great many people are stirred by. For reasons unknown, the butt is similarly as inclined to blockages in energy as bosoms seem to be, most likely in view of the extraordinary sum strain they experience when the individuals they are appended to spend by far most of their day sitting in an office. With the measure of sitting that we do, it is no big surprise that the pathways of energy in our derrieres wind up getting sponsored up.

The significant thing here is to feel your way around the territory. Blockages can happen in a few distinct pieces of the butt, so you should look around a little to discover where precisely the blockage has happened. An odd little fortuitous event is that the energy blockage is likely going to happen in a similar spot on the two cheeks, so if you discover the spot on one cheek basically begin squeezing a similar spot on the other cheek also.

Apply a similar round movement with the tips of your fingers that you used on your partner's bosom. These energy blockages may require some more pressure, notwithstanding, so if your partner can't feel anything when you are rubbing that person, simply having a go at using your thumb.

You may confront trouble finding the pressure point right now the body, particularly if your partner has been skilled with a breathtaking posterior. This is because the energy pathways are covered underneath a great deal of substance. Bosoms once in a while ever posture such an issue, regardless of whether the bosoms being referred to are very huge.

This is because the pressure points situated in bosoms are not as profound as the ones in the rear. Henceforth, if you are confronting troublesome finding your partner's pressure point, use your thumb, and it will work. If your thumb is as yet not adequate, have a go at using something inflexible like a pen to apply pressure, simply ensure you use the backside of the pen and not the pointy end!

Using such a device will assist you with providing unimaginably engaged pressure onto the energy blockage, encouraging a speedy scattering of energy and in the process most likely turning your partner on a lot.

Internal thighs: Finding the blockage in energy right now your body may end up being significantly more troublesome than discovering it on different pieces of the body. This is the reason a cursory back rub of the thighs is important before you start to test for pressure points.

The muscle rub is useful in light of the fact that it will expel a great deal of interruptions from that general region. A great deal of the time, you may be examining for the pressure point and would as far as anyone knows think that its rapidly, just to find that it was simply fundamental muscle torment and not the agony that originates from a blocked energy pathway.

However, if you have loosened up the muscles in your partner's thighs, the procedure ought to be significantly simpler. One great tip that you ought to follow is to search for the pressure point in the upper internal thigh, which implies the territory of your thigh that is legitimately beneath your partner's groin.

Attempt to crush this zone for the most part to locate a general area of the pressure point, and afterward slender it somewhere near using the tips of your fingers. When you discover the pressure point, begin applying a similar roundabout pressure that you used to both the past body parts.

Be careful while applying strain to the internal thighs. The pressure point here is significantly more sensitive than the pressure points in the butt or even the bosoms. Delicate pressure will take care of business, and apply an excess of pressure will simply wind up causing pointless agony that will likely power your partner out of the temperament.

If the round movement strategy ends up being unreasonably extraordinary for your partner, have a go at pushing your fingers ahead as you delicately knead the point. This will help by applying a lot gentler pressure than the roundabout movement, and the way that it is significantly more arousing absolutely doesn't hurt either!

Lower back: This territory of the body is totally different from the three zones talked about beforehand, thus will handle in a way that is totally unique to how that the past body parts were handled

What makes the lower back so one of a kind is that it doesn't have a solitary purpose of energy blockage that you should concentrate on. Or maybe, your partner will have one of two potential energy blockage circumstances, every one of which has its particular system that you can use to handle it.

The principal circumstance would be that there are a few dozen separate purposes of energy blockage that are peppering over your whole lower back, being centered explicitly around the segment of your lower back legitimately before your butt alongside the region of your lower back that is straightforwardly along your spine.

The subsequent circumstance would be that the energy blockage would be spread out over the aggregate of your lower back, with the energy nexuses interconnecting to shape a system of blockages like the genuine system of energy pathways that your body has.

The subsequent circumstance is regularly found in ladies with huge bosoms and individuals who do a great deal of physical work. This is because such individuals will in general put a great deal of strain on their lower back, compelling the energy pathways to get blocked in light of the fact that these strenuous exercises would intrude on their flow.

By and large, the lower back is continually going to be an intense spot of energy blockage except if your partner gets customary back rubs, and the advantage of this is even the scarcest back rub right now significantly invigorate your partner and will bring about practically moment excitement whenever done right.

To discover which of the two-energy blockage circumstances your partner is experiencing you will need to test a considerable amount. Use your fingers to see where the energy blockages are. If there are spaces between the points where your partner feels torment, this implies the energy blockages that your partner is experiencing are isolated from one another.

Nonetheless, if every last bit of your partners spinal pains when you rub it in that extraordinary bothersome, tickly way, then your partner's energy blockage circumstance is of the subsequent kind.

The principal circumstance is significantly harder to handle than the subsequent circumstance. Since the energy blockages are not associated, you will need to handle every one independently as opposed to all simultaneously. This is because endeavoring to knead a few points without a moment's delay could bring about terrible agony for your partner.

In any case, settling this energy blockage circumstance isn't that troublesome once you get its hang. Just press each pressure point and discharge the blockage by moving your hands in the roundabout movement that you will be recognizable to at this point. You will before long find that once you deal with one blockage, the ones around it will start to get more fragile consequently.

This implies concentrating on a few significant spots will permit you to scatter the energy blockages and have the energy pathways streaming openly in the blink of an eye.

The subsequent circumstance, in any case, requires an altogether different methodology. The main thing you should think about this methodology is that it includes positively no nuance. The energy blockage is serious and will hinder your partner's climax, and since the blockage is across the board and interconnected, the best thing that you can do is attempt to handle at quite a bit of it simultaneously as you can.

Warm up your partner's lower back by using your thumbs to slide the energy blockages into getting somewhat more fragile. Following a moment or two of this, you should start using your clench hands. Ply your partner's lower back as though it was batter. This may appear to be clever, however if you ply your partner's lower back precisely how you would massage mixture, with the snappy developments and not remaining in a similar spot for a really long time, your partner will before long be loose to such an extent that they'd feel as if they are drifting endlessly.

The subsequent circumstance, albeit in fact increasingly serious, is significantly simpler to disperse than the primary circumstance. Simply ensure that you don't wind up harming your partner by applying an excessive amount of pressure. Keep in mind, correspondence is fundamental if you need to ensure that the back rub experience is as pleasant as could be allowed.

You will find that no other zone will give as a lot of sexual incitement as the lower back as it is being rubbed. This is because the energy that is being discharged is making them much progressively touchy to sexual improvements. Giving your partner a full body climax will turn into significantly simpler after you have rubbed her back to the furthest reaches conceivable.

Feet and hands: Each and every body part that has been talked about right now significant. Kneading these body parts is a fundamental piece of setting up your body for the force of tantric sex. However, despite the fact that the lower back is home to the most extreme energy blockage in your whole body, there are no pieces of your body that is more critical to knead than your hands and your feet.

This is because your hands and feet contain significant energy pathways in light of the fact that so much energy is lost and increased through your furthest points. Likewise, since you use your hands and feet so much, a great deal of these energy pathways wind up getting blocked.

This is especially imperative to note because the pathway for practically each and every organ in your body is available in your grasp and feet. This implies backing the blockages out of the energy pathways in your grasp and feet will assist your body with becoming progressively touchy to improvements, making the peak of your lovemaking substantially more serious.

Since the pathways in your partner's hand are so different and near one another, you don't need to concentrate on each point independently. You can rather give your hands general back rubs as long as you ensure that you focus on all aspects of your hand during the back rub.

In any case, undoubtedly, a general back rub won't do. The foot has isolated bunches of energy pathway nexuses rather than the pointillist spread of nexuses that your hand has, which implies that a general back rub may assist you with releasing the muscles of your foot up yet likely won't do a lot to free the energy blockages.

Consequently, for your feet you will need to apply profound pressure using your thumb. The primary territory you should attempt is the upper focal point of your foot, as this region generally has a bunch of energy blockages in it since so much strain is set on it for the duration of the day.

After you have applied pressure and slackened up this energy blockage, you can start investigating for more blockages. Other regular zones incorporate the heel and the large toe, with the little toes additionally having nexuses for minor energy pathways.

You can likewise use this method on your partner's hands too. Certain regions of your hand contain blockages for nexuses serving explicit pieces of the body. The body part that you care about right currently is your partner's vagina, so normally, you are going to need to rub a piece of your partner's hand that would assist with evacuating energy blockages prompting this immensely significant piece of your partner's life forms.

The piece of your hand that interfaces through energy pathways to your partner's vagina is the impact point of her hand, which is the plump piece of her hand underneath her thumb. Pushing down here will give your partner that irritated torment that accompanies the squeezing of weight focuses, yet that is not everything it does.

Blocked energy pathways are a major supporter of your powerlessness to carry your partner to climax. If no energy is arriving at the zone that so urgently needs the energy to peak, your partner won't have a climax regardless of what number of extravagant deceives you attempt.

Henceforth, discharging the energy blockage from this piece of your partner's hand will help make her vagina significantly increasingly touchy. The significant part is that it will become delicate entirely through, which is going to make her g spot, that seldom found wellspring of interminable delight for ladies, much simpler to discover.

This simple revelation of your partner's g spot will demonstrate tremendously helpful in the following piece of the section, where a one of a kind procedure will be talked about that is going to enable you to furnish your join forces with mind blowing climaxes that will course through her whole body and possibly keep going for quite a long time!

Printed in Great Britain
by Amazon

79587636R00244